ANITA BLAKE

The Laughing Corpse

NECROMANCER

WRITER	LAURELL K. HAMILTON
ADAPTATION	JESS RUFFNER
ART	RON LIM
COLORS	JOEL SEGUIN & LAURA VILLARI
LETTERS	BILL TORTOLINI
COVER ART	RON LIM, JAKE BILBAO & HARVEY TOLIBAO
EDITOR	MICHAEL HORWITZ
SENIOR EDITOR	RALPH MACCHIO

SPECIAL THANKS TO JONATHON GREEN,
MELISSA MCALISTER, ANNE TREDWAY & MARK PANICCIA

COLLECTION EDITOR	CORY LEVINE
EDITORIAL ASSISTANT	ALEX STARBUCK
ASSISTANT EDITOR	JOHN DENNING
EDITORS, SPECIAL PROJECTS	JENNIFER GRÜNWALD & MARK D. BEAZLEY
SENIOR EDITOR, SPECIAL PROJECTS	JEFF YOUNGQUIST
SENIOR VICE PRESIDENT OF SALES	DAVID GABRIEL
SENIOR VICE PRESIDENT OF STRATEGIC DEVELOPMENT	RUWAN JAYATILLEKE
BOOK DESIGN	SPRING HOTELING
EDITOR IN CHIEF	JOE QUESADA
PUBLISHER	DAN BUCKLEY

ANITA BLAKE
The Laughing Corpse

NECROMANCER

ANITA BLAKE, VAMPIRE HUNTER: THE LAUGHING CORPSE BOOK 2 — NECROMANCER. Contains material originally published in magazine form as ANITA BLAKE: THE LAUGHING CORPSE — NEC... printing 2009. ISBN# 978-0-7851-3633-0. Published by MARVEL PUBLISHING, INC., a subsidiary of MARVEL ENTERTAINMENT, INC. OFFICE OF PUBLICATION: 417 5th Avenue, New York, NY 10... ...rrell K. Hamilton. All rights reserved. $19.99 per copy in the U.S. (GST #R127032852). Canadian Agreement #40668537. Anita Blake: Vampire Hunter and all characters featured in this issue ...s and likenesses thereof, and all related indicia are trademarks of Laurell K. Hamilton. No similarity between any of the names, characters, persons, and/or institutions in this magazine with th... ...person or institution is intended, and any such similarity which may exist is purely coincidental. Printed in the U.S.A. ALAN FINE, CEO Marvel Toys & Publishing Divisions and CMO Marvel C... ...DOWSKI, Chief Operating Officer; DAVID GABRIEL, SVP of Publishing Sales & Circulation; DAVID BOGART, SVP of Business Affairs & Talent Management; MICHAEL PASCIULLO, VP Merchandising ...KEEFE, VP of Operations & Logistics; DAN CARR, Executive Director of Publishing Technology; JUSTIN F. GABRIE, Director of Publishing & Editorial Operations; SUSAN CRESPI, Editorial Operati... ...ALES, Publishing Operations Manager; STAN LEE, Chairman Emeritus. For information regarding advertising in Marvel Comics or on Marvel.com, please contact Mitch Dane, Advertising Director... ...For Marvel subscription inquiries, please call 800-217-9158. Manufactured between 11/9/09 and 12/9/09 by WORLD COLOR PRESS INC., ST. ROMUALD, QC, CANADA.

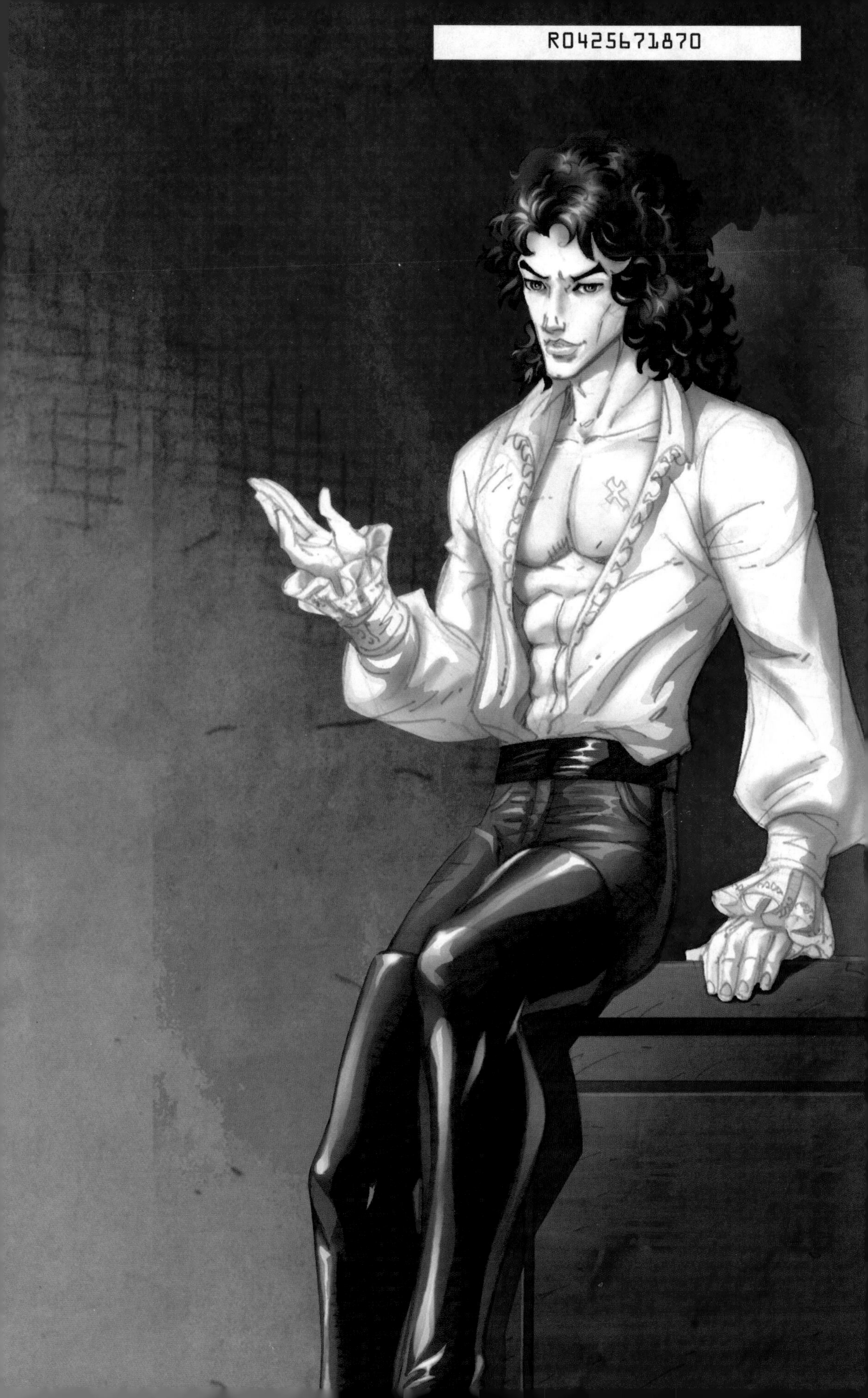

NECROMANCER

The morally absent —and mob-connected— businessman Harold Gaynor offered vampire hunter and animator Anita Blake one million dollars to raise a three-centuries-old corpse. She turned him down, but a visit from Harold's bodyguard made it clear he won't take no for an answer.

Anita found another enemy in Dominga Salvador, a voodoo priestess who wanted more than Anita was willing to give in exchange for helping her find a missing boy. In return, Dominga promised that something would come to hurt Anita when she least expects it.

The boy's corpse is discovered, mutilated by what Anita believes to be a superhumanly strong zombie. Anita swears to find the undead killer—and the mysterious animator powerful enough to raise it.

Between all of this and a run-in with the new master vampire of St. Louis, Jean-Claude, Anita is due for a good night's sleep. Which is when Dominga makes good on her promise...

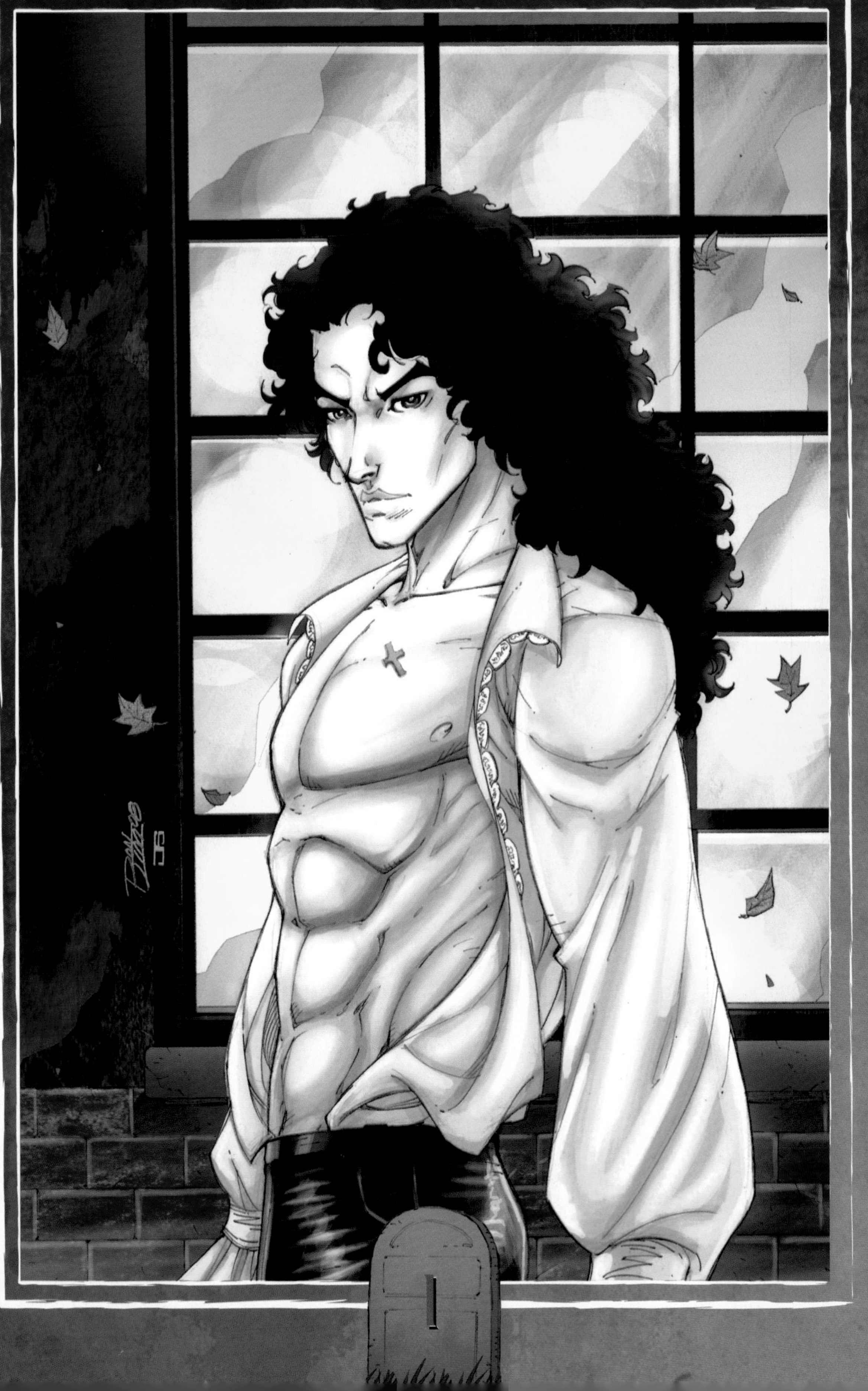

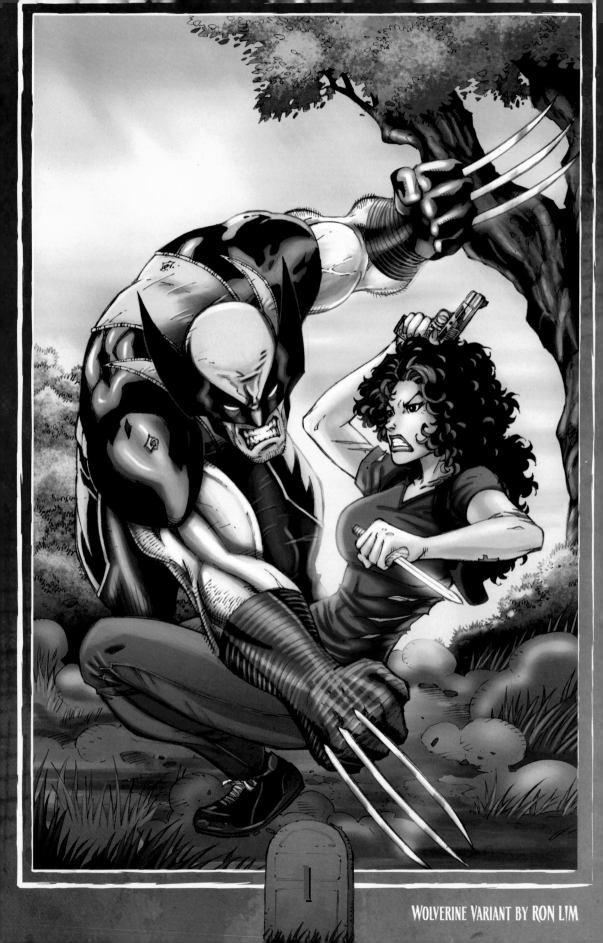

WOLVERINE VARIANT BY RON LIM

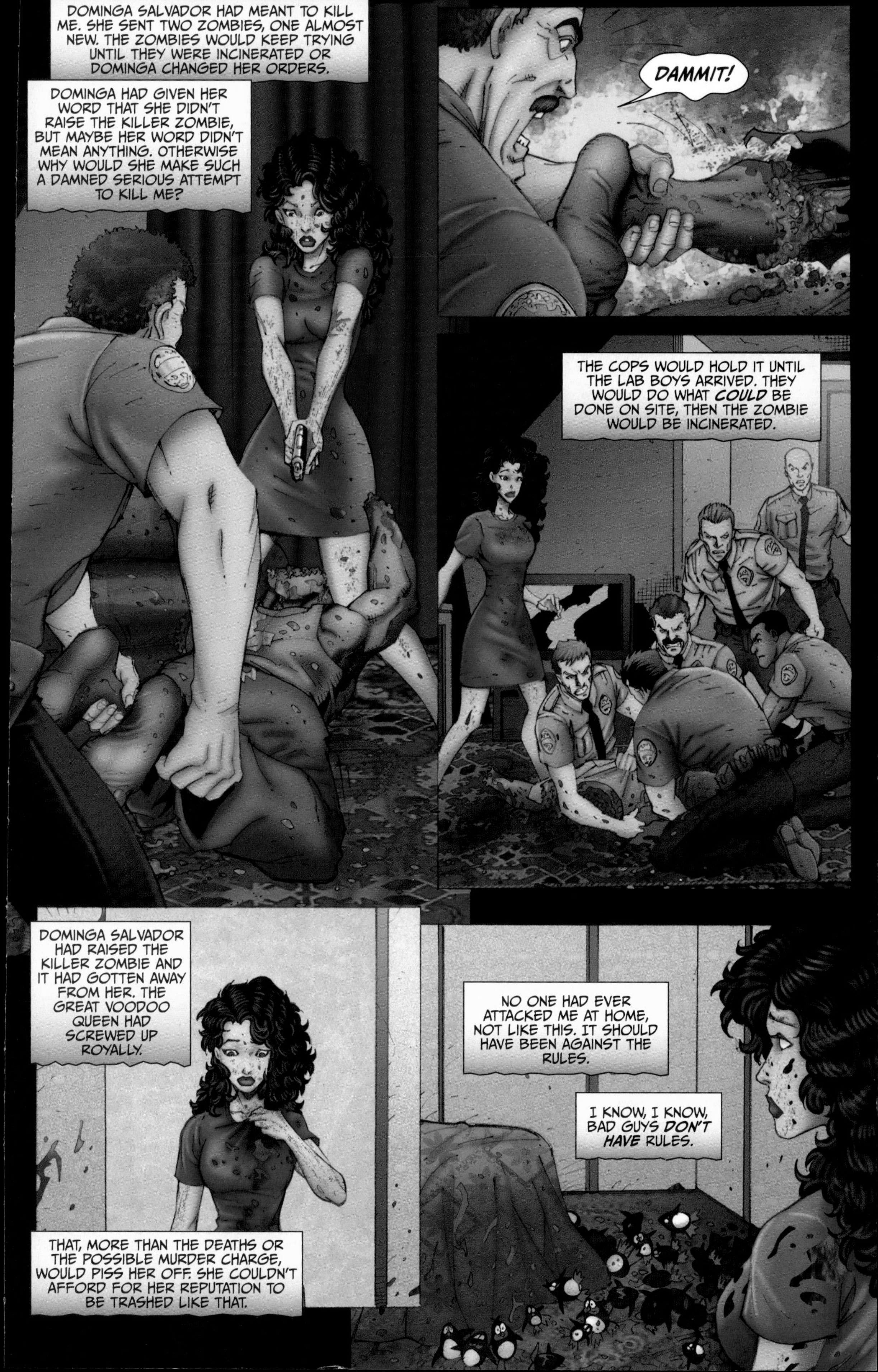
DOMINGA SALVADOR HAD MEANT TO KILL ME. SHE SENT TWO ZOMBIES, ONE ALMOST NEW. THE ZOMBIES WOULD KEEP TRYING UNTIL THEY WERE INCINERATED OR DOMINGA CHANGED HER ORDERS.
DOMINGA HAD GIVEN HER WORD THAT SHE DIDN'T RAISE THE KILLER ZOMBIE, BUT MAYBE HER WORD DIDN'T MEAN ANYTHING. OTHERWISE WHY WOULD SHE MAKE SUCH A DAMNED SERIOUS ATTEMPT TO KILL ME?
DAMMIT!
THE COPS WOULD HOLD IT UNTIL THE LAB BOYS ARRIVED. THEY WOULD DO WHAT *COULD* BE DONE ON SITE, THEN THE ZOMBIE WOULD BE INCINERATED.
DOMINGA SALVADOR HAD RAISED THE KILLER ZOMBIE AND IT HAD GOTTEN AWAY FROM HER. THE GREAT VOODOO QUEEN HAD SCREWED UP ROYALLY.
THAT, MORE THAN THE DEATHS OR THE POSSIBLE MURDER CHARGE, WOULD PISS HER OFF. SHE COULDN'T AFFORD FOR HER REPUTATION TO BE TRASHED LIKE THAT.
NO ONE HAD EVER ATTACKED ME AT HOME, NOT LIKE THIS. IT SHOULD HAVE BEEN AGAINST THE RULES.
I KNOW, I KNOW, BAD GUYS *DON'T HAVE* RULES.

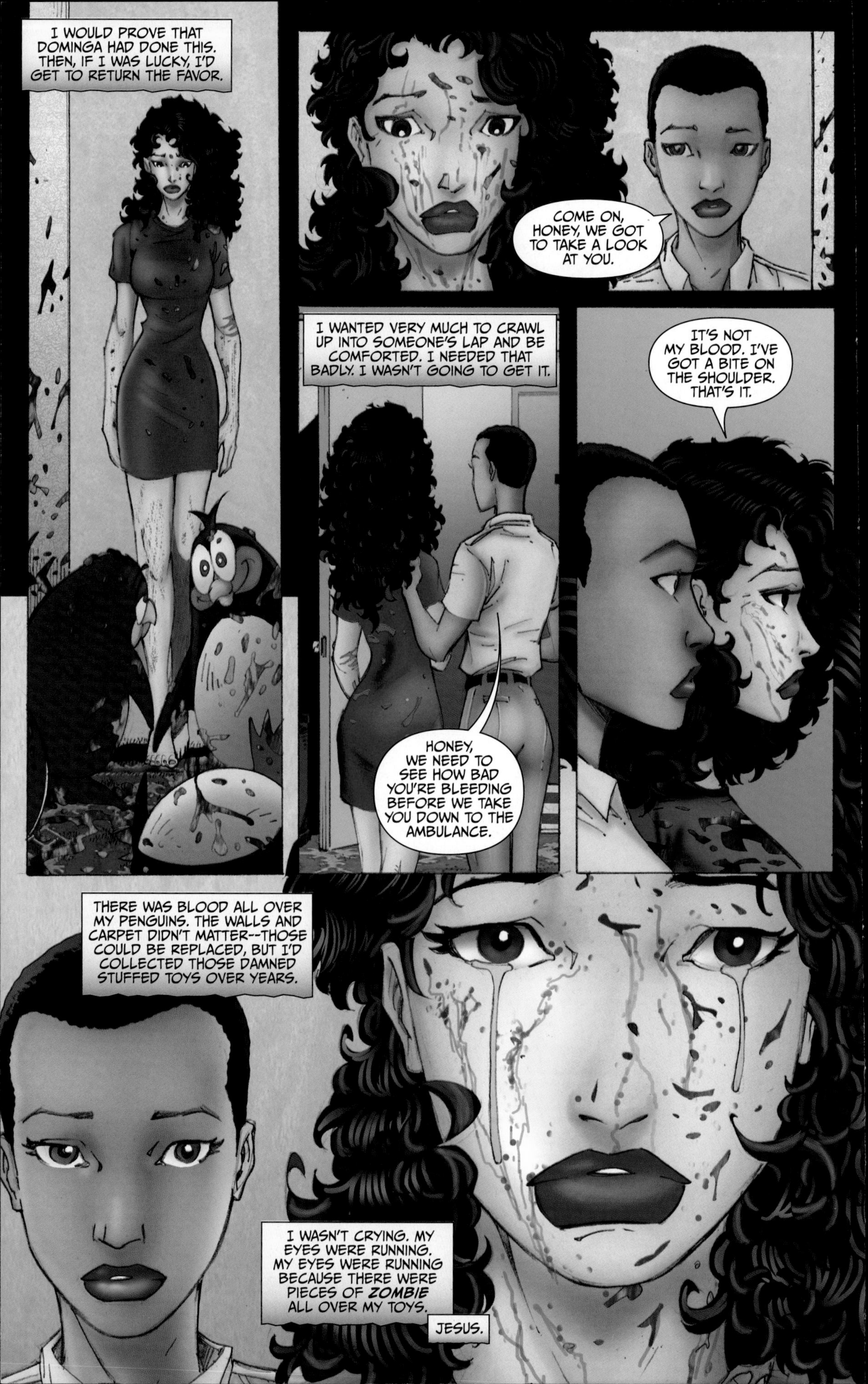
I WOULD PROVE THAT DOMINGA HAD DONE THIS. THEN, IF I WAS LUCKY, I'D GET TO RETURN THE FAVOR.
COME ON, HONEY, WE GOT TO TAKE A LOOK AT YOU.
I WANTED VERY MUCH TO CRAWL UP INTO SOMEONE'S LAP AND BE COMFORTED. I NEEDED THAT BADLY. I WASN'T GOING TO GET IT.
HONEY, WE NEED TO SEE HOW BAD YOU'RE BLEEDING BEFORE WE TAKE YOU DOWN TO THE AMBULANCE.
IT'S NOT MY BLOOD. I'VE GOT A BITE ON THE SHOULDER. THAT'S IT.
THERE WAS BLOOD ALL OVER MY PENGUINS. THE WALLS AND CARPET DIDN'T MATTER--THOSE COULD BE REPLACED, BUT I'D COLLECTED THOSE DAMNED STUFFED TOYS OVER YEARS.
I WASN'T CRYING. MY EYES WERE RUNNING. MY EYES WERE RUNNING BECAUSE THERE WERE PIECES OF ZOMBIE ALL OVER MY TOYS.
JESUS.

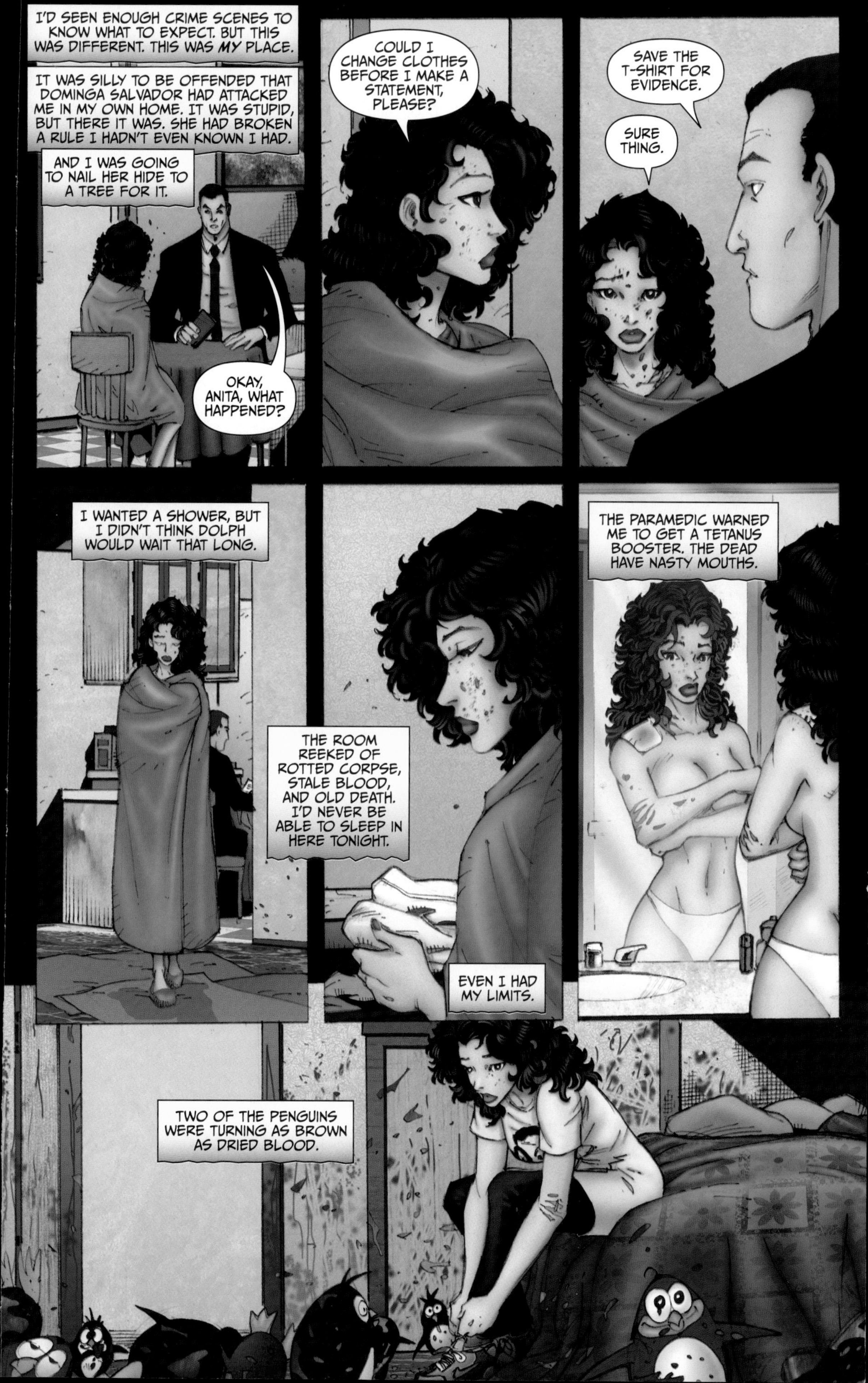
I'D SEEN ENOUGH CRIME SCENES TO KNOW WHAT TO EXPECT. BUT THIS WAS DIFFERENT. THIS WAS MY PLACE.
IT WAS SILLY TO BE OFFENDED THAT DOMINGA SALVADOR HAD ATTACKED ME IN MY OWN HOME. IT WAS STUPID, BUT THERE IT WAS. SHE HAD BROKEN A RULE I HADN'T EVEN KNOWN I HAD.
AND I WAS GOING TO NAIL HER HIDE TO A TREE FOR IT.
OKAY, ANITA, WHAT HAPPENED?
COULD I CHANGE CLOTHES BEFORE I MAKE A STATEMENT, PLEASE?
SAVE THE T-SHIRT FOR EVIDENCE.
SURE THING.
I WANTED A SHOWER, BUT I DIDN'T THINK DOLPH WOULD WAIT THAT LONG.
THE ROOM REEKED OF ROTTED CORPSE, STALE BLOOD, AND OLD DEATH. I'D NEVER BE ABLE TO SLEEP IN HERE TONIGHT.
EVEN I HAD MY LIMITS.
THE PARAMEDIC WARNED ME TO GET A TETANUS BOOSTER. THE DEAD HAVE NASTY MOUTHS.
TWO OF THE PENGUINS WERE TURNING AS BROWN AS DRIED BLOOD.

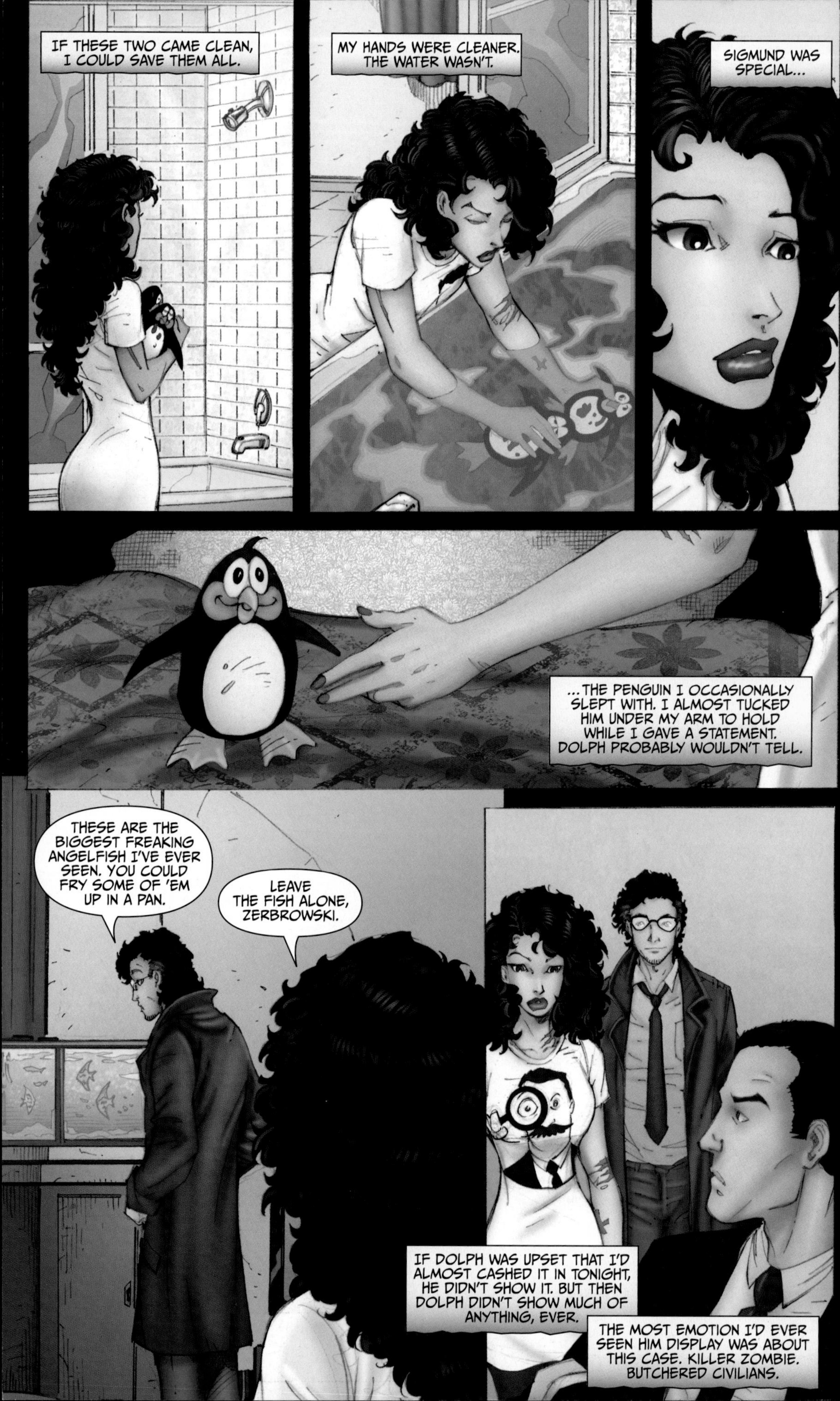
IF THESE TWO CAME CLEAN, I COULD SAVE THEM ALL.
MY HANDS WERE CLEANER. THE WATER WASN'T.
SIGMUND WAS SPECIAL...
...THE PENGUIN I OCCASIONALLY SLEPT WITH. I ALMOST TUCKED HIM UNDER MY ARM TO HOLD WHILE I GAVE A STATEMENT. DOLPH PROBABLY WOULDN'T TELL.
THESE ARE THE BIGGEST FREAKING ANGELFISH I'VE EVER SEEN. YOU COULD FRY SOME OF 'EM UP IN A PAN.
LEAVE THE FISH ALONE, ZERBROWSKI.
IF DOLPH WAS UPSET THAT I'D ALMOST CASHED IT IN TONIGHT, HE DIDN'T SHOW IT. BUT THEN DOLPH DIDN'T SHOW MUCH OF ANYTHING, EVER.
THE MOST EMOTION I'D EVER SEEN HIM DISPLAY WAS ABOUT THIS CASE. KILLER ZOMBIE. BUTCHERED CIVILIANS.

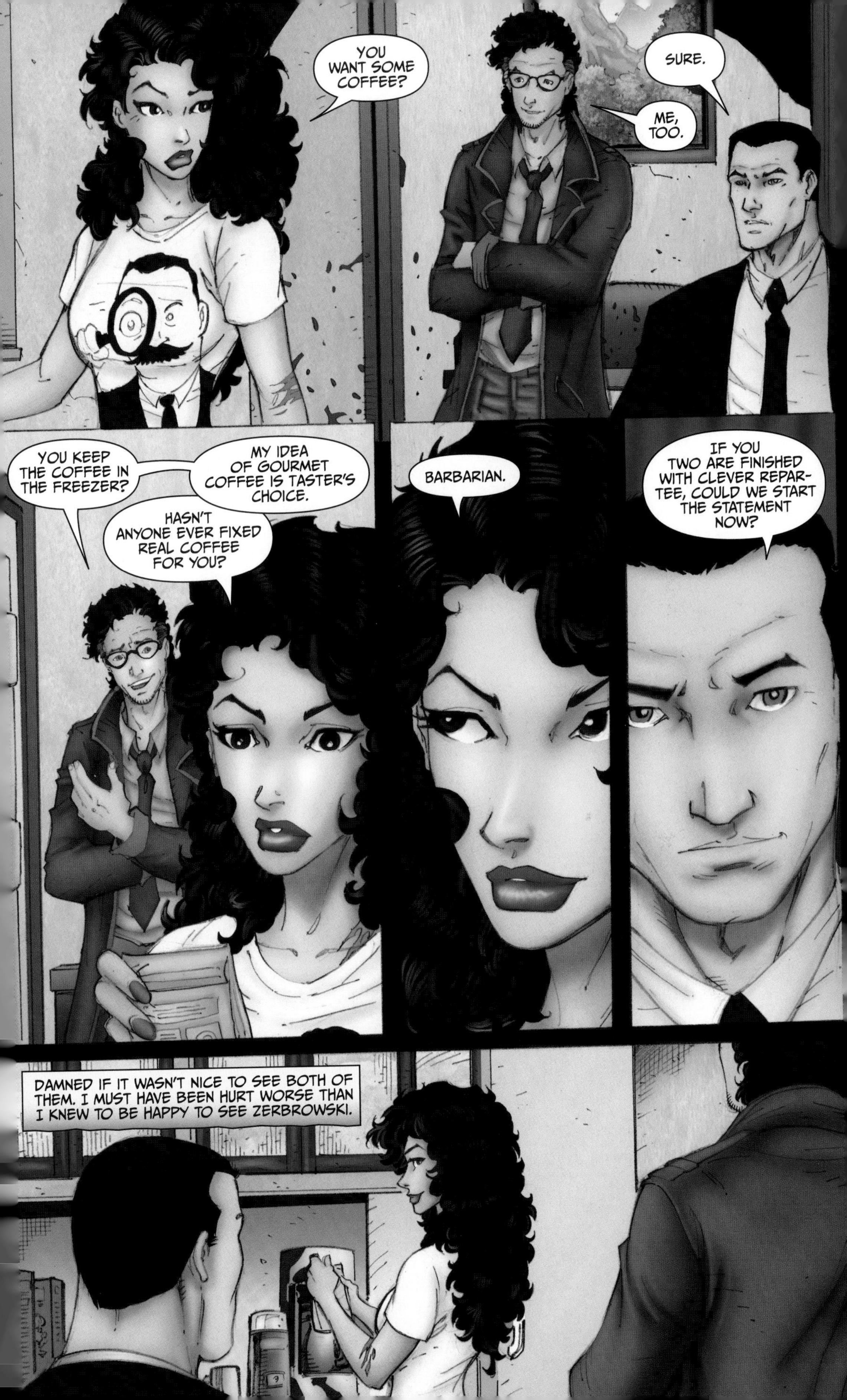
YOU WANT SOME COFFEE?
SURE.
ME, TOO.
YOU KEEP THE COFFEE IN THE FREEZER?
MY IDEA OF GOURMET COFFEE IS TASTER'S CHOICE.
HASN'T ANYONE EVER FIXED REAL COFFEE FOR YOU?
BARBARIAN.
IF YOU TWO ARE FINISHED WITH CLEVER REPARTEE, COULD WE START THE STATEMENT NOW?
DAMNED IF IT WASN'T NICE TO SEE BOTH OF THEM. I MUST HAVE BEEN HURT WORSE THAN I KNEW TO BE HAPPY TO SEE ZERBROWSKI.

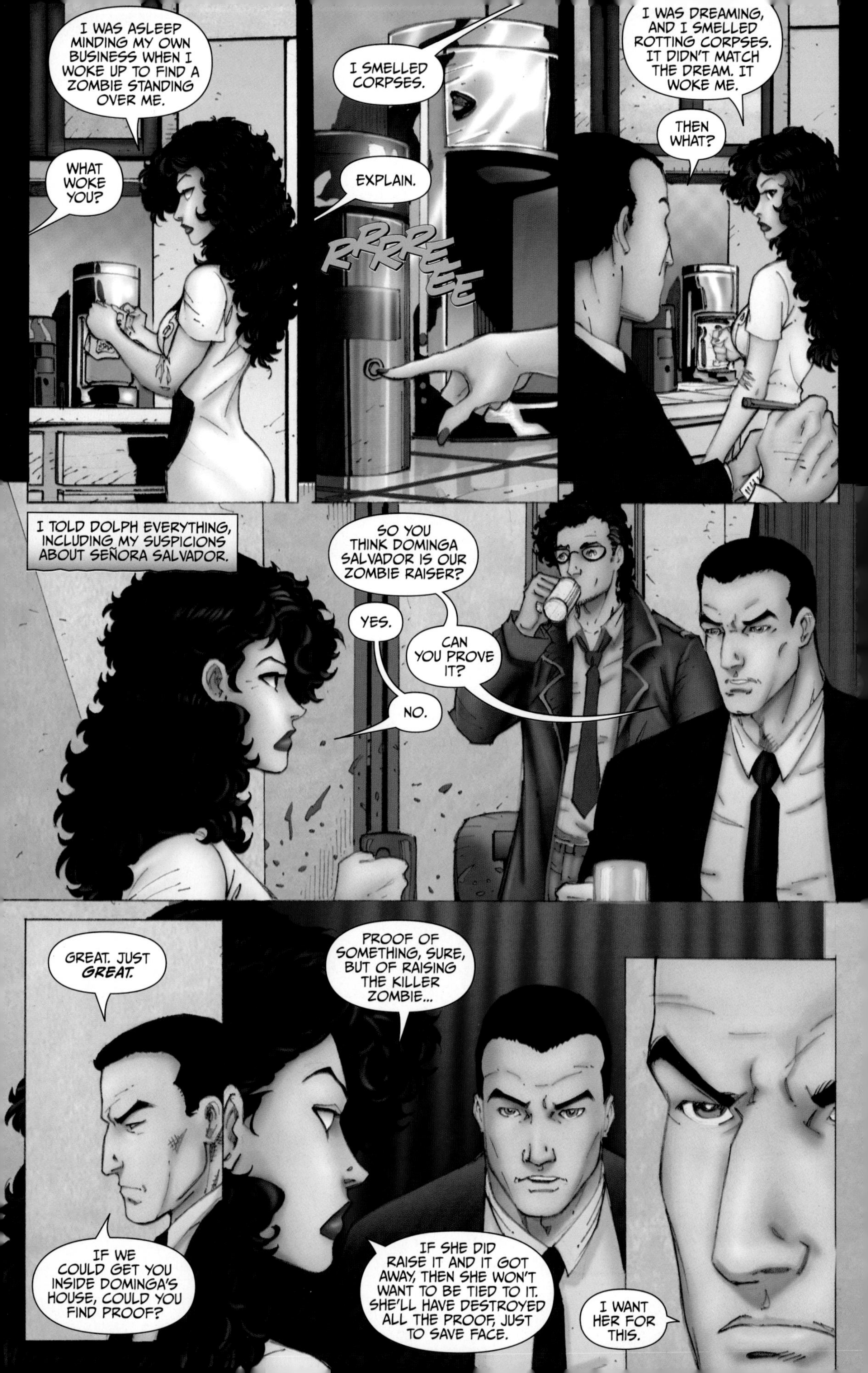

I WAS ASLEEP MINDING MY OWN BUSINESS WHEN I WOKE UP TO FIND A ZOMBIE STANDING OVER ME.
WHAT WOKE YOU?
I SMELLED CORPSES.
EXPLAIN.
RRRREEEE
I WAS DREAMING, AND I SMELLED ROTTING CORPSES. IT DIDN'T MATCH THE DREAM. IT WOKE ME.
THEN WHAT?
I TOLD DOLPH EVERYTHING, INCLUDING MY SUSPICIONS ABOUT SEÑORA SALVADOR.
SO YOU THINK DOMINGA SALVADOR IS OUR ZOMBIE RAISER?
YES.
CAN YOU PROVE IT?
NO.
GREAT. JUST GREAT.
PROOF OF SOMETHING, SURE, BUT OF RAISING THE KILLER ZOMBIE...
IF WE COULD GET YOU INSIDE DOMINGA'S HOUSE, COULD YOU FIND PROOF?
IF SHE DID RAISE IT AND IT GOT AWAY, THEN SHE WON'T WANT TO BE TIED TO IT. SHE'LL HAVE DESTROYED ALL THE PROOF, JUST TO SAVE FACE.
I WANT HER FOR THIS.

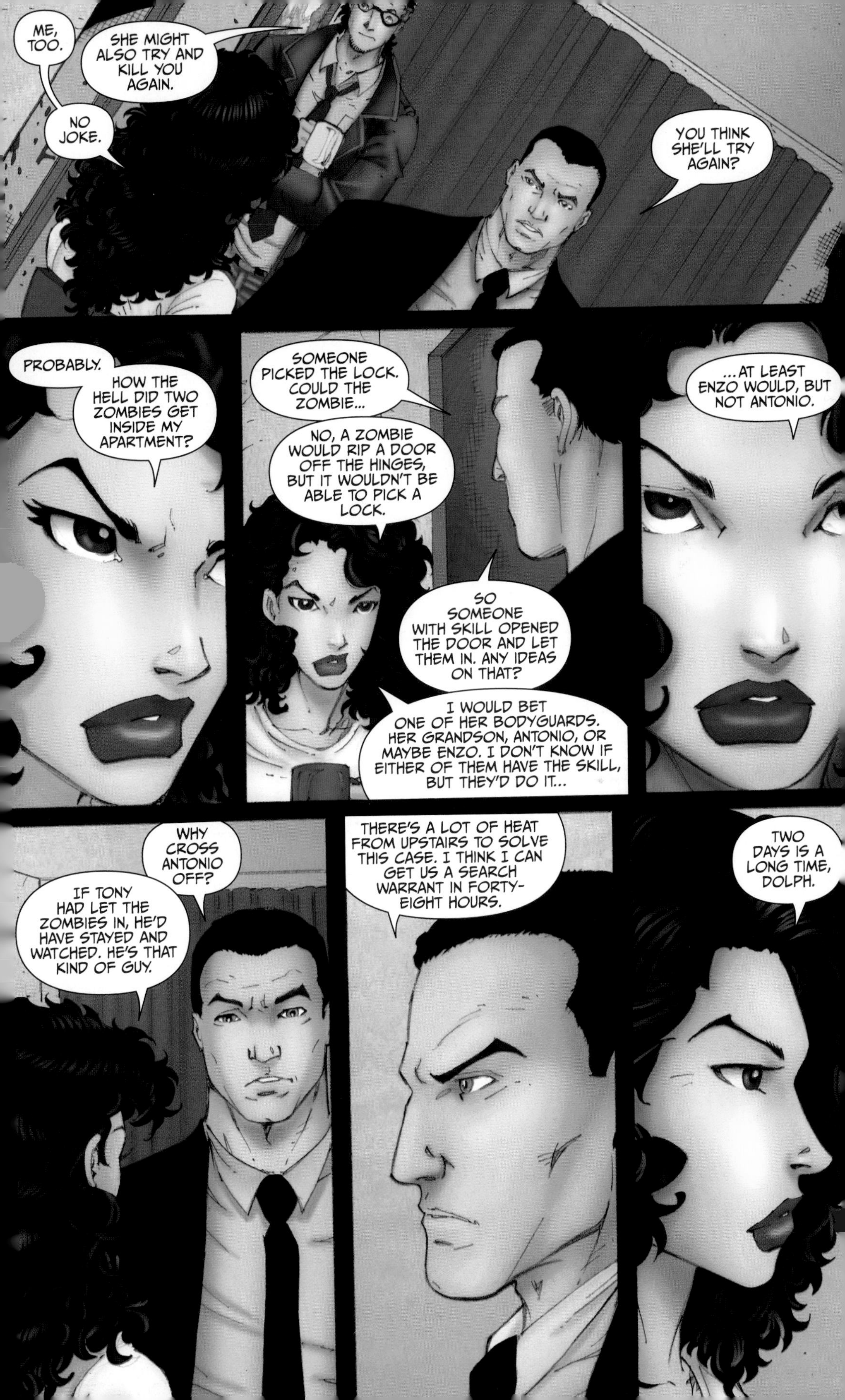
ME, TOO.
SHE MIGHT ALSO TRY AND KILL YOU AGAIN.
NO JOKE.
YOU THINK SHE'LL TRY AGAIN?
PROBABLY.
HOW THE HELL DID TWO ZOMBIES GET INSIDE MY APARTMENT?
SOMEONE PICKED THE LOCK. COULD THE ZOMBIE...
NO, A ZOMBIE WOULD RIP A DOOR OFF THE HINGES, BUT IT WOULDN'T BE ABLE TO PICK A LOCK.
SO SOMEONE WITH SKILL OPENED THE DOOR AND LET THEM IN. ANY IDEAS ON THAT?
I WOULD BET ONE OF HER BODYGUARDS. HER GRANDSON, ANTONIO, OR MAYBE ENZO. I DON'T KNOW IF EITHER OF THEM HAVE THE SKILL, BUT THEY'D DO IT...
...AT LEAST ENZO WOULD, BUT NOT ANTONIO.
WHY CROSS ANTONIO OFF?
IF TONY HAD LET THE ZOMBIES IN, HE'D HAVE STAYED AND WATCHED. HE'S THAT KIND OF GUY.
THERE'S A LOT OF HEAT FROM UPSTAIRS TO SOLVE THIS CASE. I THINK I CAN GET US A SEARCH WARRANT IN FORTY-EIGHT HOURS.
TWO DAYS IS A LONG TIME, DOLPH.

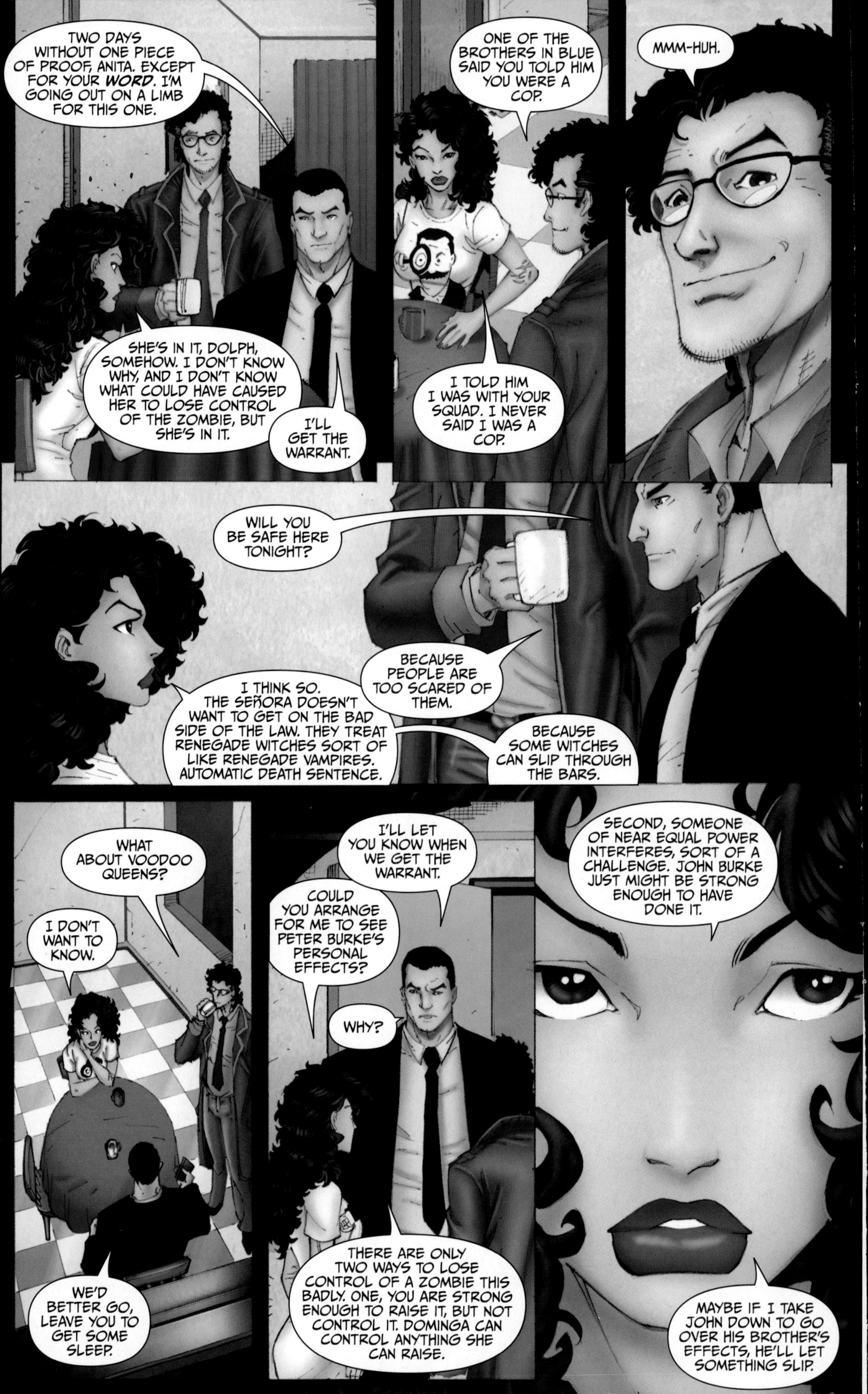
TWO DAYS WITHOUT ONE PIECE OF PROOF, ANITA. EXCEPT FOR YOUR **WORD**. I'M GOING OUT ON A LIMB FOR THIS ONE.
SHE'S IN IT, DOLPH, SOMEHOW. I DON'T KNOW WHY, AND I DON'T KNOW WHAT COULD HAVE CAUSED HER TO LOSE CONTROL OF THE ZOMBIE, BUT SHE'S IN IT.
I'LL GET THE WARRANT.
ONE OF THE BROTHERS IN BLUE SAID YOU TOLD HIM YOU WERE A COP.
I TOLD HIM I WAS WITH YOUR SQUAD. I NEVER SAID I WAS A COP.
MMM-HUH.
WILL YOU BE SAFE HERE TONIGHT?
I THINK SO. THE SEÑORA DOESN'T WANT TO GET ON THE BAD SIDE OF THE LAW. THEY TREAT RENEGADE WITCHES SORT OF LIKE RENEGADE VAMPIRES. AUTOMATIC DEATH SENTENCE.
BECAUSE PEOPLE ARE TOO SCARED OF THEM.
BECAUSE SOME WITCHES CAN SLIP THROUGH THE BARS.
WHAT ABOUT VOODOO QUEENS?
I DON'T WANT TO KNOW.
WE'D BETTER GO, LEAVE YOU TO GET SOME SLEEP.
I'LL LET YOU KNOW WHEN WE GET THE WARRANT.
COULD YOU ARRANGE FOR ME TO SEE PETER BURKE'S PERSONAL EFFECTS?
WHY?
THERE ARE ONLY TWO WAYS TO LOSE CONTROL OF A ZOMBIE THIS BADLY. ONE, YOU ARE STRONG ENOUGH TO RAISE IT, BUT NOT CONTROL IT. DOMINGA CAN CONTROL ANYTHING SHE CAN RAISE.
SECOND, SOMEONE OF NEAR EQUAL POWER INTERFERES, SORT OF A CHALLENGE. JOHN BURKE JUST MIGHT BE STRONG ENOUGH TO HAVE DONE IT.
MAYBE IF I TAKE JOHN DOWN TO GO OVER HIS BROTHER'S EFFECTS, HE'LL LET SOMETHING SLIP.

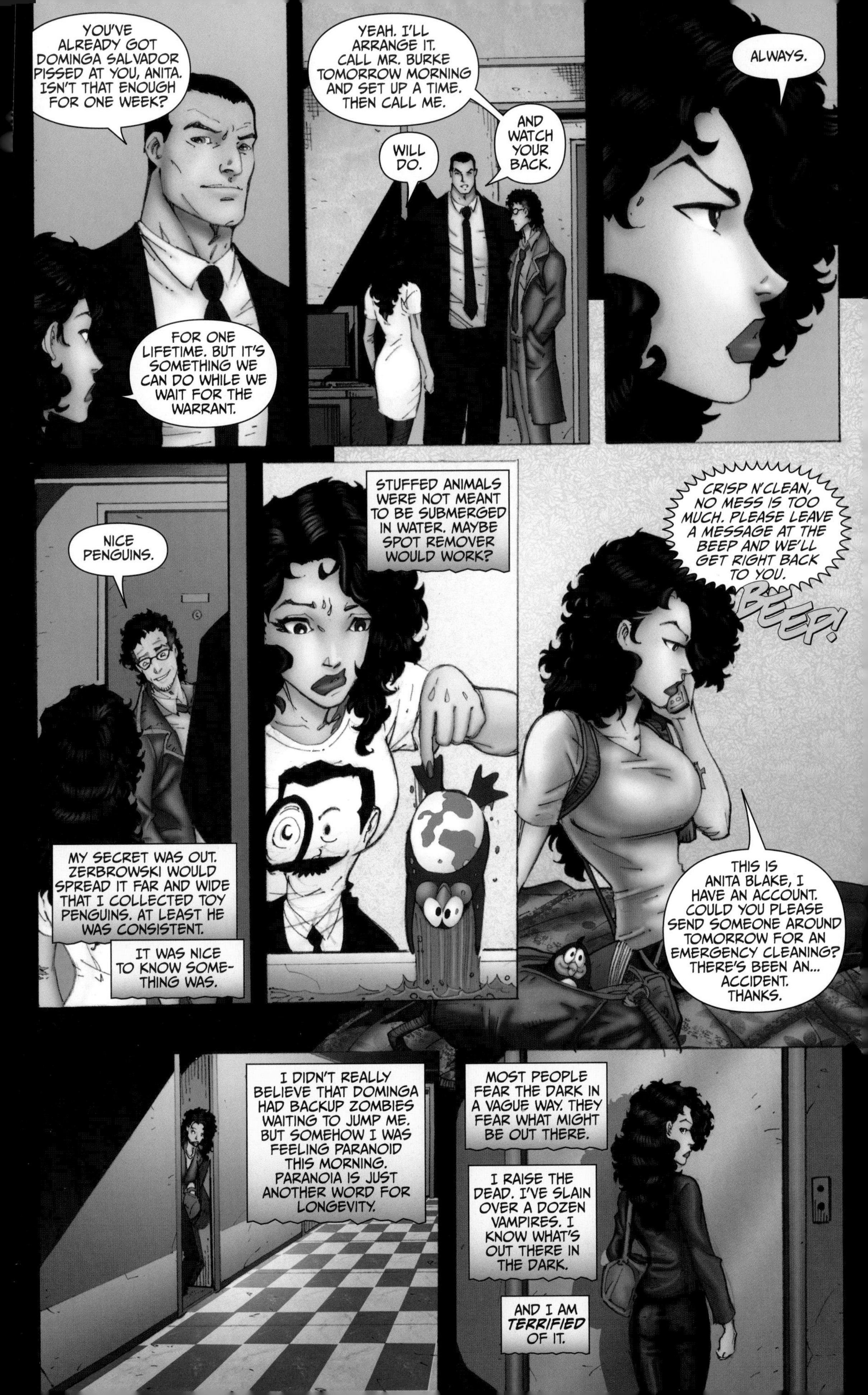
YOU'VE ALREADY GOT DOMINGA SALVADOR PISSED AT YOU, ANITA. ISN'T THAT ENOUGH FOR ONE WEEK?
FOR ONE LIFETIME. BUT IT'S SOMETHING WE CAN DO WHILE WE WAIT FOR THE WARRANT.
YEAH. I'LL ARRANGE IT. CALL MR. BURKE TOMORROW MORNING AND SET UP A TIME. THEN CALL ME.
WILL DO.
AND WATCH YOUR BACK.
ALWAYS.
NICE PENGUINS.
MY SECRET WAS OUT. ZERBROWSKI WOULD SPREAD IT FAR AND WIDE THAT I COLLECTED TOY PENGUINS. AT LEAST HE WAS CONSISTENT.
IT WAS NICE TO KNOW SOME-THING WAS.
STUFFED ANIMALS WERE NOT MEANT TO BE SUBMERGED IN WATER. MAYBE SPOT REMOVER WOULD WORK?
CRISP N'CLEAN, NO MESS IS TOO MUCH. PLEASE LEAVE A MESSAGE AT THE BEEP AND WE'LL GET RIGHT BACK TO YOU.
BEEP!
THIS IS ANITA BLAKE, I HAVE AN ACCOUNT. COULD YOU PLEASE SEND SOMEONE AROUND TOMORROW FOR AN EMERGENCY CLEANING? THERE'S BEEN AN... ACCIDENT. THANKS.
I DIDN'T REALLY BELIEVE THAT DOMINGA HAD BACKUP ZOMBIES WAITING TO JUMP ME. BUT SOMEHOW I WAS FEELING PARANOID THIS MORNING. PARANOIA IS JUST ANOTHER WORD FOR LONGEVITY.
MOST PEOPLE FEAR THE DARK IN A VAGUE WAY. THEY FEAR WHAT MIGHT BE OUT THERE.
I RAISE THE DEAD. I'VE SLAIN OVER A DOZEN VAMPIRES. I KNOW WHAT'S OUT THERE IN THE DARK.
AND I AM TERRIFIED OF IT.

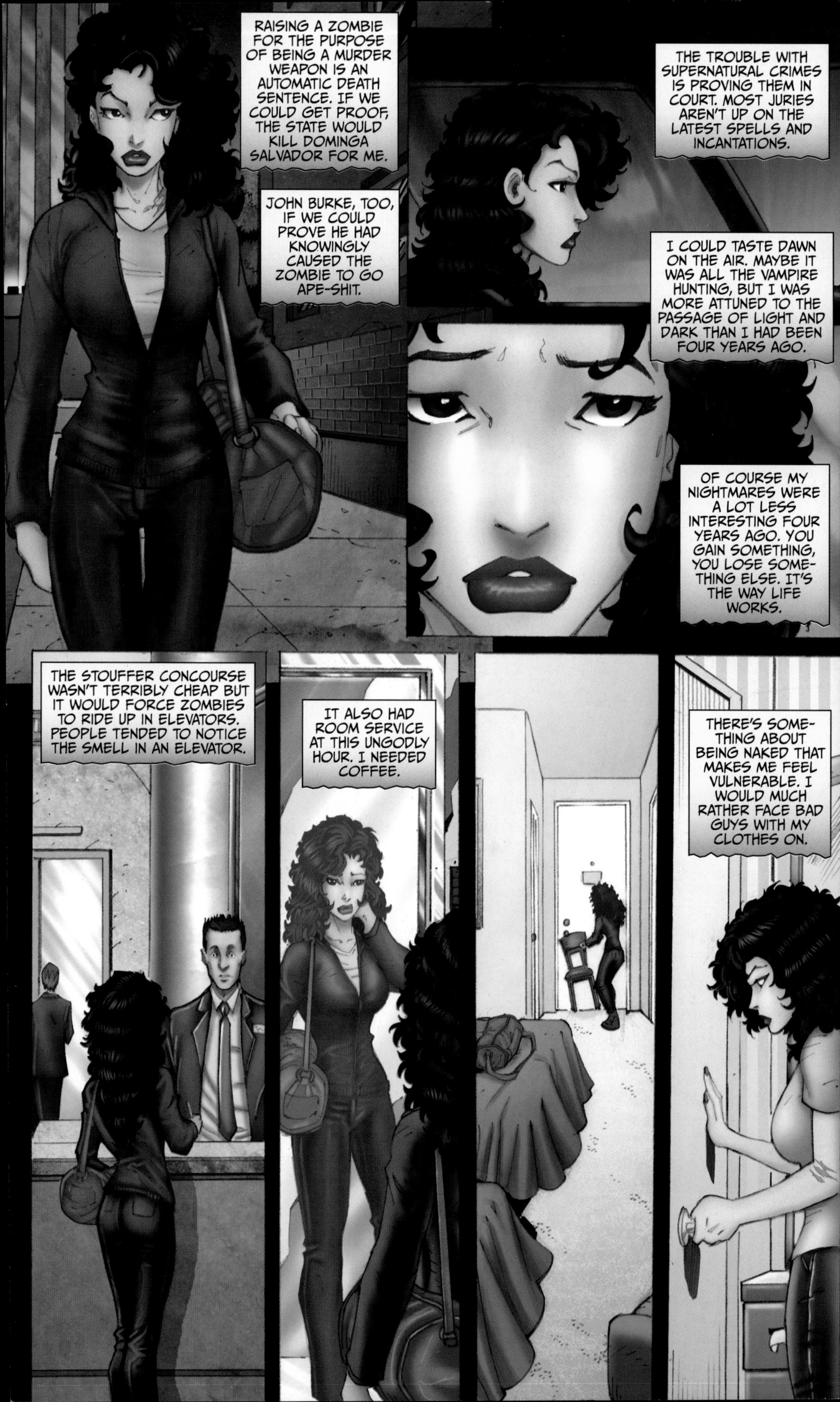
RAISING A ZOMBIE FOR THE PURPOSE OF BEING A MURDER WEAPON IS AN AUTOMATIC DEATH SENTENCE. IF WE COULD GET PROOF, THE STATE WOULD KILL DOMINGA SALVADOR FOR ME.
JOHN BURKE, TOO, IF WE COULD PROVE HE HAD KNOWINGLY CAUSED THE ZOMBIE TO GO APE-SHIT.
THE TROUBLE WITH SUPERNATURAL CRIMES IS PROVING THEM IN COURT. MOST JURIES AREN'T UP ON THE LATEST SPELLS AND INCANTATIONS.
I COULD TASTE DAWN ON THE AIR. MAYBE IT WAS ALL THE VAMPIRE HUNTING, BUT I WAS MORE ATTUNED TO THE PASSAGE OF LIGHT AND DARK THAN I HAD BEEN FOUR YEARS AGO.
OF COURSE MY NIGHTMARES WERE A LOT LESS INTERESTING FOUR YEARS AGO. YOU GAIN SOMETHING, YOU LOSE SOMETHING ELSE. IT'S THE WAY LIFE WORKS.
THE STOUFFER CONCOURSE WASN'T TERRIBLY CHEAP BUT IT WOULD FORCE ZOMBIES TO RIDE UP IN ELEVATORS. PEOPLE TENDED TO NOTICE THE SMELL IN AN ELEVATOR.
IT ALSO HAD ROOM SERVICE AT THIS UNGODLY HOUR. I NEEDED COFFEE.
THERE'S SOMETHING ABOUT BEING NAKED THAT MAKES ME FEEL VULNERABLE. I WOULD MUCH RATHER FACE BAD GUYS WITH MY CLOTHES ON.

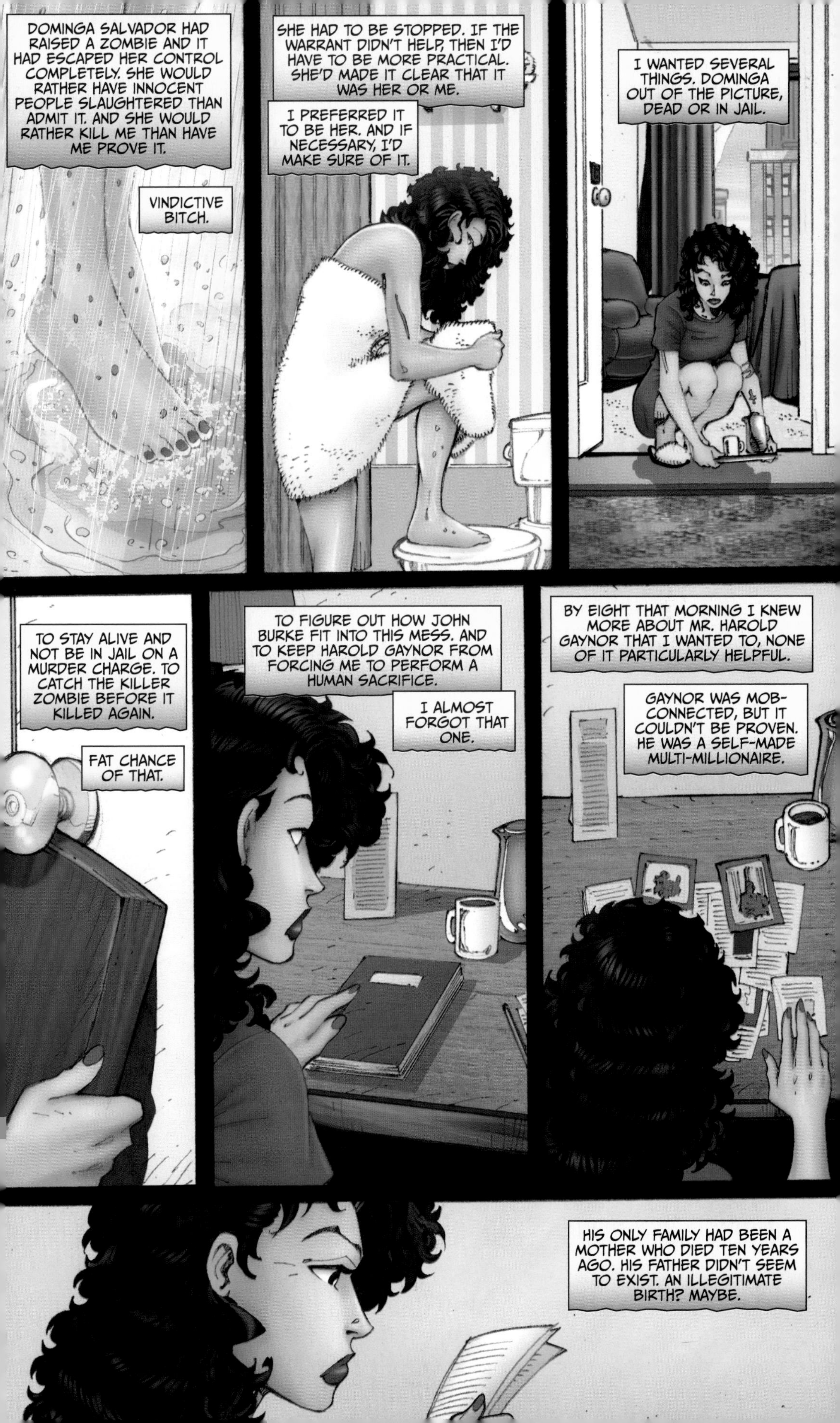
DOMINGA SALVADOR HAD RAISED A ZOMBIE AND IT HAD ESCAPED HER CONTROL COMPLETELY. SHE WOULD RATHER HAVE INNOCENT PEOPLE SLAUGHTERED THAN ADMIT IT. AND SHE WOULD RATHER KILL ME THAN HAVE ME PROVE IT.
VINDICTIVE BITCH.
SHE HAD TO BE STOPPED. IF THE WARRANT DIDN'T HELP, THEN I'D HAVE TO BE MORE PRACTICAL. SHE'D MADE IT CLEAR THAT IT WAS HER OR ME.
I PREFERRED IT TO BE HER. AND IF NECESSARY, I'D MAKE SURE OF IT.
I WANTED SEVERAL THINGS. DOMINGA OUT OF THE PICTURE, DEAD OR IN JAIL.
TO STAY ALIVE AND NOT BE IN JAIL ON A MURDER CHARGE. TO CATCH THE KILLER ZOMBIE BEFORE IT KILLED AGAIN.
FAT CHANCE OF THAT.
TO FIGURE OUT HOW JOHN BURKE FIT INTO THIS MESS. AND TO KEEP HAROLD GAYNOR FROM FORCING ME TO PERFORM A HUMAN SACRIFICE.
I ALMOST FORGOT THAT ONE.
BY EIGHT THAT MORNING I KNEW MORE ABOUT MR. HAROLD GAYNOR THAT I WANTED TO, NONE OF IT PARTICULARLY HELPFUL.
GAYNOR WAS MOB-CONNECTED, BUT IT COULDN'T BE PROVEN. HE WAS A SELF-MADE MULTI-MILLIONAIRE.
HIS ONLY FAMILY HAD BEEN A MOTHER WHO DIED TEN YEARS AGO. HIS FATHER DIDN'T SEEM TO EXIST. AN ILLEGITIMATE BIRTH? MAYBE.

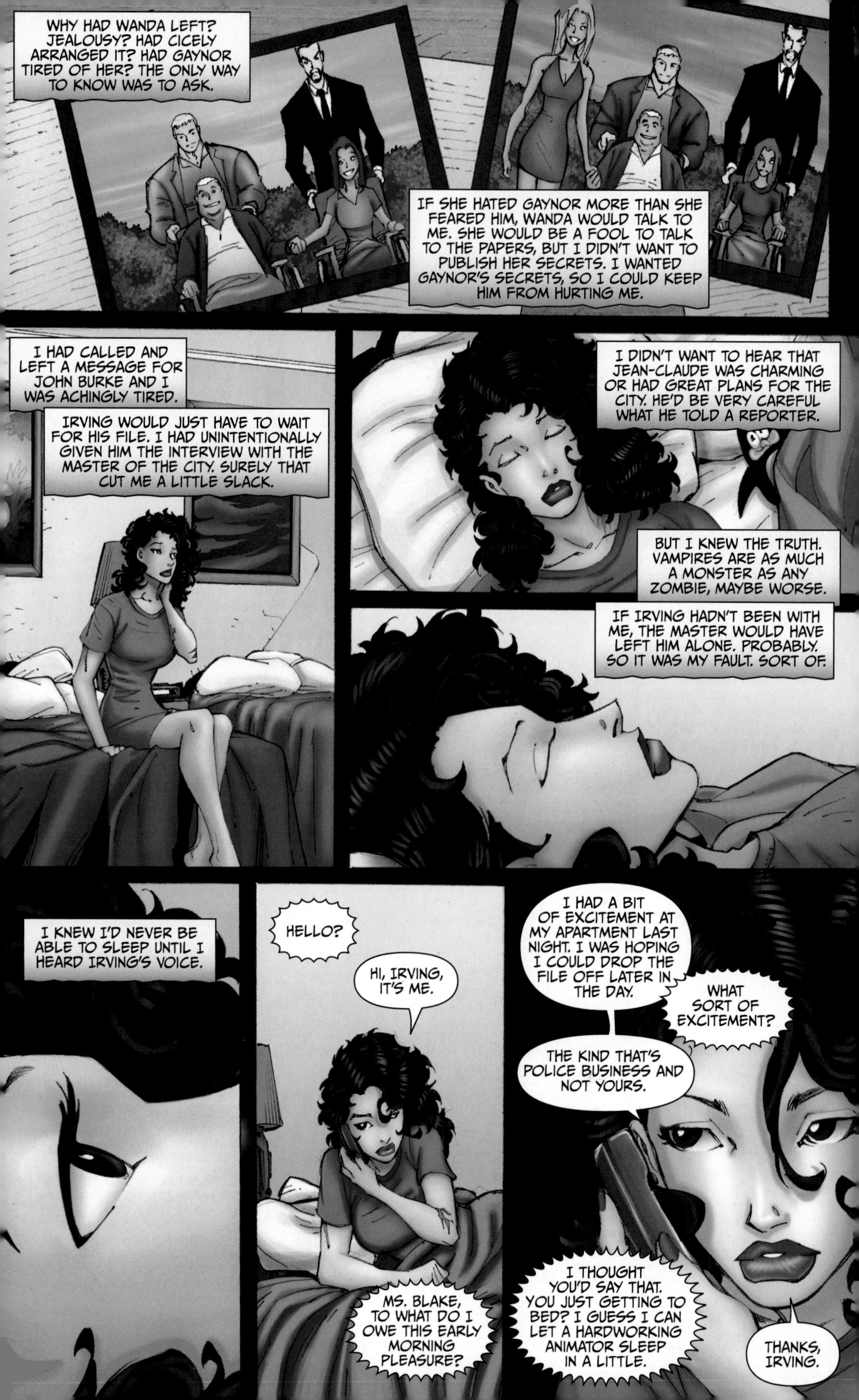
WHY HAD WANDA LEFT? JEALOUSY? HAD CICELY ARRANGED IT? HAD GAYNOR TIRED OF HER? THE ONLY WAY TO KNOW WAS TO ASK.
IF SHE HATED GAYNOR MORE THAN SHE FEARED HIM, WANDA WOULD TALK TO ME. SHE WOULD BE A FOOL TO TALK TO THE PAPERS, BUT I DIDN'T WANT TO PUBLISH HER SECRETS. I WANTED GAYNOR'S SECRETS, SO I COULD KEEP HIM FROM HURTING ME.
I HAD CALLED AND LEFT A MESSAGE FOR JOHN BURKE AND I WAS ACHINGLY TIRED.
IRVING WOULD JUST HAVE TO WAIT FOR HIS FILE. I HAD UNINTENTIONALLY GIVEN HIM THE INTERVIEW WITH THE MASTER OF THE CITY. SURELY THAT CUT ME A LITTLE SLACK.
I DIDN'T WANT TO HEAR THAT JEAN-CLAUDE WAS CHARMING OR HAD GREAT PLANS FOR THE CITY. HE'D BE VERY CAREFUL WHAT HE TOLD A REPORTER.
BUT I KNEW THE TRUTH. VAMPIRES ARE AS MUCH A MONSTER AS ANY ZOMBIE, MAYBE WORSE.
IF IRVING HADN'T BEEN WITH ME, THE MASTER WOULD HAVE LEFT HIM ALONE. PROBABLY. SO IT WAS MY FAULT. SORT OF.
I KNEW I'D NEVER BE ABLE TO SLEEP UNTIL I HEARD IRVING'S VOICE.
HELLO?
HI, IRVING, IT'S ME.
MS. BLAKE, TO WHAT DO I OWE THIS EARLY MORNING PLEASURE?
I HAD A BIT OF EXCITEMENT AT MY APARTMENT LAST NIGHT. I WAS HOPING I COULD DROP THE FILE OFF LATER IN THE DAY.
WHAT SORT OF EXCITEMENT?
THE KIND THAT'S POLICE BUSINESS AND NOT YOURS.
I THOUGHT YOU'D SAY THAT. YOU JUST GETTING TO BED? I GUESS I CAN LET A HARDWORKING ANIMATOR SLEEP IN A LITTLE.
THANKS, IRVING.

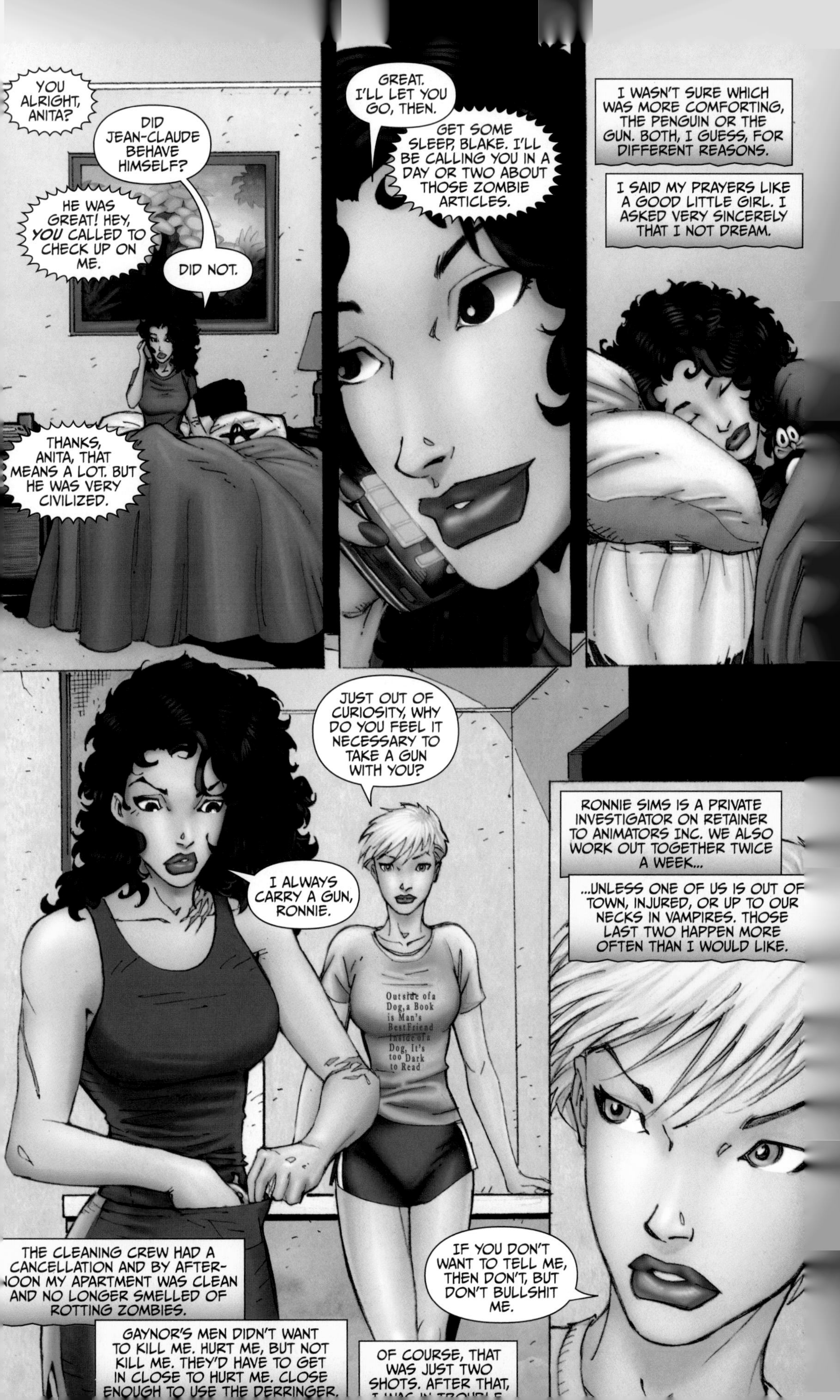

YOU ALRIGHT, ANITA?
DID JEAN-CLAUDE BEHAVE HIMSELF?
HE WAS GREAT! HEY, *YOU* CALLED TO CHECK UP ON ME.
DID NOT.
THANKS, ANITA, THAT MEANS A LOT. BUT HE WAS VERY CIVILIZED.
GREAT. I'LL LET YOU GO, THEN.
GET SOME SLEEP, BLAKE. I'LL BE CALLING YOU IN A DAY OR TWO ABOUT THOSE ZOMBIE ARTICLES.
I WASN'T SURE WHICH WAS MORE COMFORTING, THE PENGUIN OR THE GUN. BOTH, I GUESS, FOR DIFFERENT REASONS.
I SAID MY PRAYERS LIKE A GOOD LITTLE GIRL. I ASKED VERY SINCERELY THAT I NOT DREAM.
JUST OUT OF CURIOSITY, WHY DO YOU FEEL IT NECESSARY TO TAKE A GUN WITH YOU?
I ALWAYS CARRY A GUN, RONNIE.
RONNIE SIMS IS A PRIVATE INVESTIGATOR ON RETAINER TO ANIMATORS INC. WE ALSO WORK OUT TOGETHER TWICE A WEEK...
...UNLESS ONE OF US IS OUT OF TOWN, INJURED, OR UP TO OUR NECKS IN VAMPIRES. THOSE LAST TWO HAPPEN MORE OFTEN THAN I WOULD LIKE.
Outside of a Dog, a Book is Man's Best Friend Inside of a Dog, It's too Dark to Read
THE CLEANING CREW HAD A CANCELLATION AND BY AFTER-NOON MY APARTMENT WAS CLEAN AND NO LONGER SMELLED OF ROTTING ZOMBIES.
GAYNOR'S MEN DIDN'T WANT TO KILL ME. HURT ME, BUT NOT KILL ME. THEY'D HAVE TO GET IN CLOSE TO HURT ME. CLOSE ENOUGH TO USE THE DERRINGER.
IF YOU DON'T WANT TO TELL ME, THEN DON'T, BUT DON'T BULLSHIT ME.
OF COURSE, THAT WAS JUST TWO SHOTS. AFTER THAT,

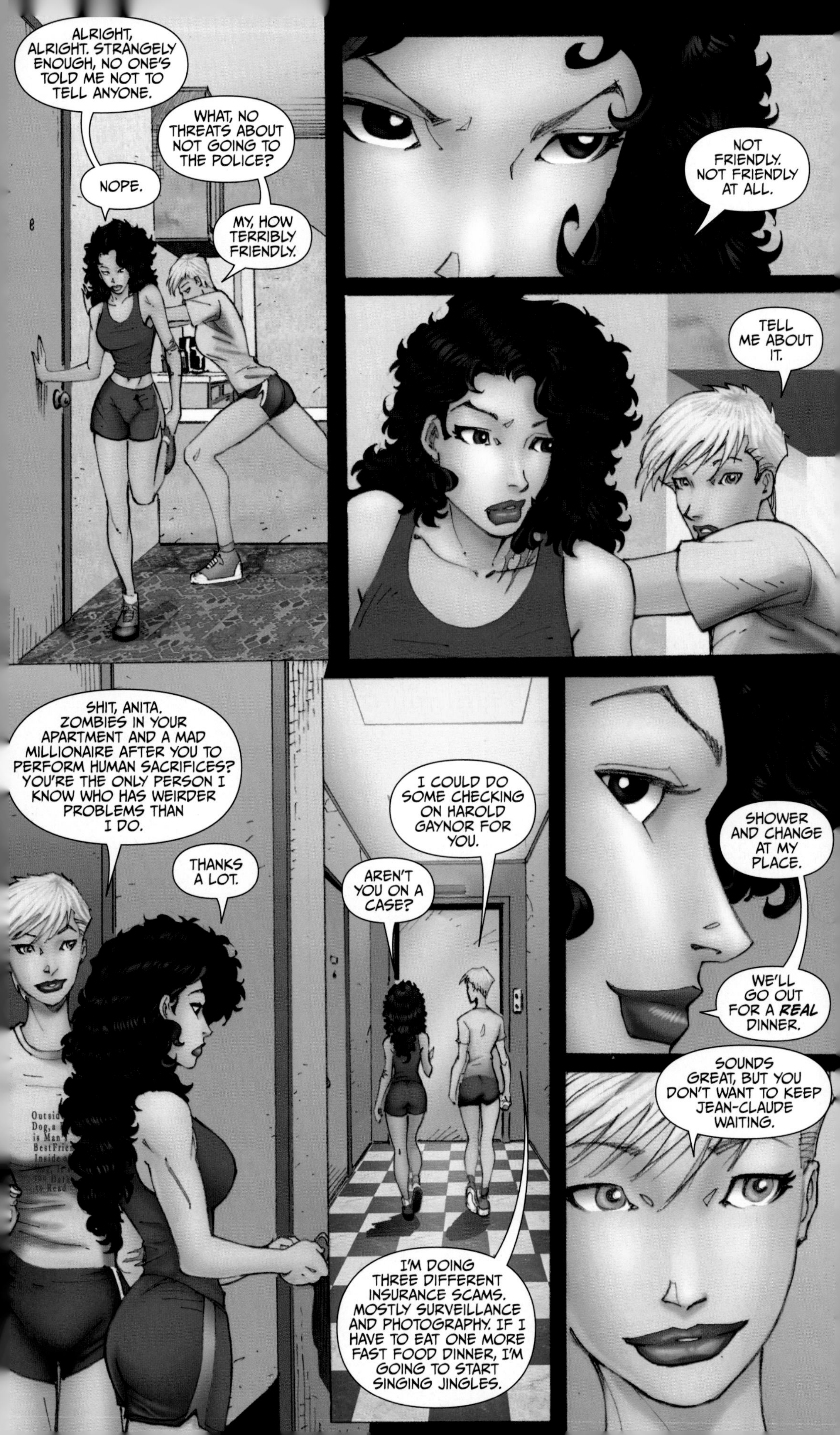
ALRIGHT, ALRIGHT. STRANGELY ENOUGH, NO ONE'S TOLD ME NOT TO TELL ANYONE.
WHAT, NO THREATS ABOUT NOT GOING TO THE POLICE?
NOPE.
MY, HOW TERRIBLY FRIENDLY.
NOT FRIENDLY. NOT FRIENDLY AT ALL.
TELL ME ABOUT IT.
SHIT, ANITA. ZOMBIES IN YOUR APARTMENT AND A MAD MILLIONAIRE AFTER YOU TO PERFORM HUMAN SACRIFICES? YOU'RE THE ONLY PERSON I KNOW WHO HAS WEIRDER PROBLEMS THAN I DO.
THANKS A LOT.
I COULD DO SOME CHECKING ON HAROLD GAYNOR FOR YOU.
AREN'T YOU ON A CASE?
I'M DOING THREE DIFFERENT INSURANCE SCAMS. MOSTLY SURVEILLANCE AND PHOTOGRAPHY. IF I HAVE TO EAT ONE MORE FAST FOOD DINNER, I'M GOING TO START SINGING JINGLES.
SHOWER AND CHANGE AT MY PLACE.
WE'LL GO OUT FOR A *REAL* DINNER.
SOUNDS GREAT, BUT YOU DON'T WANT TO KEEP JEAN-CLAUDE WAITING.

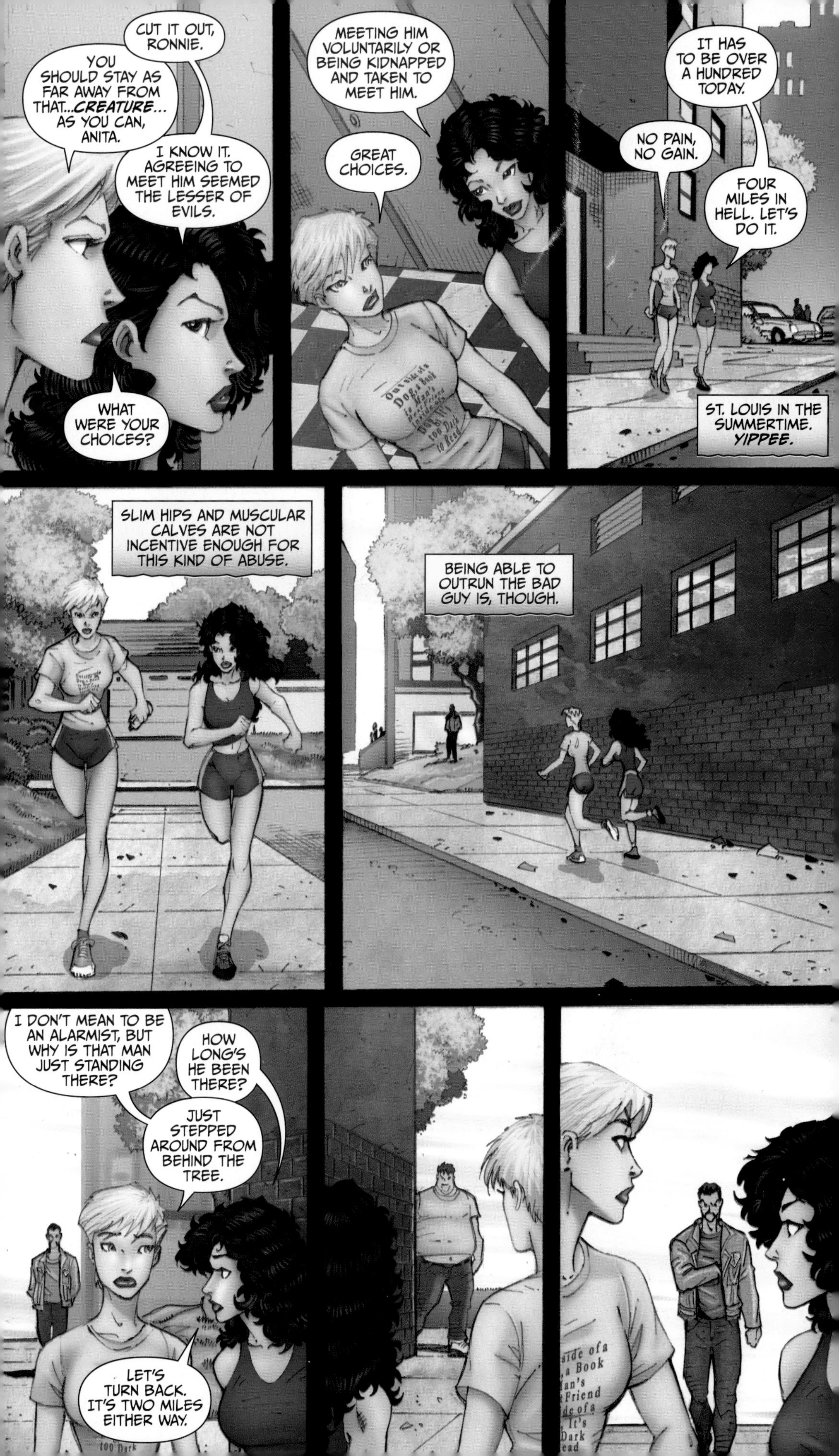
YOU SHOULD STAY AS FAR AWAY FROM THAT...CREATURE... AS YOU CAN, ANITA.
CUT IT OUT, RONNIE.
I KNOW IT. AGREEING TO MEET HIM SEEMED THE LESSER OF EVILS.
WHAT WERE YOUR CHOICES?
MEETING HIM VOLUNTARILY OR BEING KIDNAPPED AND TAKEN TO MEET HIM.
GREAT CHOICES.
IT HAS TO BE OVER A HUNDRED TODAY.
NO PAIN, NO GAIN.
FOUR MILES IN HELL. LET'S DO IT.
ST. LOUIS IN THE SUMMERTIME. YIPPEE.
SLIM HIPS AND MUSCULAR CALVES ARE NOT INCENTIVE ENOUGH FOR THIS KIND OF ABUSE.
BEING ABLE TO OUTRUN THE BAD GUY IS, THOUGH.
I DON'T MEAN TO BE AN ALARMIST, BUT WHY IS THAT MAN JUST STANDING THERE?
HOW LONG'S HE BEEN THERE?
JUST STEPPED AROUND FROM BEHIND THE TREE.
LET'S TURN BACK. IT'S TWO MILES EITHER WAY.

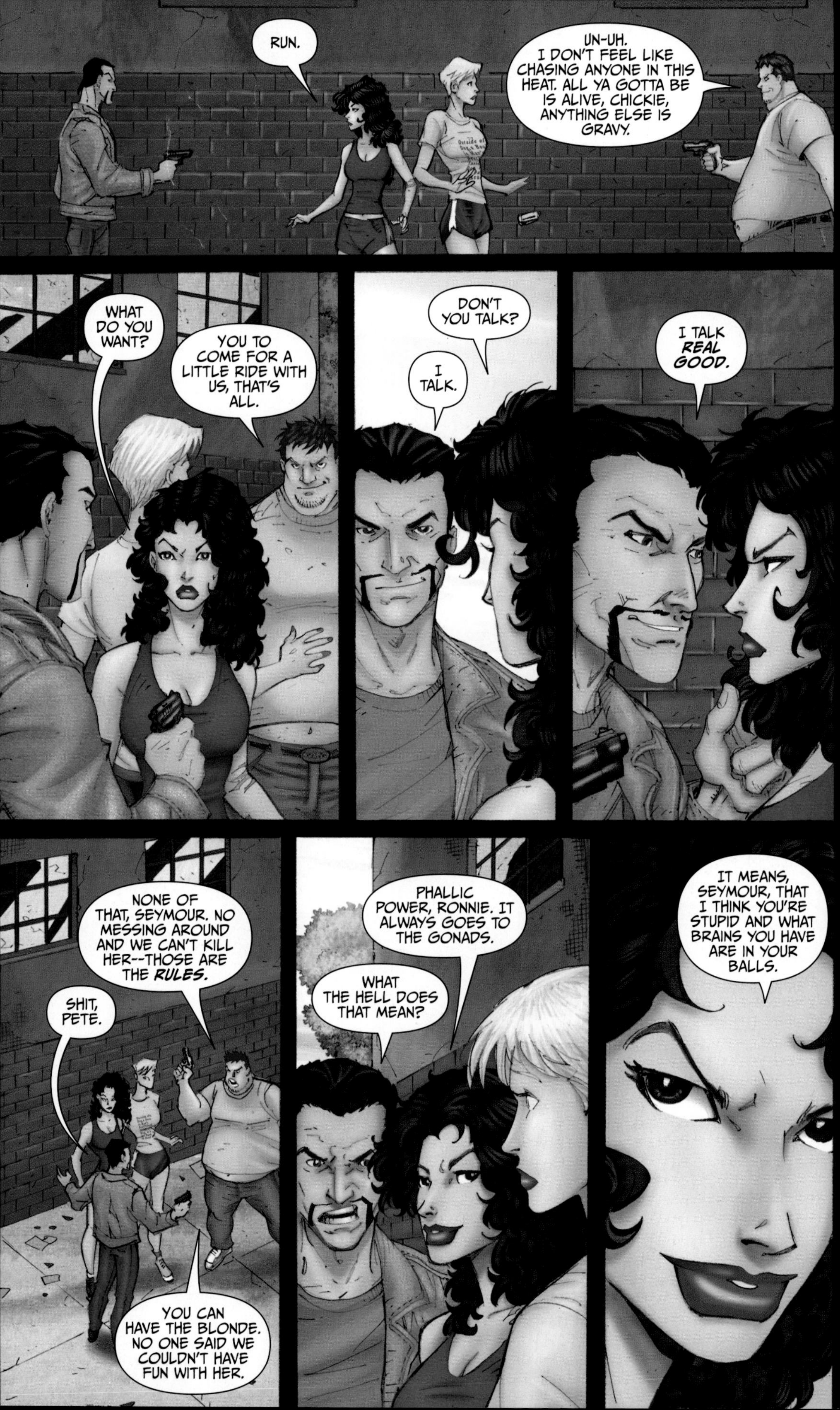
RUN.
UN-UH. I DON'T FEEL LIKE CHASING ANYONE IN THIS HEAT. ALL YA GOTTA BE IS ALIVE, CHICKIE, ANYTHING ELSE IS GRAVY.
WHAT DO YOU WANT?
YOU TO COME FOR A LITTLE RIDE WITH US, THAT'S ALL.
DON'T YOU TALK?
I TALK.
I TALK *REAL GOOD.*
NONE OF THAT, SEYMOUR. NO MESSING AROUND AND WE CAN'T KILL HER--THOSE ARE THE *RULES.*
SHIT, PETE.
YOU CAN HAVE THE BLONDE. NO ONE SAID WE COULDN'T HAVE FUN WITH HER.
PHALLIC POWER, RONNIE. IT ALWAYS GOES TO THE GONADS.
WHAT THE HELL DOES THAT MEAN?
IT MEANS, SEYMOUR, THAT I THINK YOU'RE STUPID AND WHAT BRAINS YOU HAVE ARE IN YOUR BALLS.

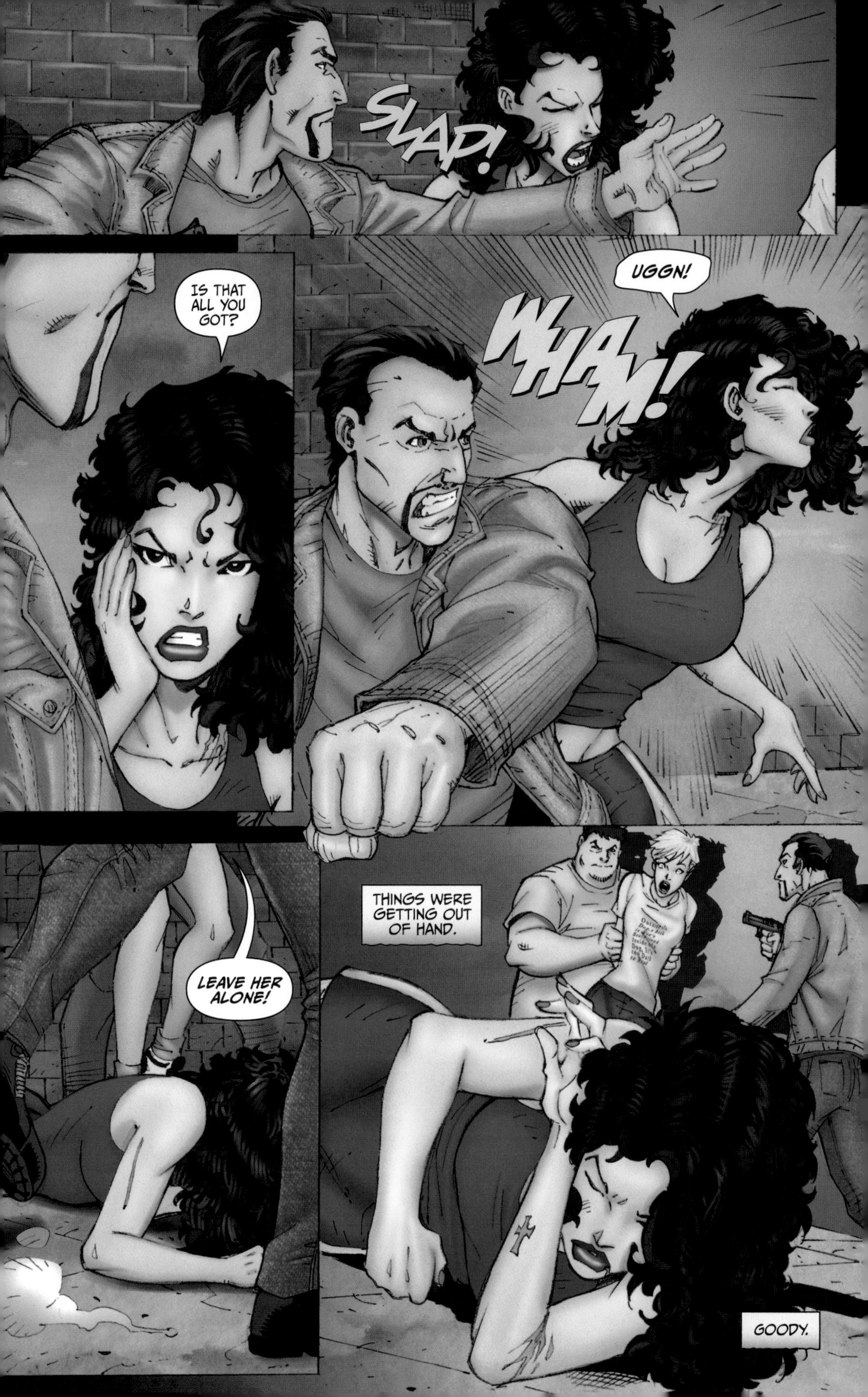
SLAP!
IS THAT ALL YOU GOT?
UGGN!
WHAM!
LEAVE HER ALONE!
THINGS WERE GETTING OUT OF HAND.
GOODY.

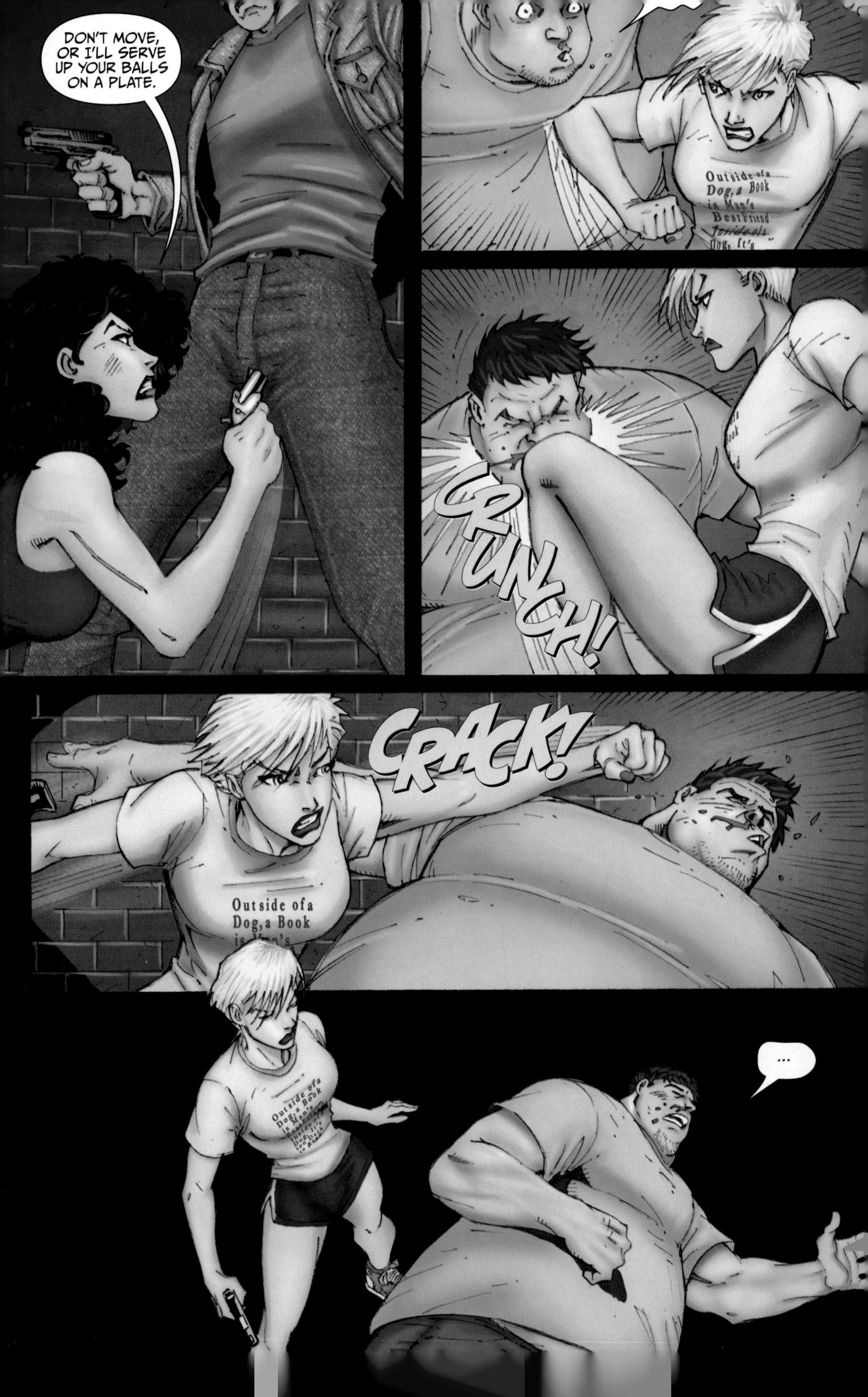
DON'T MOVE, OR I'LL SERVE UP YOUR BALLS ON A PLATE.
Outside of a Dog, a Book is Man's Best Friend
CRUNCH!
CRACK!
Outside of a Dog, a Book
...

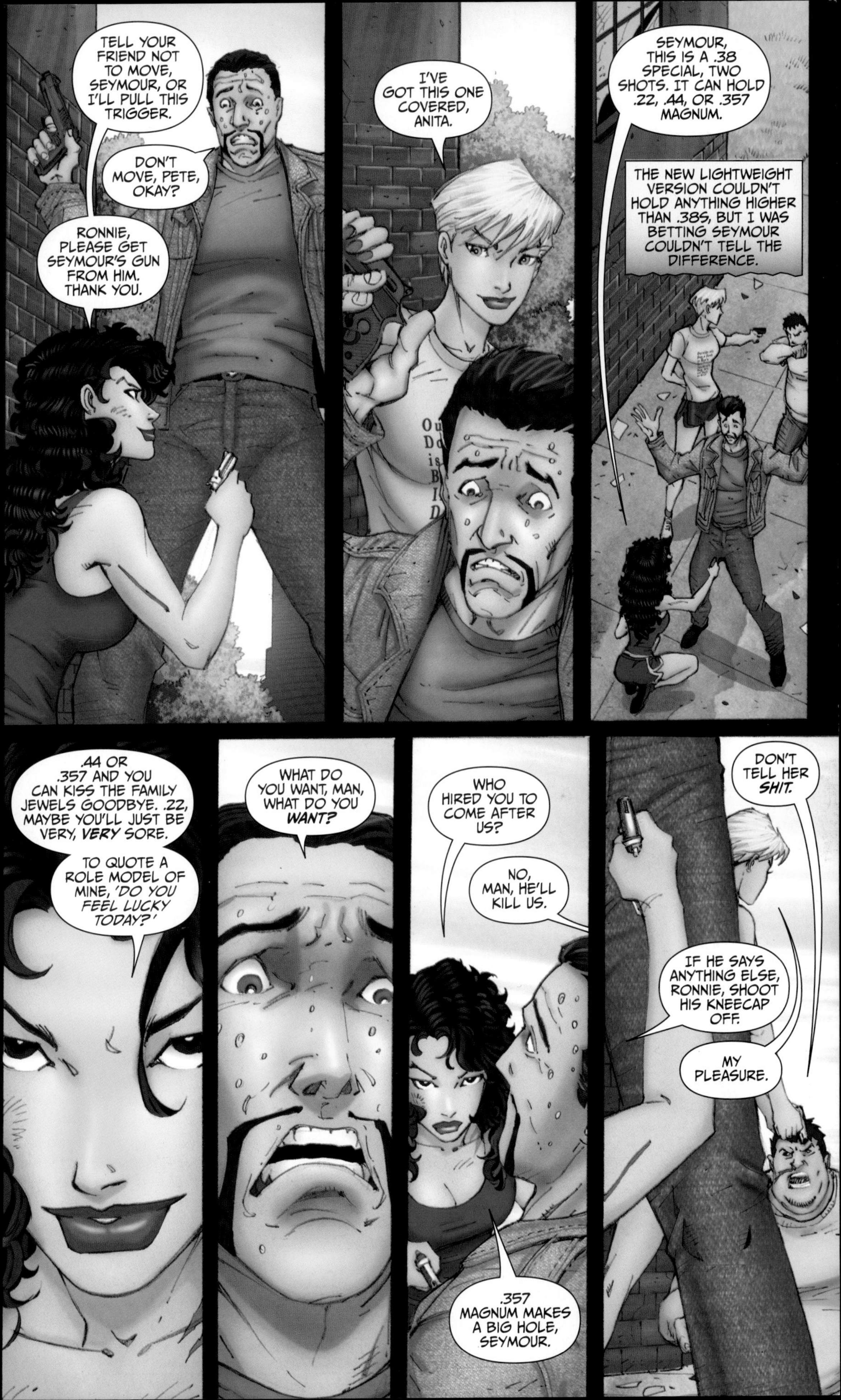

TELL YOUR FRIEND NOT TO MOVE, SEYMOUR, OR I'LL PULL THIS TRIGGER.
DON'T MOVE, PETE, OKAY?
RONNIE, PLEASE GET SEYMOUR'S GUN FROM HIM. THANK YOU.
I'VE GOT THIS ONE COVERED, ANITA.
SEYMOUR, THIS IS A .38 SPECIAL, TWO SHOTS. IT CAN HOLD .22, .44, OR .357 MAGNUM.
THE NEW LIGHTWEIGHT VERSION COULDN'T HOLD ANYTHING HIGHER THAN .38S, BUT I WAS BETTING SEYMOUR COULDN'T TELL THE DIFFERENCE.
.44 OR .357 AND YOU CAN KISS THE FAMILY JEWELS GOODBYE. .22, MAYBE YOU'LL JUST BE VERY, *VERY* SORE.
TO QUOTE A ROLE MODEL OF MINE, 'DO YOU FEEL LUCKY TODAY?'
WHAT DO YOU WANT, MAN, WHAT DO YOU *WANT?*
WHO HIRED YOU TO COME AFTER US?
NO, MAN, HE'LL KILL US.
.357 MAGNUM MAKES A BIG HOLE, SEYMOUR.
DON'T TELL HER *SHIT.*
IF HE SAYS ANYTHING ELSE, RONNIE, SHOOT HIS KNEECAP OFF.
MY PLEASURE.

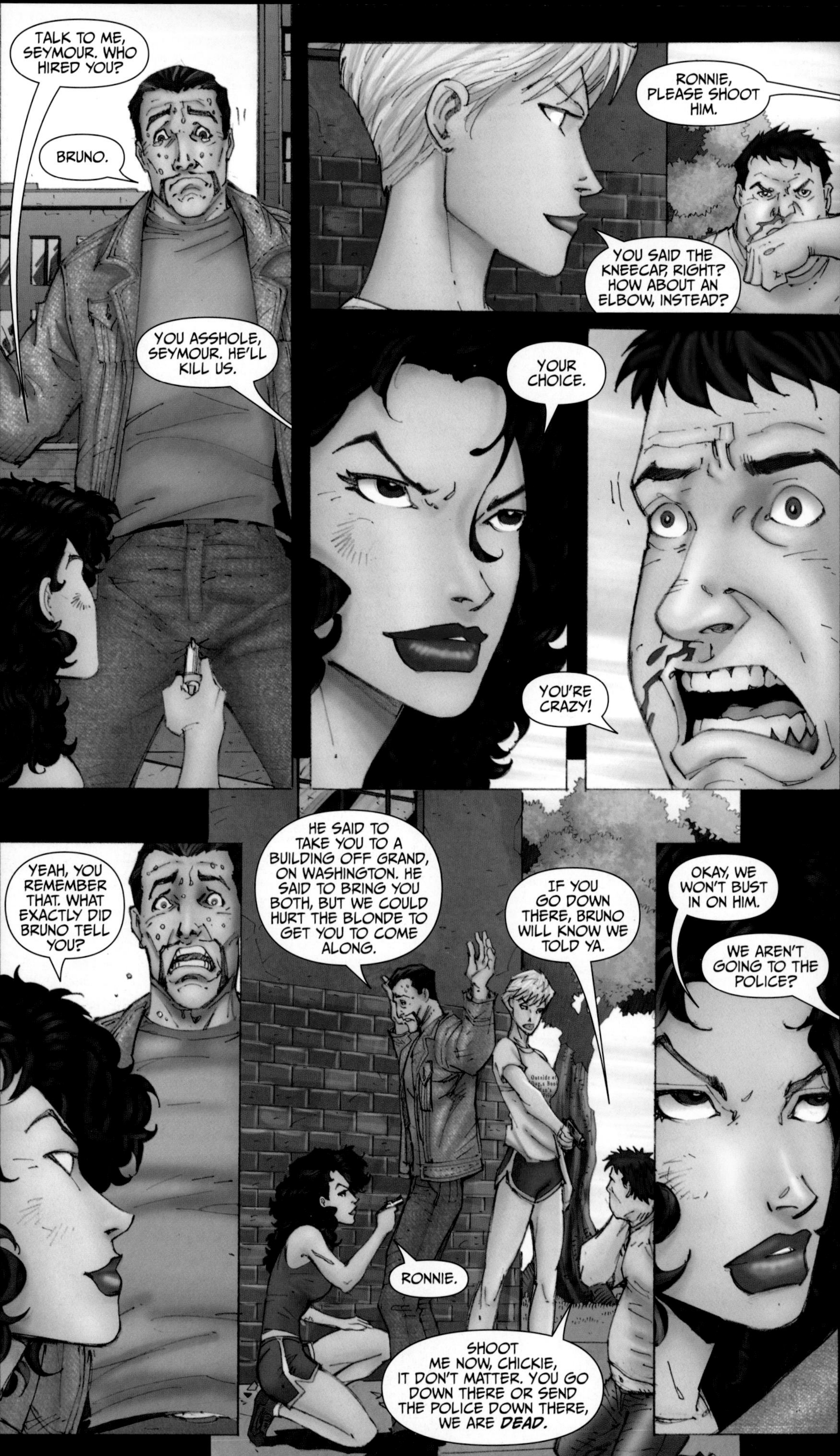
TALK TO ME, SEYMOUR. WHO HIRED YOU?
BRUNO.
YOU ASSHOLE, SEYMOUR. HE'LL KILL US.
RONNIE, PLEASE SHOOT HIM.
YOU SAID THE KNEECAP, RIGHT? HOW ABOUT AN ELBOW, INSTEAD?
YOUR CHOICE.
YOU'RE CRAZY!
YEAH, YOU REMEMBER THAT. WHAT EXACTLY DID BRUNO TELL YOU?
HE SAID TO TAKE YOU TO A BUILDING OFF GRAND, ON WASHINGTON. HE SAID TO BRING YOU BOTH, BUT WE COULD HURT THE BLONDE TO GET YOU TO COME ALONG.
IF YOU GO DOWN THERE, BRUNO WILL KNOW WE TOLD YA.
RONNIE.
SHOOT ME NOW, CHICKIE, IT DON'T MATTER. YOU GO DOWN THERE OR SEND THE POLICE DOWN THERE, WE ARE ***DEAD.***
OKAY, WE WON'T BUST IN ON HIM.
WE AREN'T GOING TO THE POLICE?

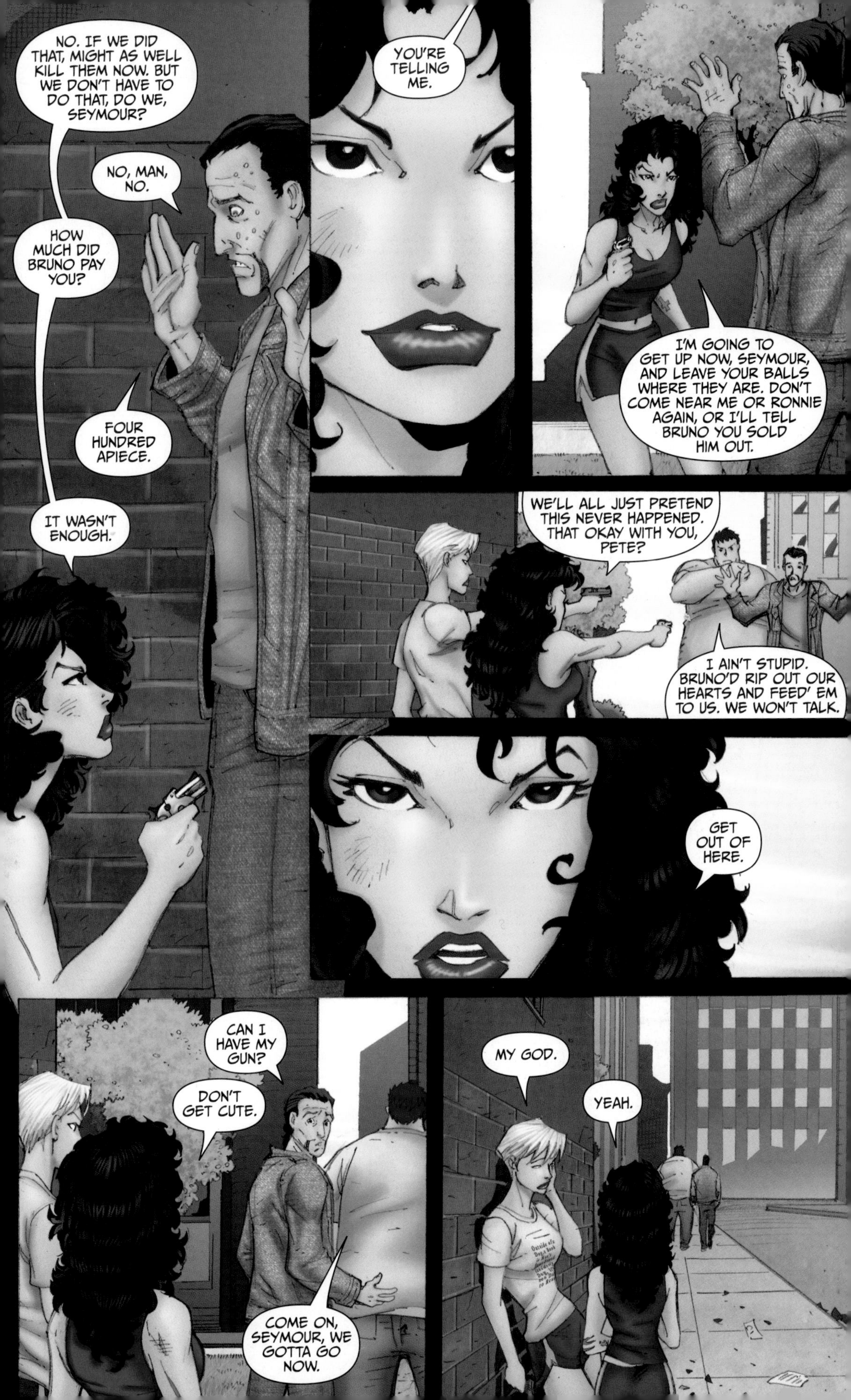
NO. IF WE DID THAT, MIGHT AS WELL KILL THEM NOW. BUT WE DON'T HAVE TO DO THAT, DO WE, SEYMOUR?
NO, MAN, NO.
HOW MUCH DID BRUNO PAY YOU?
FOUR HUNDRED APIECE.
IT WASN'T ENOUGH.
YOU'RE TELLING ME.
I'M GOING TO GET UP NOW, SEYMOUR, AND LEAVE YOUR BALLS WHERE THEY ARE. DON'T COME NEAR ME OR RONNIE AGAIN, OR I'LL TELL BRUNO YOU SOLD HIM OUT.
WE'LL ALL JUST PRETEND THIS NEVER HAPPENED. THAT OKAY WITH YOU, PETE?
I AIN'T STUPID. BRUNO'D RIP OUT OUR HEARTS AND FEED' EM TO US. WE WON'T TALK.
GET OUT OF HERE.
CAN I HAVE MY GUN?
DON'T GET CUTE.
COME ON, SEYMOUR, WE GOTTA GO NOW.
MY GOD.
YEAH.

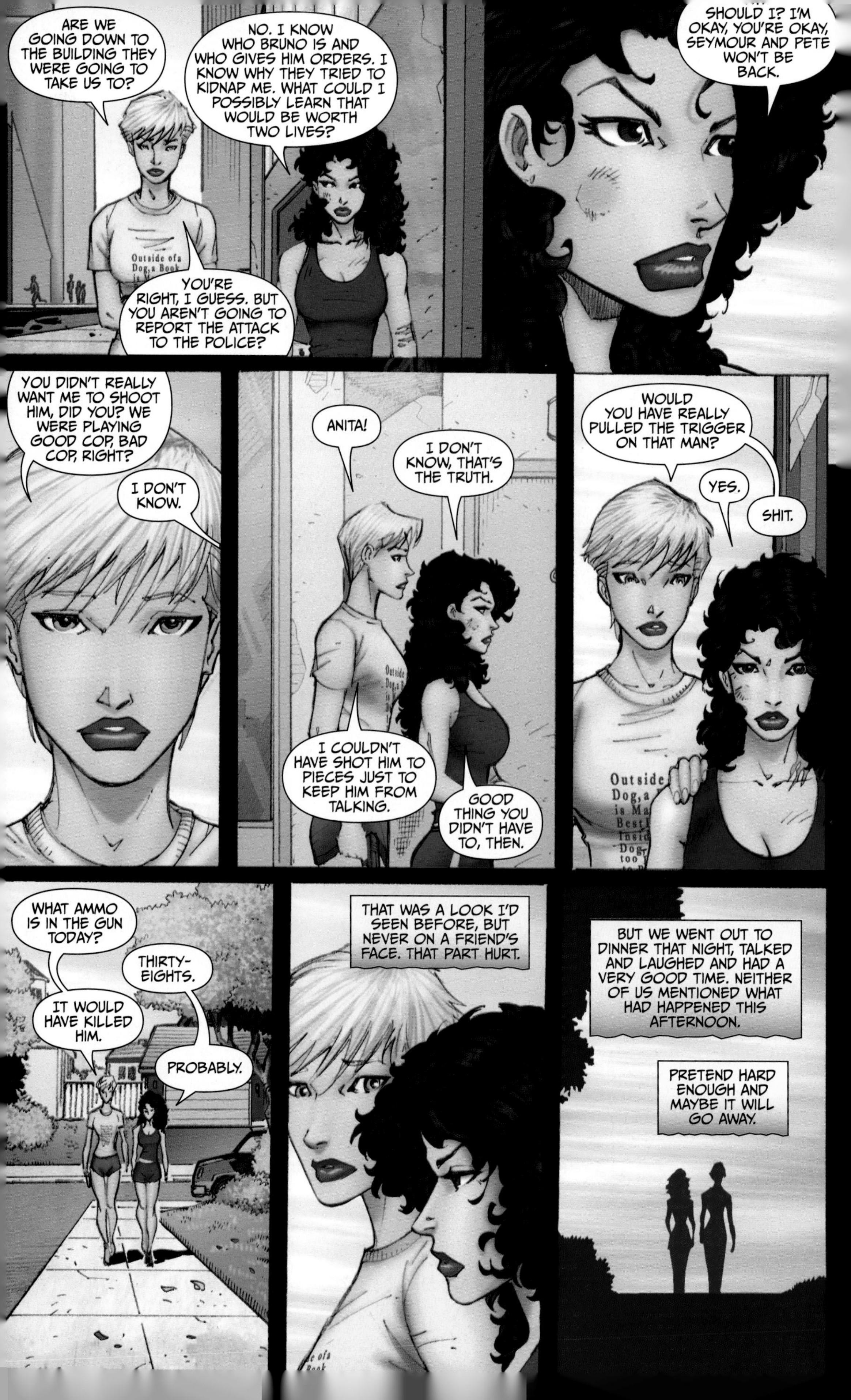
ARE WE GOING DOWN TO THE BUILDING THEY WERE GOING TO TAKE US TO?
NO. I KNOW WHO BRUNO IS AND WHO GIVES HIM ORDERS. I KNOW WHY THEY TRIED TO KIDNAP ME. WHAT COULD I POSSIBLY LEARN THAT WOULD BE WORTH TWO LIVES?
YOU'RE RIGHT, I GUESS. BUT YOU AREN'T GOING TO REPORT THE ATTACK TO THE POLICE?
SHOULD I? I'M OKAY, YOU'RE OKAY, SEYMOUR AND PETE WON'T BE BACK.
YOU DIDN'T REALLY WANT ME TO SHOOT HIM, DID YOU? WE WERE PLAYING GOOD COP, BAD COP, RIGHT?
I DON'T KNOW.
ANITA!
I DON'T KNOW, THAT'S THE TRUTH.
I COULDN'T HAVE SHOT HIM TO PIECES JUST TO KEEP HIM FROM TALKING.
GOOD THING YOU DIDN'T HAVE TO, THEN.
WOULD YOU HAVE REALLY PULLED THE TRIGGER ON THAT MAN?
YES.
SHIT.
WHAT AMMO IS IN THE GUN TODAY?
THIRTY-EIGHTS.
IT WOULD HAVE KILLED HIM.
PROBABLY.
THAT WAS A LOOK I'D SEEN BEFORE, BUT NEVER ON A FRIEND'S FACE. THAT PART HURT.
BUT WE WENT OUT TO DINNER THAT NIGHT, TALKED AND LAUGHED AND HAD A VERY GOOD TIME. NEITHER OF US MENTIONED WHAT HAD HAPPENED THIS AFTERNOON.
PRETEND HARD ENOUGH AND MAYBE IT WILL GO AWAY.

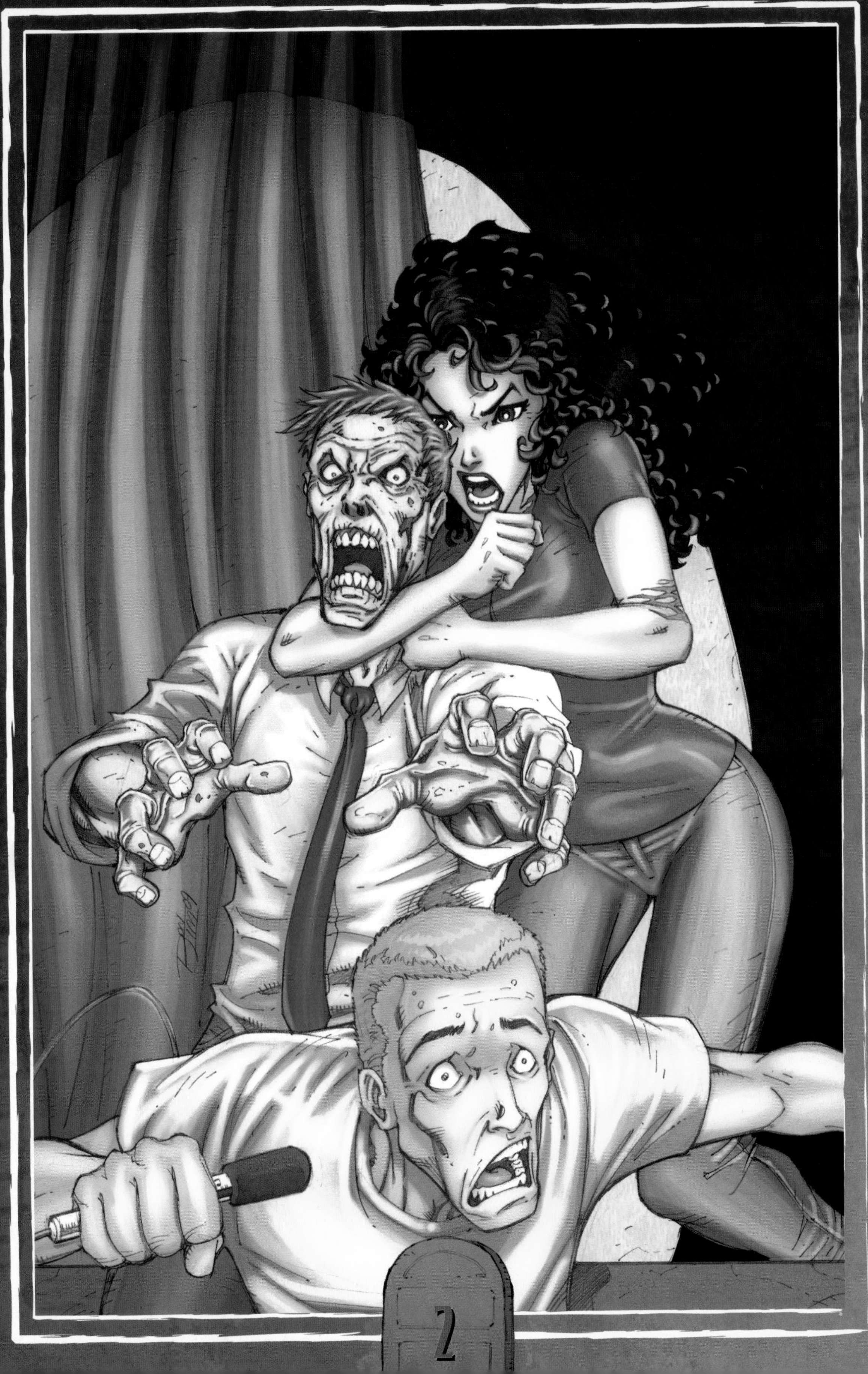
2

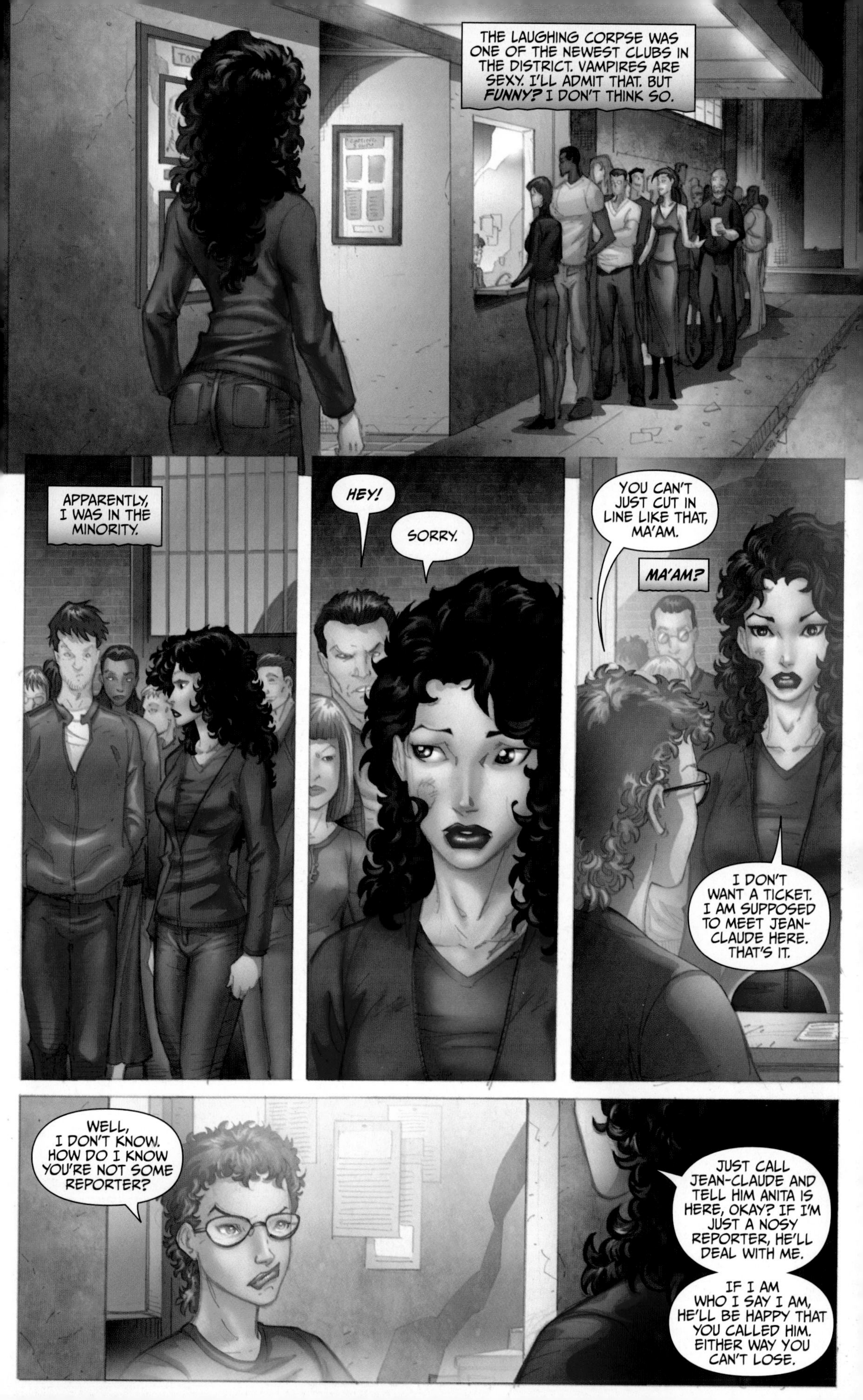
THE LAUGHING CORPSE WAS ONE OF THE NEWEST CLUBS IN THE DISTRICT. VAMPIRES ARE SEXY. I'LL ADMIT THAT. BUT *FUNNY?* I DON'T THINK SO.
APPARENTLY, I WAS IN THE MINORITY.
HEY!
SORRY.
YOU CAN'T JUST CUT IN LINE LIKE THAT, MA'AM.
MA'AM?
I DON'T WANT A TICKET. I AM SUPPOSED TO MEET JEAN-CLAUDE HERE. THAT'S IT.
WELL, I DON'T KNOW. HOW DO I KNOW YOU'RE NOT SOME REPORTER?
JUST CALL JEAN-CLAUDE AND TELL HIM ANITA IS HERE, OKAY? IF I'M JUST A NOSY REPORTER, HE'LL DEAL WITH ME.
IF I AM WHO I SAY I AM, HE'LL BE HAPPY THAT YOU CALLED HIM. EITHER WAY YOU CAN'T LOSE.

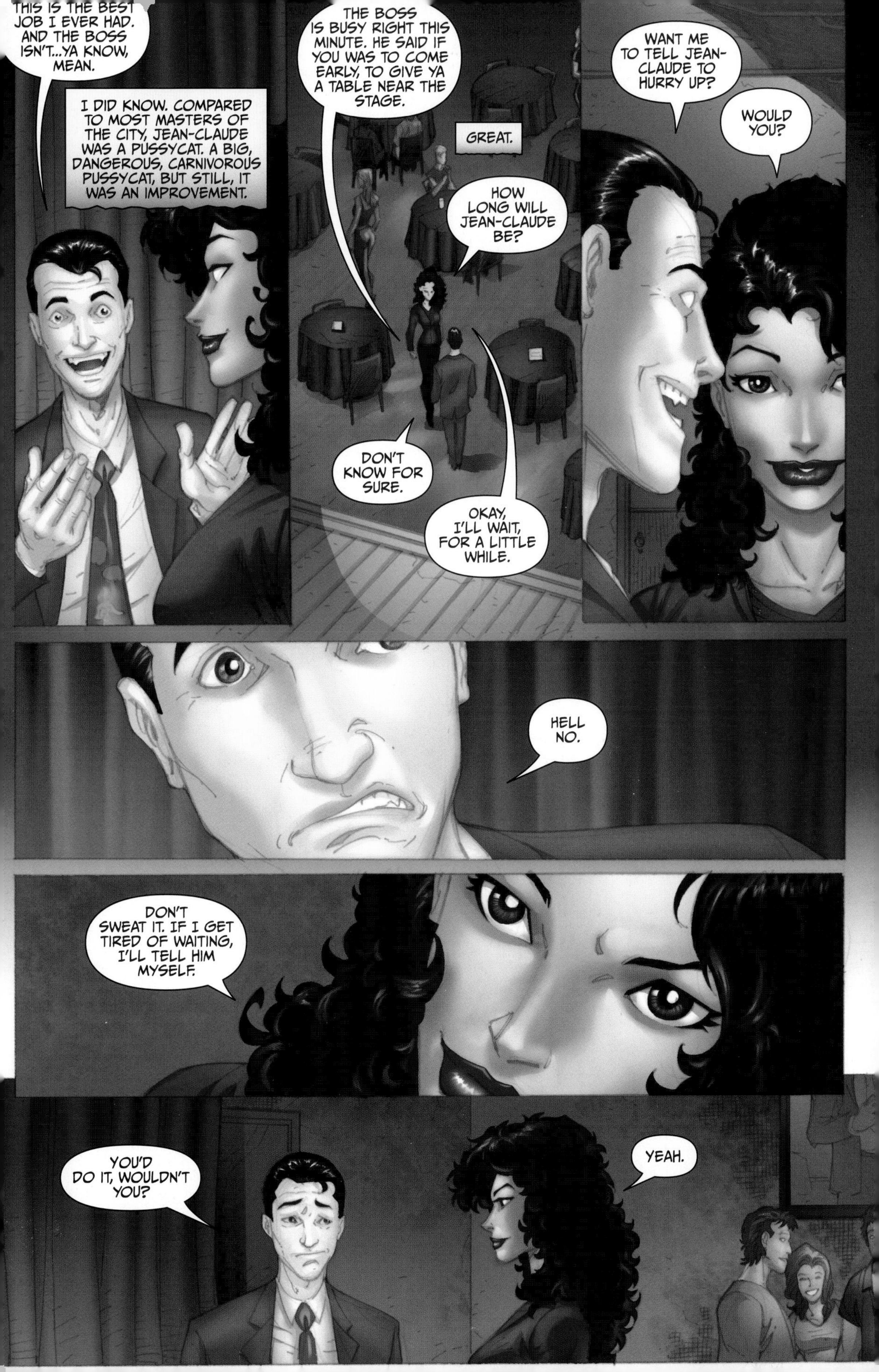
THIS IS THE BEST JOB I EVER HAD. AND THE BOSS ISN'T...YA KNOW, MEAN.
I DID KNOW. COMPARED TO MOST MASTERS OF THE CITY, JEAN-CLAUDE WAS A PUSSYCAT. A BIG, DANGEROUS, CARNIVOROUS PUSSYCAT, BUT STILL, IT WAS AN IMPROVEMENT.
THE BOSS IS BUSY RIGHT THIS MINUTE. HE SAID IF YOU WAS TO COME EARLY, TO GIVE YA A TABLE NEAR THE STAGE.
GREAT.
HOW LONG WILL JEAN-CLAUDE BE?
DON'T KNOW FOR SURE.
OKAY, I'LL WAIT, FOR A LITTLE WHILE.
WANT ME TO TELL JEAN-CLAUDE TO HURRY UP?
WOULD YOU?
HELL NO.
DON'T SWEAT IT. IF I GET TIRED OF WAITING, I'LL TELL HIM MYSELF.
YOU'D DO IT, WOULDN'T YOU?
YEAH.

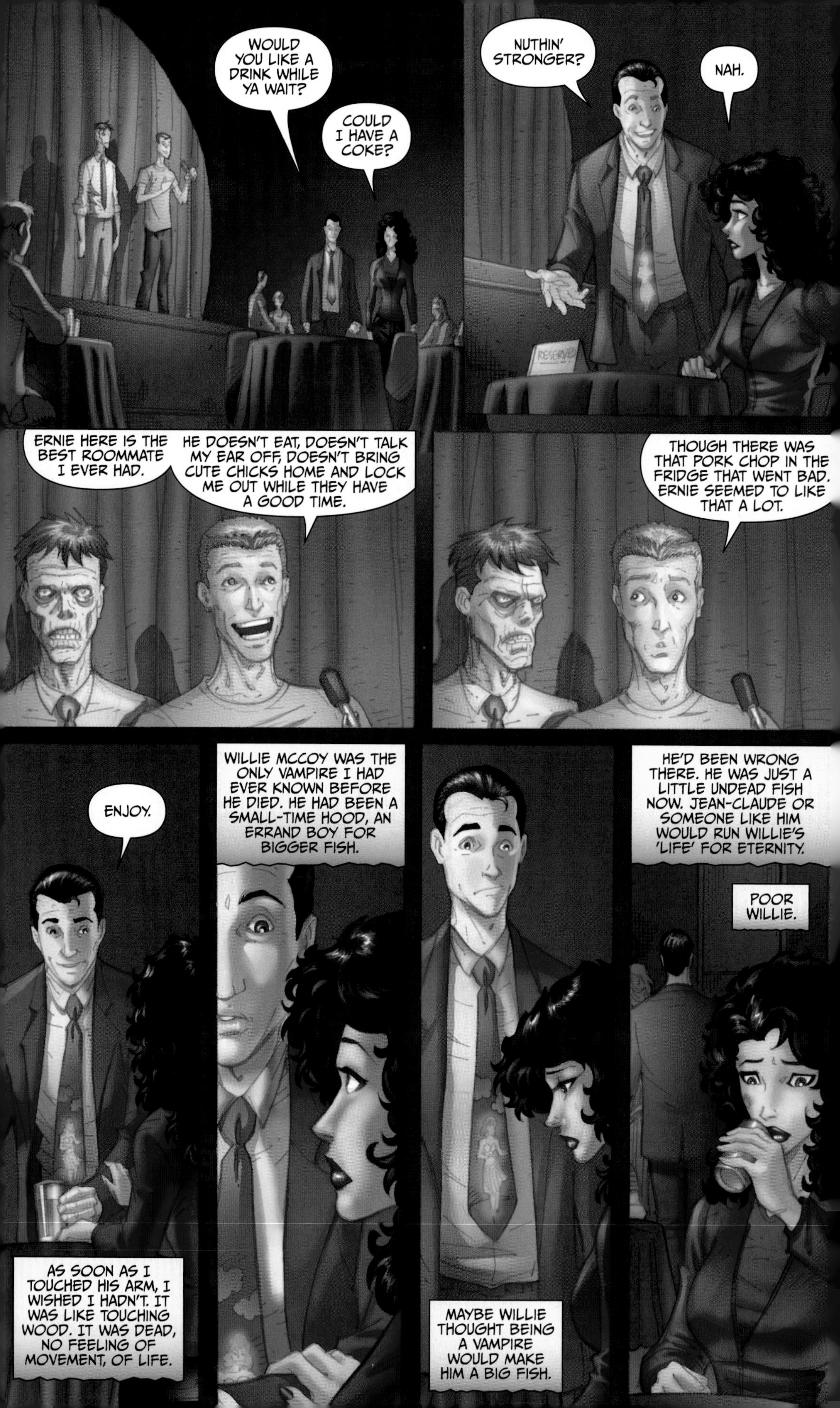

WOULD YOU LIKE A DRINK WHILE YA WAIT?
COULD I HAVE A COKE?
NUTHIN' STRONGER?
NAH.
ERNIE HERE IS THE BEST ROOMMATE I EVER HAD.
HE DOESN'T EAT, DOESN'T TALK MY EAR OFF, DOESN'T BRING CUTE CHICKS HOME AND LOCK ME OUT WHILE THEY HAVE A GOOD TIME.
THOUGH THERE WAS THAT PORK CHOP IN THE FRIDGE THAT WENT BAD. ERNIE SEEMED TO LIKE THAT A LOT.
ENJOY.
AS SOON AS I TOUCHED HIS ARM, I WISHED I HADN'T. IT WAS LIKE TOUCHING WOOD. IT WAS DEAD, NO FEELING OF MOVEMENT, OF LIFE.
WILLIE MCCOY WAS THE ONLY VAMPIRE I HAD EVER KNOWN BEFORE HE DIED. HE HAD BEEN A SMALL-TIME HOOD, AN ERRAND BOY FOR BIGGER FISH.
MAYBE WILLIE THOUGHT BEING A VAMPIRE WOULD MAKE HIM A BIG FISH.
HE'D BEEN WRONG THERE. HE WAS JUST A LITTLE UNDEAD FISH NOW. JEAN-CLAUDE OR SOMEONE LIKE HIM WOULD RUN WILLIE'S 'LIFE' FOR ETERNITY.
POOR WILLIE.

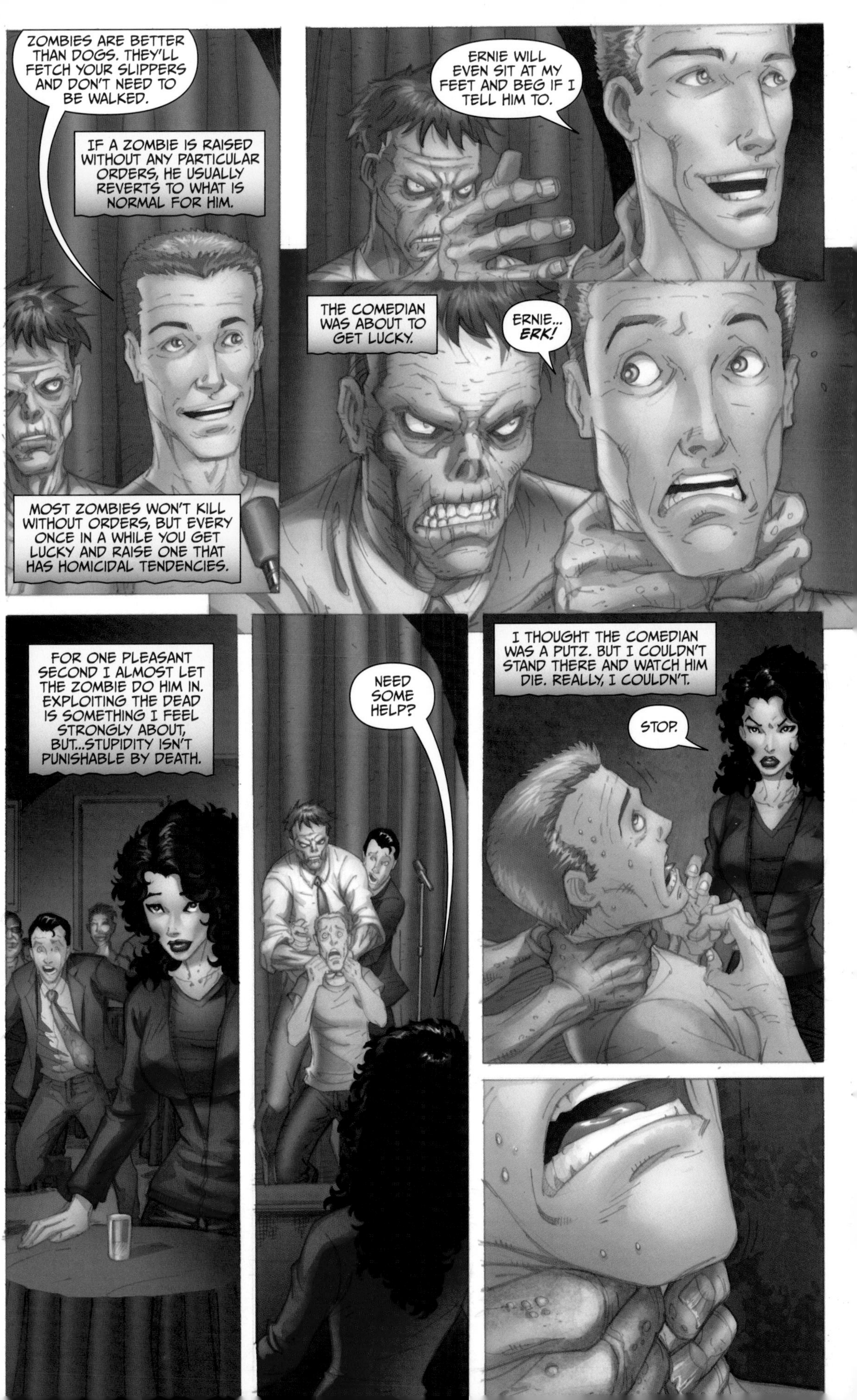
ZOMBIES ARE BETTER THAN DOGS. THEY'LL FETCH YOUR SLIPPERS AND DON'T NEED TO BE WALKED.
IF A ZOMBIE IS RAISED WITHOUT ANY PARTICULAR ORDERS, HE USUALLY REVERTS TO WHAT IS NORMAL FOR HIM.
MOST ZOMBIES WON'T KILL WITHOUT ORDERS, BUT EVERY ONCE IN A WHILE YOU GET LUCKY AND RAISE ONE THAT HAS HOMICIDAL TENDENCIES.
ERNIE WILL EVEN SIT AT MY FEET AND BEG IF I TELL HIM TO.
THE COMEDIAN WAS ABOUT TO GET LUCKY.
ERNIE... *ERK!*
FOR ONE PLEASANT SECOND I ALMOST LET THE ZOMBIE DO HIM IN. EXPLOITING THE DEAD IS SOMETHING I FEEL STRONGLY ABOUT, BUT...STUPIDITY ISN'T PUNISHABLE BY DEATH.
NEED SOME HELP?
I THOUGHT THE COMEDIAN WAS A PUTZ. BUT I COULDN'T STAND THERE AND WATCH HIM DIE. REALLY, I COULDN'T.
STOP.

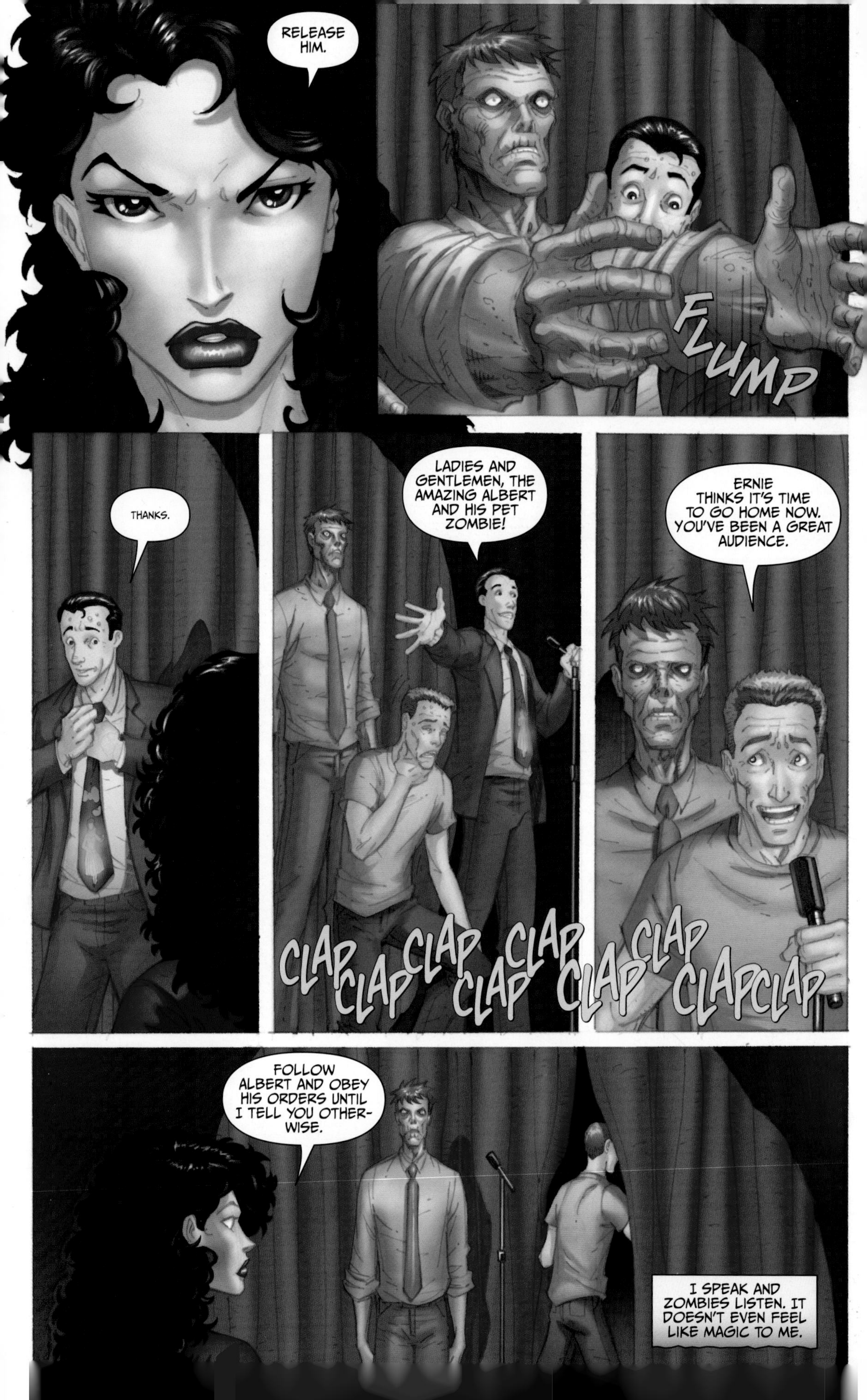
RELEASE HIM.
FLUMP
THANKS.
LADIES AND GENTLEMEN, THE AMAZING ALBERT AND HIS PET ZOMBIE!
ERNIE THINKS IT'S TIME TO GO HOME NOW. YOU'VE BEEN A GREAT AUDIENCE.
CLAP CLAP CLAP CLAP CLAP CLAP CLAP CLAP CLAPCLAP
FOLLOW ALBERT AND OBEY HIS ORDERS UNTIL I TELL YOU OTHER-WISE.
I SPEAK AND ZOMBIES LISTEN. IT DOESN'T EVEN FEEL LIKE MAGIC TO ME.

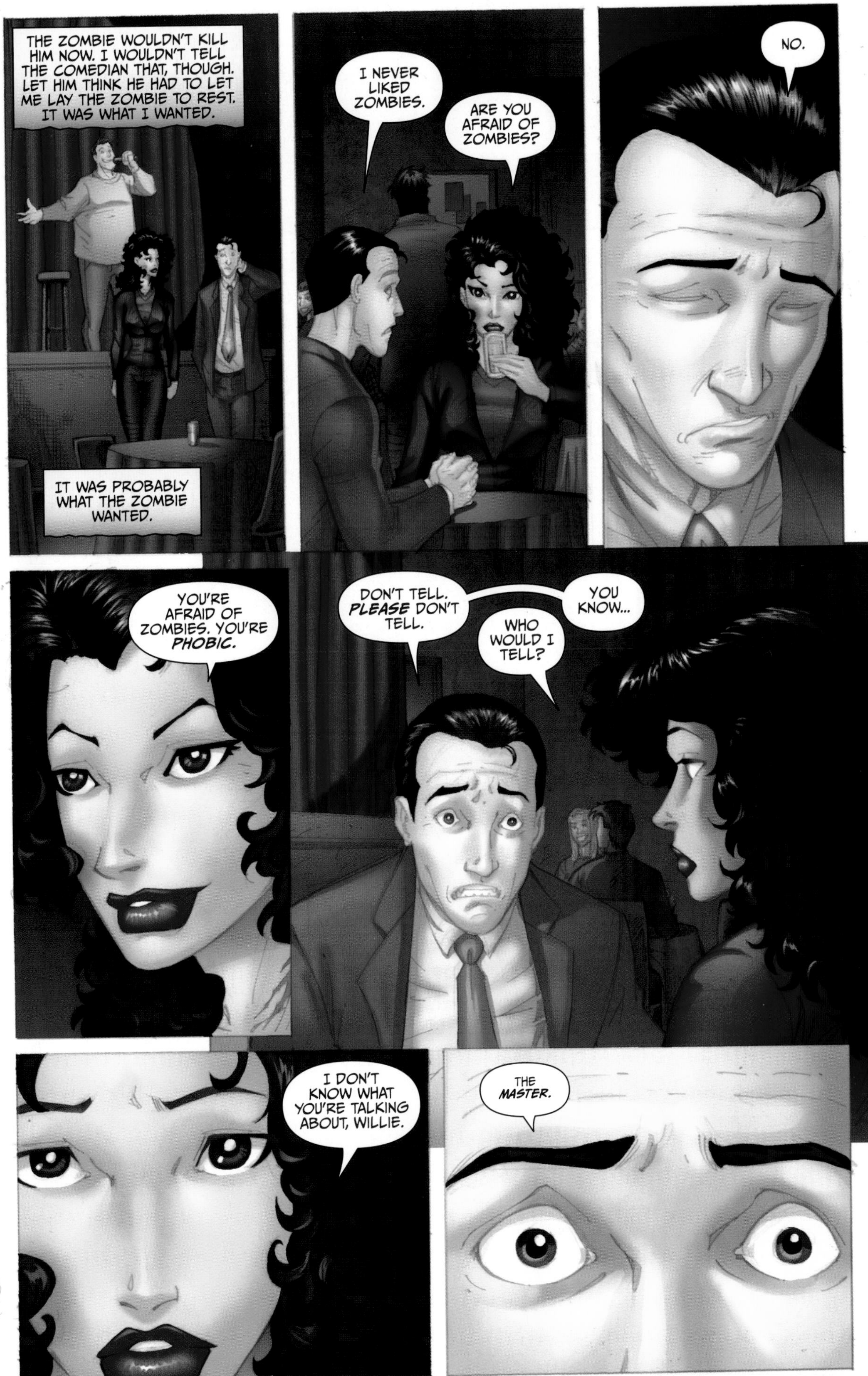
THE ZOMBIE WOULDN'T KILL HIM NOW. I WOULDN'T TELL THE COMEDIAN THAT, THOUGH. LET HIM THINK HE HAD TO LET ME LAY THE ZOMBIE TO REST. IT WAS WHAT I WANTED.
IT WAS PROBABLY WHAT THE ZOMBIE WANTED.
I NEVER LIKED ZOMBIES.
ARE YOU AFRAID OF ZOMBIES?
NO.
YOU'RE AFRAID OF ZOMBIES. YOU'RE PHOBIC.
DON'T TELL. PLEASE DON'T TELL.
WHO WOULD I TELL?
YOU KNOW...
I DON'T KNOW WHAT YOU'RE TALKING ABOUT, WILLIE.
THE MASTER.

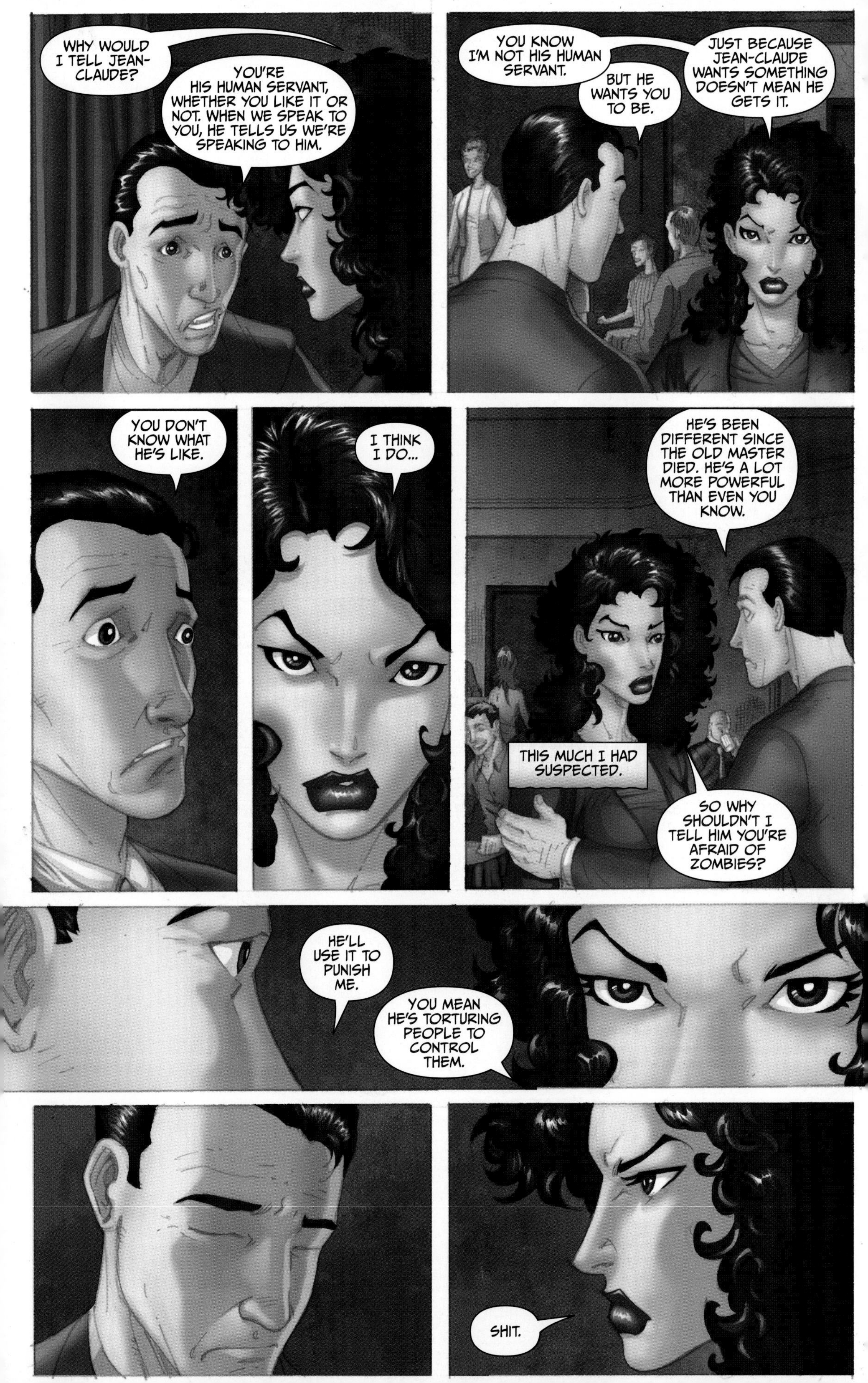
WHY WOULD I TELL JEAN-CLAUDE?
YOU'RE HIS HUMAN SERVANT, WHETHER YOU LIKE IT OR NOT. WHEN WE SPEAK TO YOU, HE TELLS US WE'RE SPEAKING TO HIM.
YOU KNOW I'M NOT HIS HUMAN SERVANT.
BUT HE WANTS YOU TO BE.
JUST BECAUSE JEAN-CLAUDE WANTS SOMETHING DOESN'T MEAN HE GETS IT.
YOU DON'T KNOW WHAT HE'S LIKE.
I THINK I DO...
HE'S BEEN DIFFERENT SINCE THE OLD MASTER DIED. HE'S A LOT MORE POWERFUL THAN EVEN YOU KNOW.
THIS MUCH I HAD SUSPECTED.
SO WHY SHOULDN'T I TELL HIM YOU'RE AFRAID OF ZOMBIES?
HE'LL USE IT TO PUNISH ME.
YOU MEAN HE'S TORTURING PEOPLE TO CONTROL THEM.
SHIT.

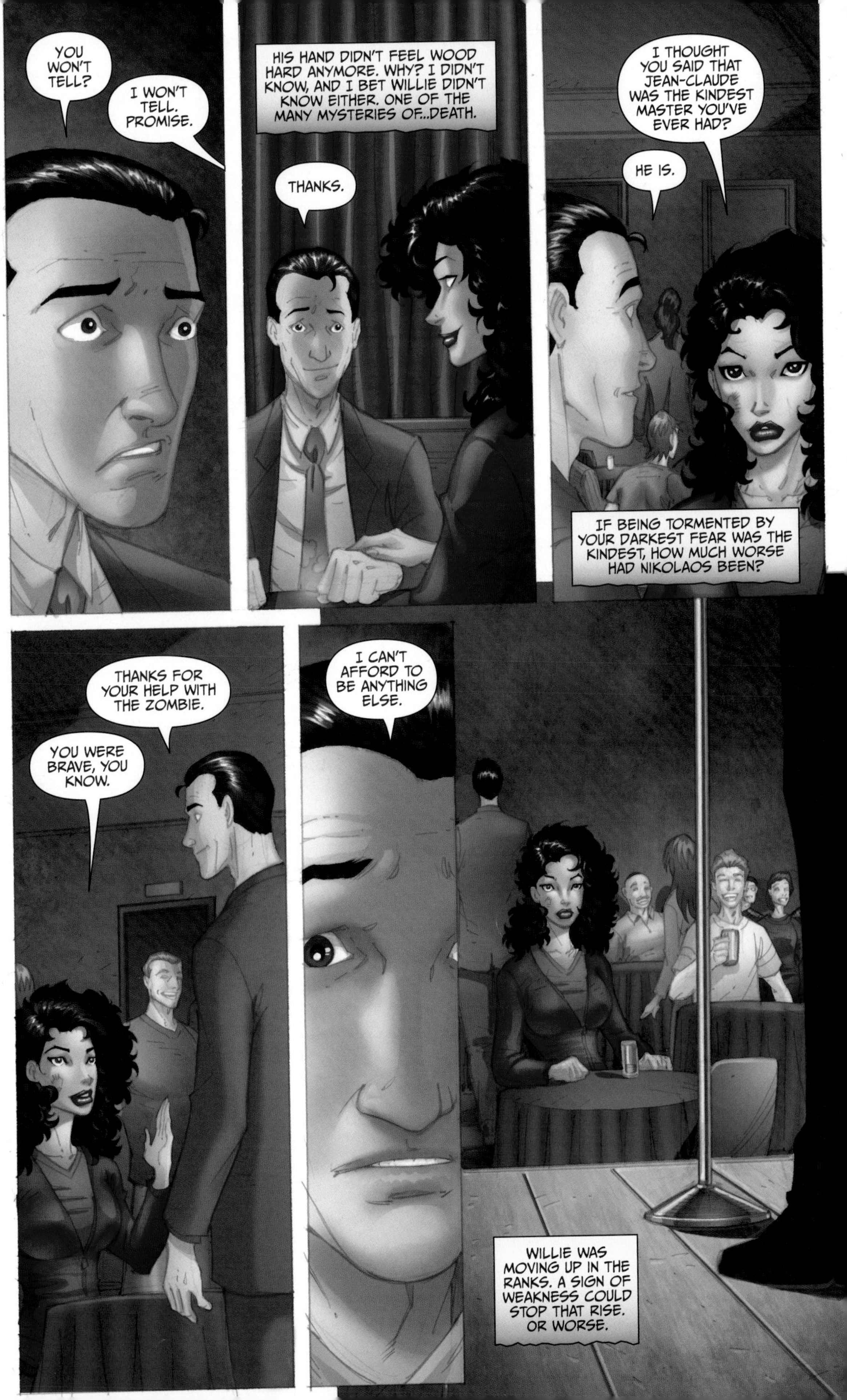
YOU WON'T TELL?
I WON'T TELL. PROMISE.
HIS HAND DIDN'T FEEL WOOD HARD ANYMORE. WHY? I DIDN'T KNOW, AND I BET WILLIE DIDN'T KNOW EITHER. ONE OF THE MANY MYSTERIES OF...DEATH.
THANKS.
I THOUGHT YOU SAID THAT JEAN-CLAUDE WAS THE KINDEST MASTER YOU'VE EVER HAD?
HE IS.
IF BEING TORMENTED BY YOUR DARKEST FEAR WAS THE KINDEST, HOW MUCH WORSE HAD NIKOLAOS BEEN?
THANKS FOR YOUR HELP WITH THE ZOMBIE.
YOU WERE BRAVE, YOU KNOW.
I CAN'T AFFORD TO BE ANYTHING ELSE.
WILLIE WAS MOVING UP IN THE RANKS. A SIGN OF WEAKNESS COULD STOP THAT RISE. OR WORSE.

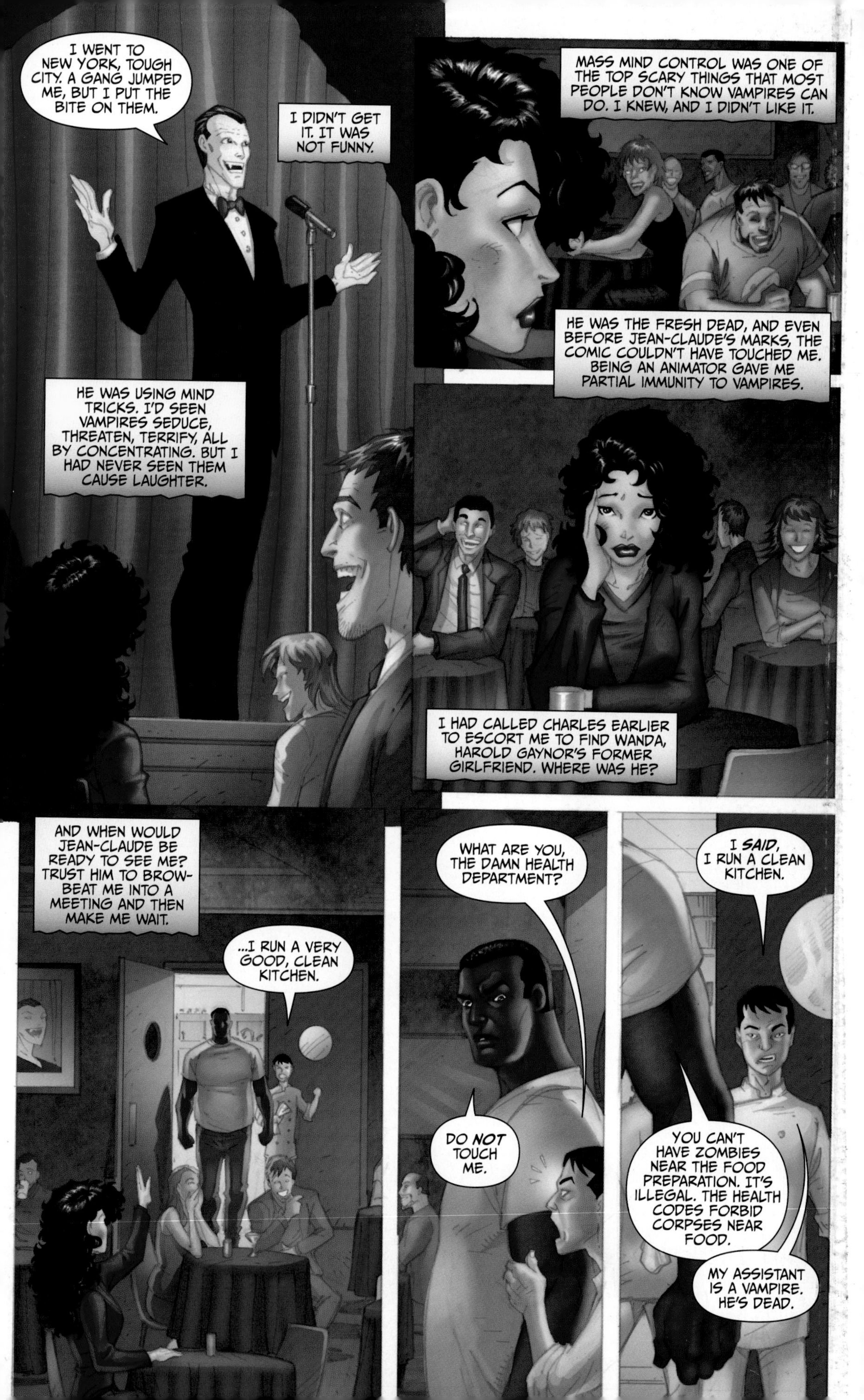

I WENT TO NEW YORK, TOUGH CITY. A GANG JUMPED ME, BUT I PUT THE BITE ON THEM.
I DIDN'T GET IT. IT WAS NOT FUNNY.
HE WAS USING MIND TRICKS. I'D SEEN VAMPIRES SEDUCE, THREATEN, TERRIFY, ALL BY CONCENTRATING. BUT I HAD NEVER SEEN THEM CAUSE LAUGHTER.
MASS MIND CONTROL WAS ONE OF THE TOP SCARY THINGS THAT MOST PEOPLE DON'T KNOW VAMPIRES CAN DO. I KNEW, AND I DIDN'T LIKE IT.
HE WAS THE FRESH DEAD, AND EVEN BEFORE JEAN-CLAUDE'S MARKS, THE COMIC COULDN'T HAVE TOUCHED ME. BEING AN ANIMATOR GAVE ME PARTIAL IMMUNITY TO VAMPIRES.
I HAD CALLED CHARLES EARLIER TO ESCORT ME TO FIND WANDA, HAROLD GAYNOR'S FORMER GIRLFRIEND. WHERE WAS HE?
AND WHEN WOULD JEAN-CLAUDE BE READY TO SEE ME? TRUST HIM TO BROW-BEAT ME INTO A MEETING AND THEN MAKE ME WAIT.
...I RUN A VERY GOOD, CLEAN KITCHEN.
WHAT ARE YOU, THE DAMN HEALTH DEPARTMENT?
DO *NOT* TOUCH ME.
I *SAID*, I RUN A CLEAN KITCHEN.
YOU CAN'T HAVE ZOMBIES NEAR THE FOOD PREPARATION. IT'S ILLEGAL. THE HEALTH CODES FORBID CORPSES NEAR FOOD.
MY ASSISTANT IS A VAMPIRE. HE'S DEAD.

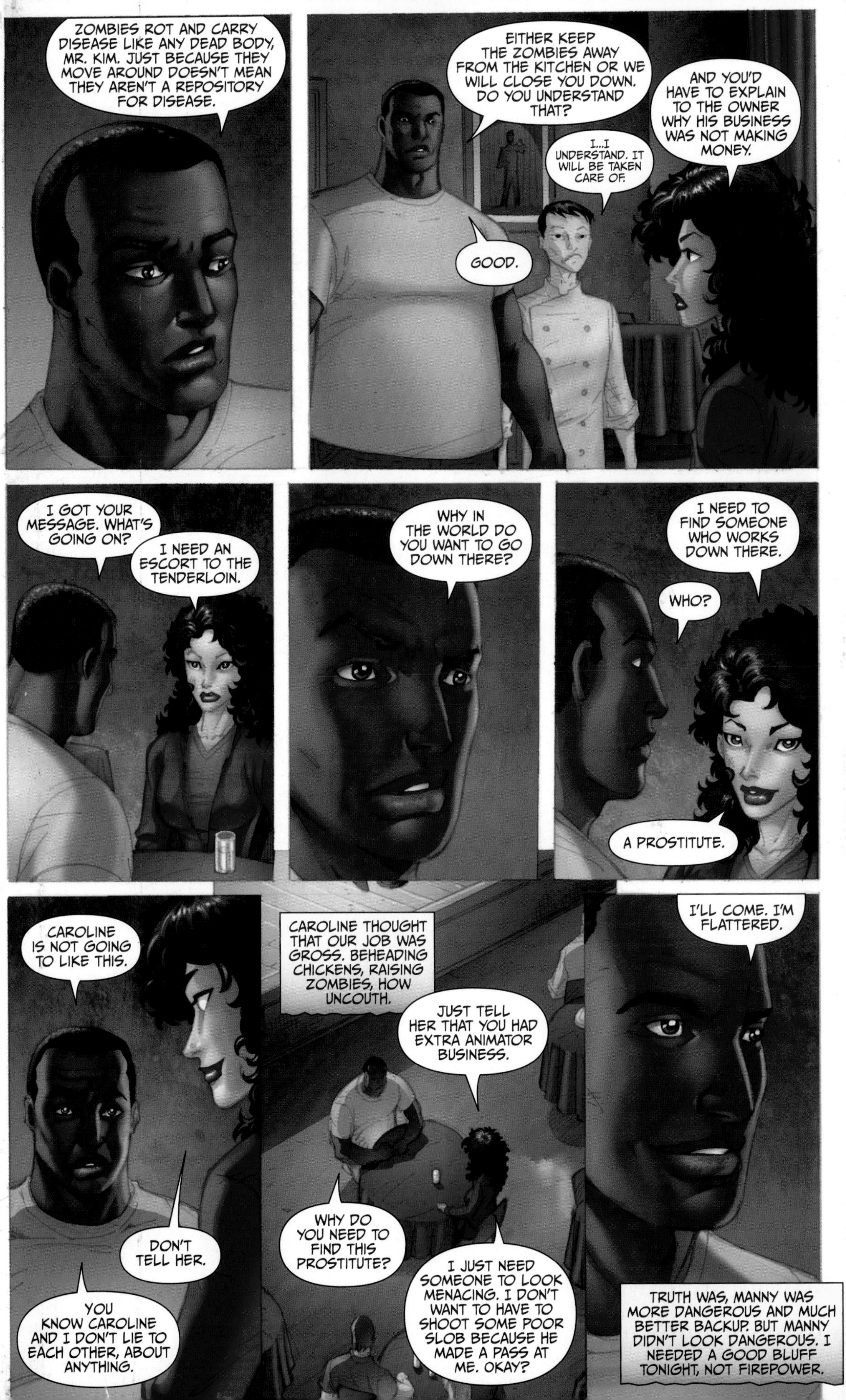
ZOMBIES ROT AND CARRY DISEASE LIKE ANY DEAD BODY, MR. KIM. JUST BECAUSE THEY MOVE AROUND DOESN'T MEAN THEY AREN'T A REPOSITORY FOR DISEASE.
EITHER KEEP THE ZOMBIES AWAY FROM THE KITCHEN OR WE WILL CLOSE YOU DOWN. DO YOU UNDERSTAND THAT?
AND YOU'D HAVE TO EXPLAIN TO THE OWNER WHY HIS BUSINESS WAS NOT MAKING MONEY.
I...I UNDERSTAND. IT WILL BE TAKEN CARE OF.
GOOD.
I GOT YOUR MESSAGE. WHAT'S GOING ON?
I NEED AN ESCORT TO THE TENDERLOIN.
WHY IN THE WORLD DO YOU WANT TO GO DOWN THERE?
I NEED TO FIND SOMEONE WHO WORKS DOWN THERE.
WHO?
A PROSTITUTE.
CAROLINE IS NOT GOING TO LIKE THIS.
DON'T TELL HER.
YOU KNOW CAROLINE AND I DON'T LIE TO EACH OTHER, ABOUT ANYTHING.
CAROLINE THOUGHT THAT OUR JOB WAS GROSS. BEHEADING CHICKENS, RAISING ZOMBIES, HOW UNCOUTH.
JUST TELL HER THAT YOU HAD EXTRA ANIMATOR BUSINESS.
WHY DO YOU NEED TO FIND THIS PROSTITUTE?
I JUST NEED SOMEONE TO LOOK MENACING. I DON'T WANT TO HAVE TO SHOOT SOME POOR SLOB BECAUSE HE MADE A PASS AT ME. OKAY?
I'LL COME. I'M FLATTERED.
TRUTH WAS, MANNY WAS MORE DANGEROUS AND MUCH BETTER BACKUP. BUT MANNY DIDN'T LOOK DANGEROUS. I NEEDED A GOOD BLUFF TONIGHT, NOT FIREPOWER.

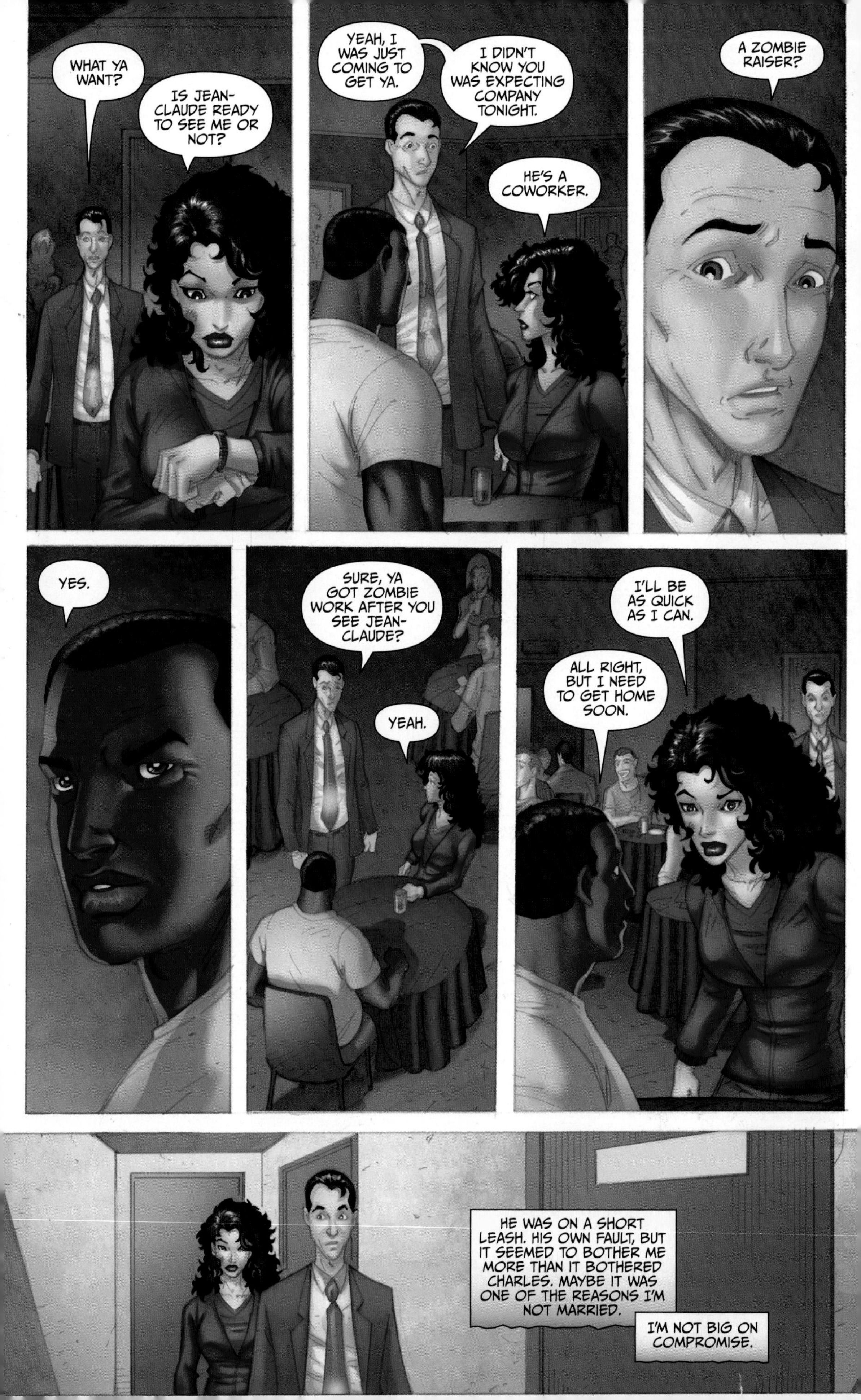
WHAT YA WANT?
IS JEAN-CLAUDE READY TO SEE ME OR NOT?
YEAH, I WAS JUST COMING TO GET YA.
I DIDN'T KNOW YOU WAS EXPECTING COMPANY TONIGHT.
HE'S A COWORKER.
A ZOMBIE RAISER?
YES.
SURE, YA GOT ZOMBIE WORK AFTER YOU SEE JEAN-CLAUDE?
YEAH.
I'LL BE AS QUICK AS I CAN.
ALL RIGHT, BUT I NEED TO GET HOME SOON.
HE WAS ON A SHORT LEASH. HIS OWN FAULT, BUT IT SEEMED TO BOTHER ME MORE THAN IT BOTHERED CHARLES. MAYBE IT WAS ONE OF THE REASONS I'M NOT MARRIED.
I'M NOT BIG ON COMPROMISE.

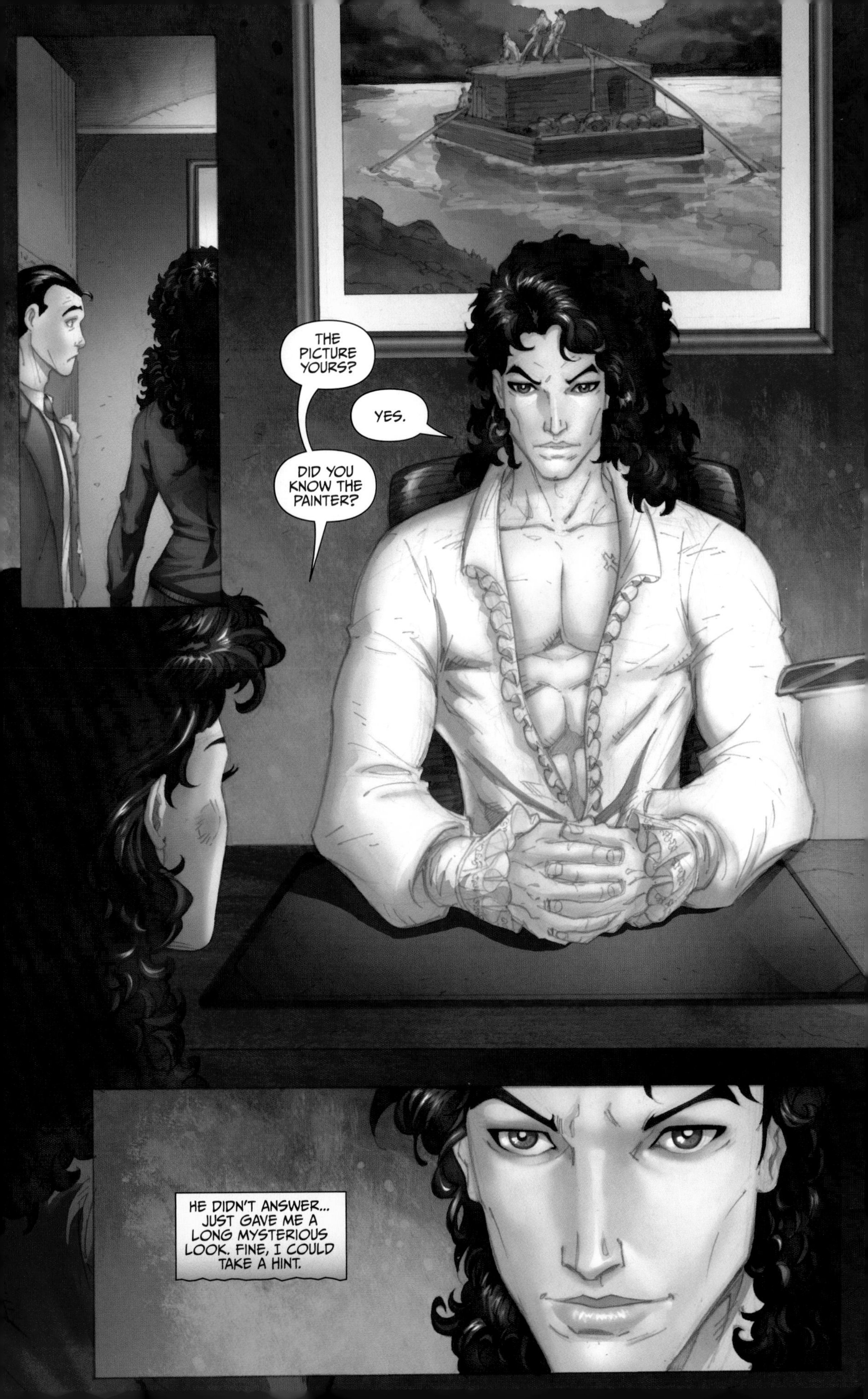
THE PICTURE YOURS?
YES.
DID YOU KNOW THE PAINTER?
HE DIDN'T ANSWER... JUST GAVE ME A LONG MYSTERIOUS LOOK. FINE, I COULD TAKE A HINT.

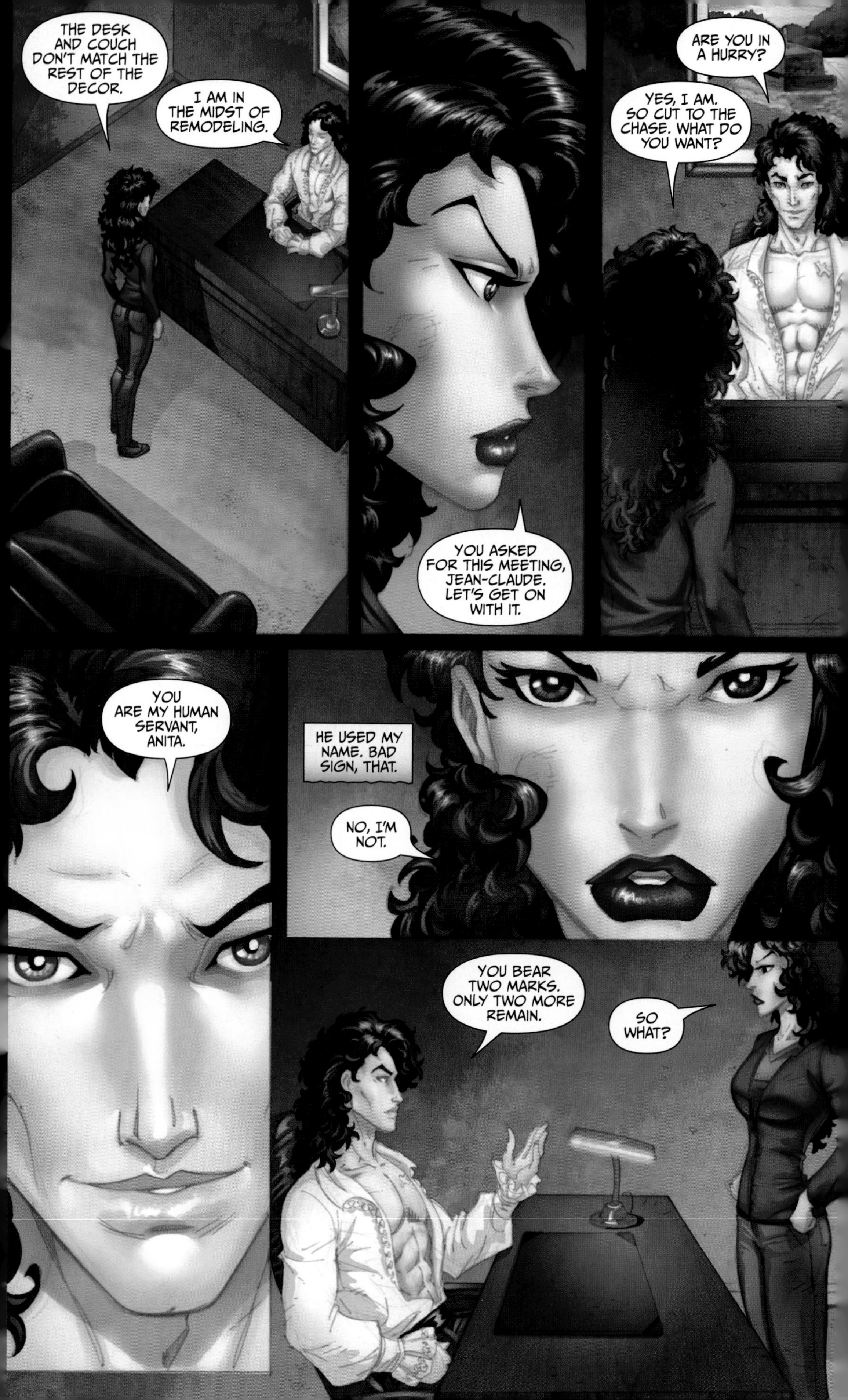
THE DESK AND COUCH DON'T MATCH THE REST OF THE DECOR.
I AM IN THE MIDST OF REMODELING.
YOU ASKED FOR THIS MEETING, JEAN-CLAUDE. LET'S GET ON WITH IT.
ARE YOU IN A HURRY?
YES, I AM. SO CUT TO THE CHASE. WHAT DO YOU WANT?
YOU ARE MY HUMAN SERVANT, ANITA.
HE USED MY NAME. BAD SIGN, THAT.
NO, I'M NOT.
YOU BEAR TWO MARKS. ONLY TWO MORE REMAIN.
SO WHAT?

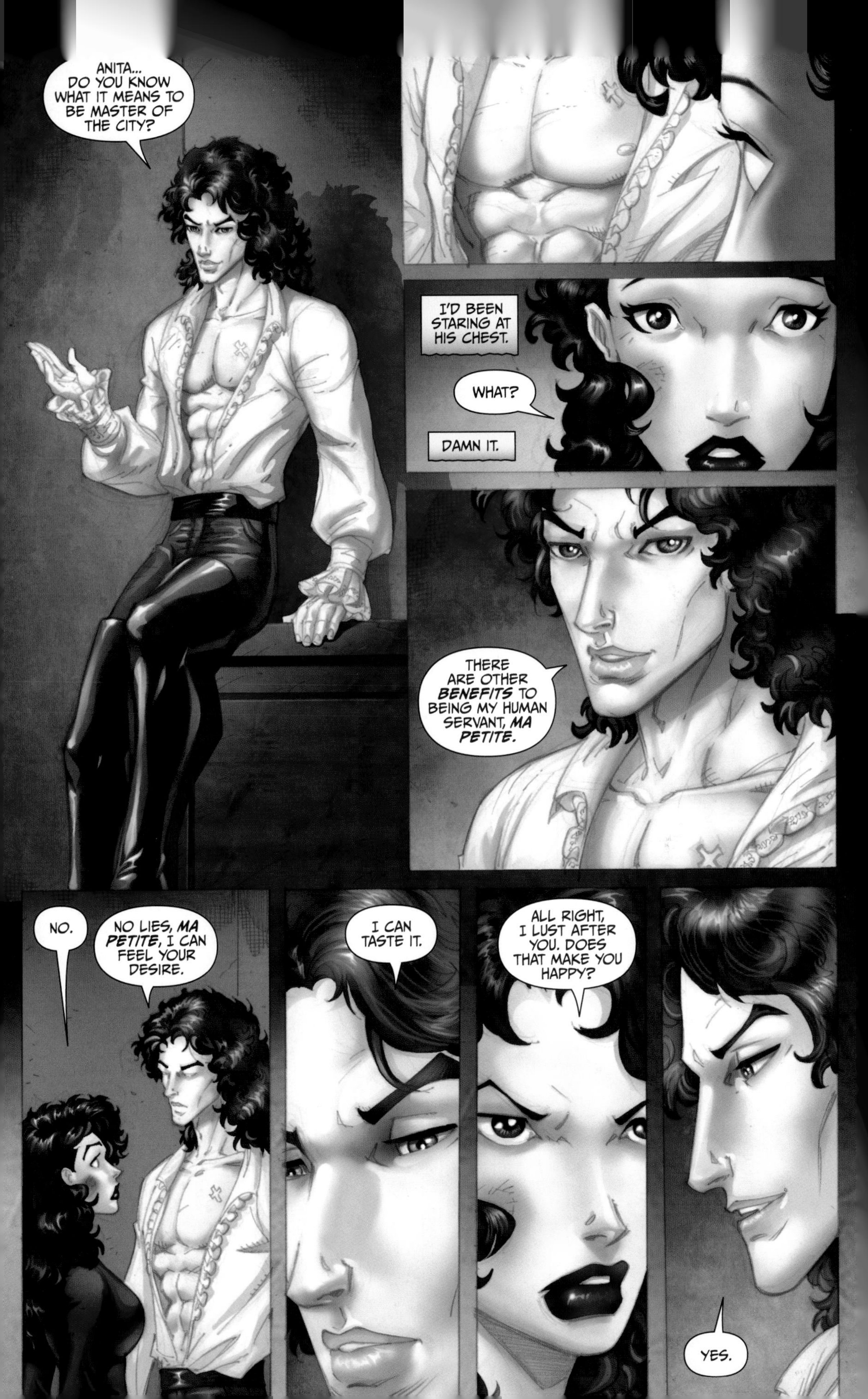
ANITA... DO YOU KNOW WHAT IT MEANS TO BE MASTER OF THE CITY?
I'D BEEN STARING AT HIS CHEST.
WHAT?
DAMN IT.
THERE ARE OTHER **BENEFITS** TO BEING MY HUMAN SERVANT, ***MA PETITE.***
NO.
NO LIES, ***MA PETITE***, I CAN FEEL YOUR DESIRE.
I CAN TASTE IT.
ALL RIGHT, I LUST AFTER YOU. DOES THAT MAKE YOU HAPPY?
YES.

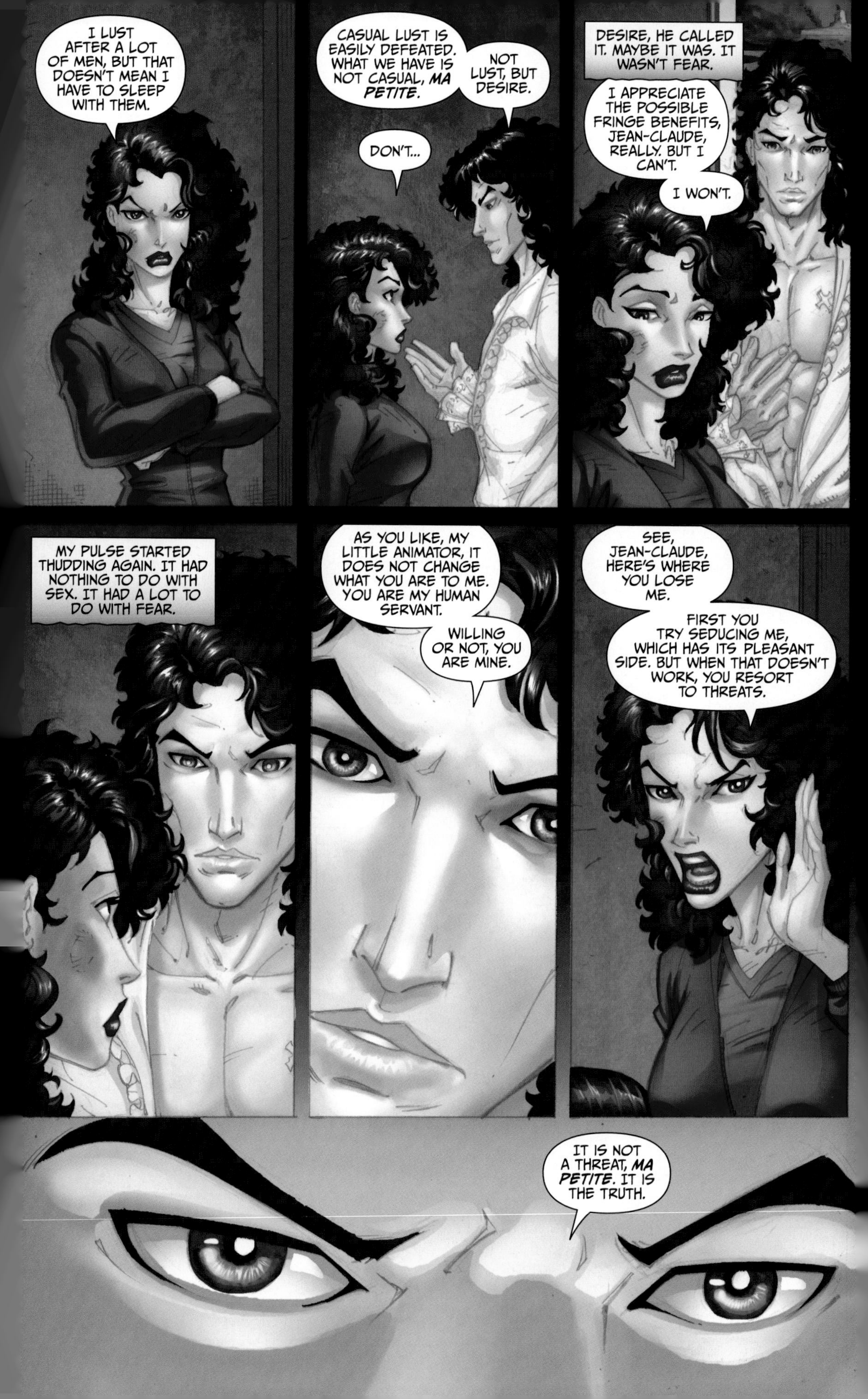
I LUST AFTER A LOT OF MEN, BUT THAT DOESN'T MEAN I HAVE TO SLEEP WITH THEM.
CASUAL LUST IS EASILY DEFEATED. WHAT WE HAVE IS NOT CASUAL, *MA PETITE*.
NOT LUST, BUT DESIRE.
DON'T...
DESIRE, HE CALLED IT. MAYBE IT WAS. IT WASN'T FEAR.
I APPRECIATE THE POSSIBLE FRINGE BENEFITS, JEAN-CLAUDE, REALLY. BUT I CAN'T.
I WON'T.
MY PULSE STARTED THUDDING AGAIN. IT HAD NOTHING TO DO WITH SEX. IT HAD A LOT TO DO WITH FEAR.
AS YOU LIKE, MY LITTLE ANIMATOR, IT DOES NOT CHANGE WHAT YOU ARE TO ME. YOU ARE MY HUMAN SERVANT.
WILLING OR NOT, YOU ARE MINE.
SEE, JEAN-CLAUDE, HERE'S WHERE YOU LOSE ME.
FIRST YOU TRY SEDUCING ME, WHICH HAS ITS PLEASANT SIDE. BUT WHEN THAT DOESN'T WORK, YOU RESORT TO THREATS.
IT IS NOT A THREAT, *MA PETITE*. IT IS THE TRUTH.

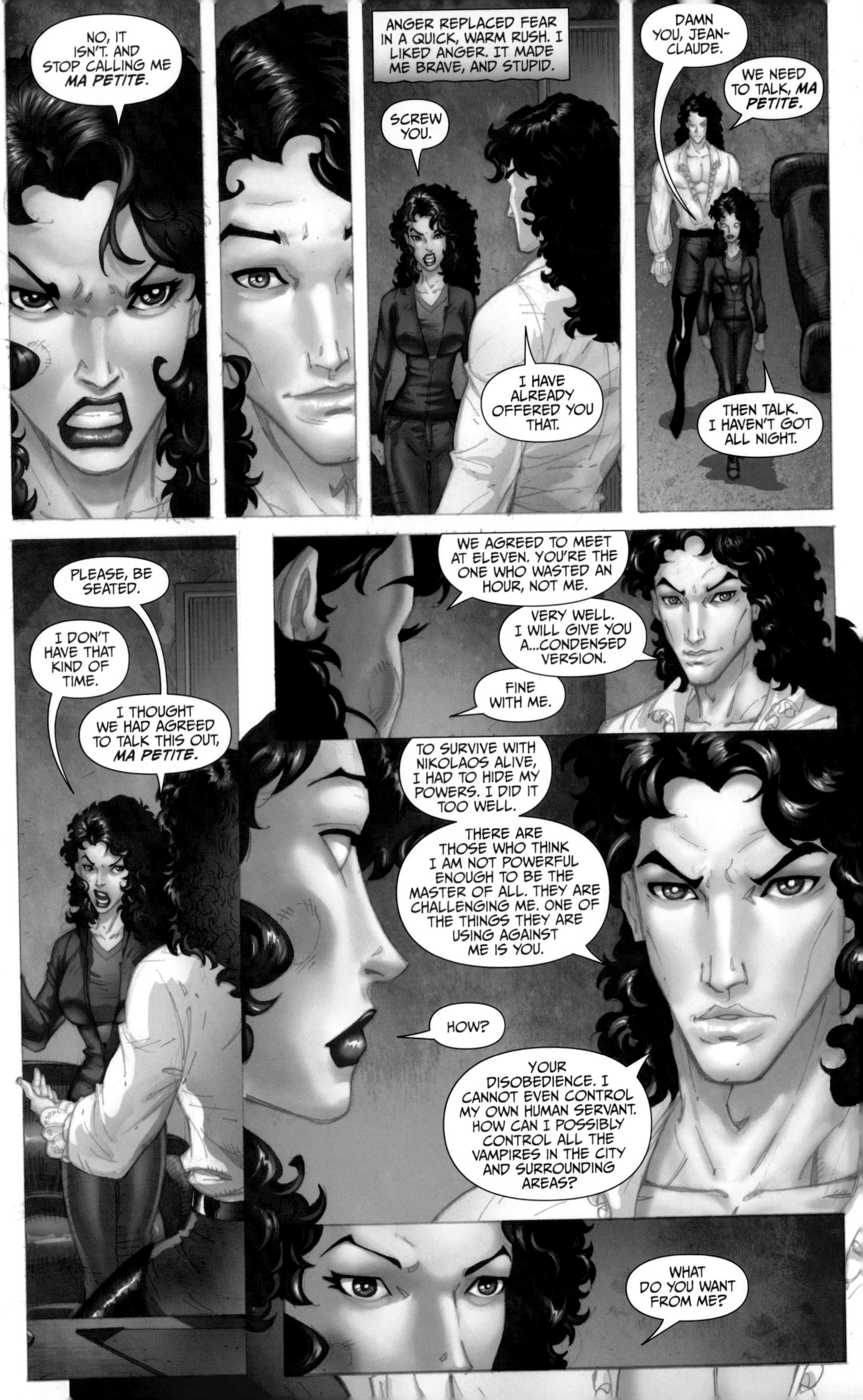
NO, IT ISN'T. AND STOP CALLING ME *MA PETITE*.
ANGER REPLACED FEAR IN A QUICK, WARM RUSH. I LIKED ANGER. IT MADE ME BRAVE, AND STUPID.
SCREW YOU.
I HAVE ALREADY OFFERED YOU THAT.
DAMN YOU, JEAN-CLAUDE.
WE NEED TO TALK, *MA PETITE*.
THEN TALK. I HAVEN'T GOT ALL NIGHT.
PLEASE, BE SEATED.
I DON'T HAVE THAT KIND OF TIME.
I THOUGHT WE HAD AGREED TO TALK THIS OUT, *MA PETITE*.
WE AGREED TO MEET AT ELEVEN. YOU'RE THE ONE WHO WASTED AN HOUR, NOT ME.
VERY WELL. I WILL GIVE YOU A...CONDENSED VERSION.
FINE WITH ME.
TO SURVIVE WITH NIKOLAOS ALIVE, I HAD TO HIDE MY POWERS. I DID IT TOO WELL.
THERE ARE THOSE WHO THINK I AM NOT POWERFUL ENOUGH TO BE THE MASTER OF ALL. THEY ARE CHALLENGING ME. ONE OF THE THINGS THEY ARE USING AGAINST ME IS YOU.
HOW?
YOUR DISOBEDIENCE. I CANNOT EVEN CONTROL MY OWN HUMAN SERVANT. HOW CAN I POSSIBLY CONTROL ALL THE VAMPIRES IN THE CITY AND SURROUNDING AREAS?
WHAT DO YOU WANT FROM ME?

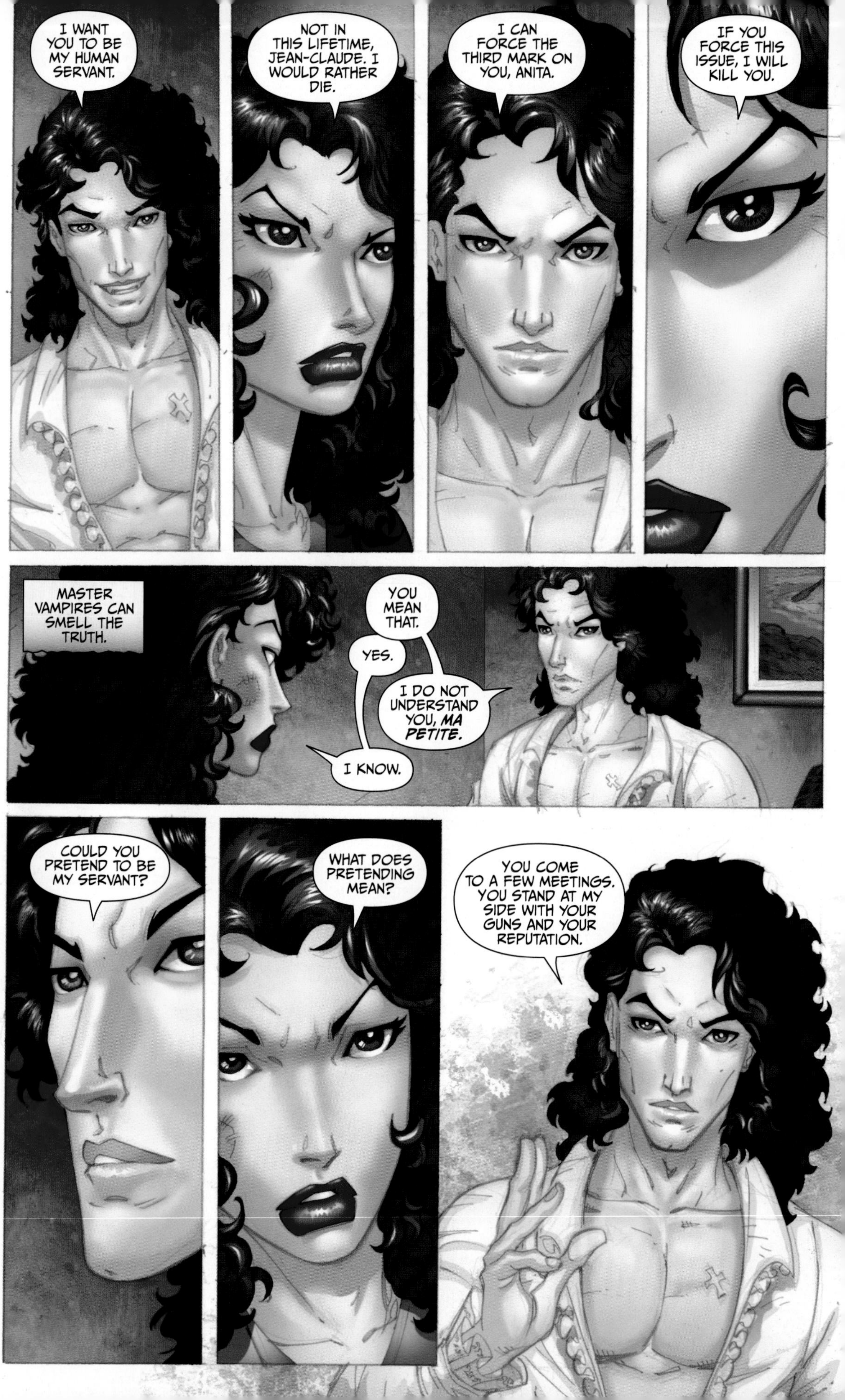
I WANT YOU TO BE MY HUMAN SERVANT.
NOT IN THIS LIFETIME, JEAN-CLAUDE. I WOULD RATHER DIE.
I CAN FORCE THE THIRD MARK ON YOU, ANITA.
IF YOU FORCE THIS ISSUE, I WILL KILL YOU.
MASTER VAMPIRES CAN SMELL THE TRUTH.
YOU MEAN THAT.
YES.
I DO NOT UNDERSTAND YOU, *MA PETITE.*
I KNOW.
COULD YOU PRETEND TO BE MY SERVANT?
WHAT DOES PRETENDING MEAN?
YOU COME TO A FEW MEETINGS. YOU STAND AT MY SIDE WITH YOUR GUNS AND YOUR REPUTATION.

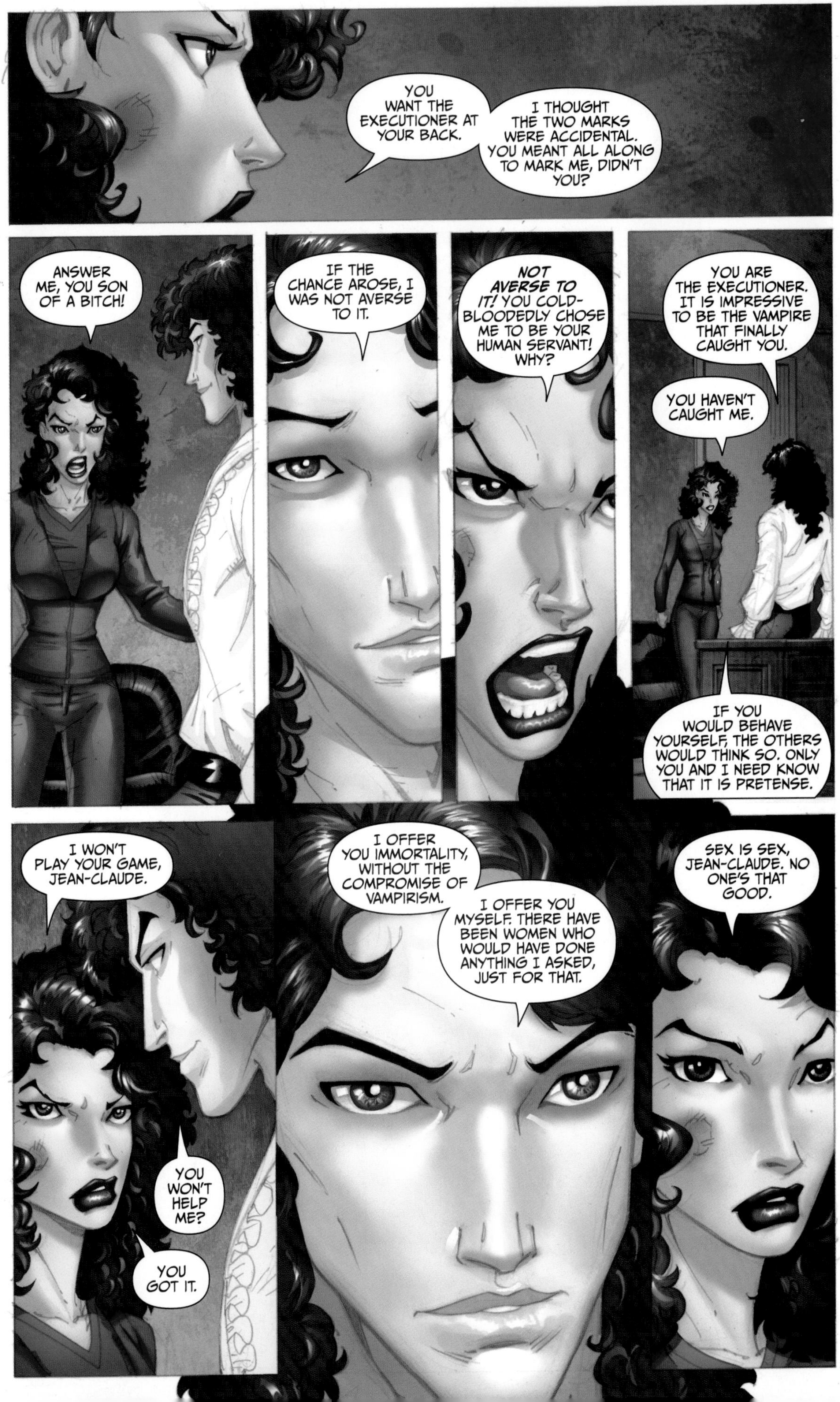
YOU WANT THE EXECUTIONER AT YOUR BACK.
I THOUGHT THE TWO MARKS WERE ACCIDENTAL. YOU MEANT ALL ALONG TO MARK ME, DIDN'T YOU?
ANSWER ME, YOU SON OF A BITCH!
IF THE CHANCE AROSE, I WAS NOT AVERSE TO IT.
NOT AVERSE TO IT! YOU COLD-BLOODEDLY CHOSE ME TO BE YOUR HUMAN SERVANT! WHY?
YOU ARE THE EXECUTIONER. IT IS IMPRESSIVE TO BE THE VAMPIRE THAT FINALLY CAUGHT YOU.
YOU HAVEN'T CAUGHT ME.
IF YOU WOULD BEHAVE YOURSELF, THE OTHERS WOULD THINK SO. ONLY YOU AND I NEED KNOW THAT IT IS PRETENSE.
I WON'T PLAY YOUR GAME, JEAN-CLAUDE.
YOU WON'T HELP ME?
YOU GOT IT.
I OFFER YOU IMMORTALITY, WITHOUT THE COMPROMISE OF VAMPIRISM.
I OFFER YOU MYSELF. THERE HAVE BEEN WOMEN WHO WOULD HAVE DONE ANYTHING I ASKED, JUST FOR THAT.
SEX IS SEX, JEAN-CLAUDE. NO ONE'S THAT GOOD.

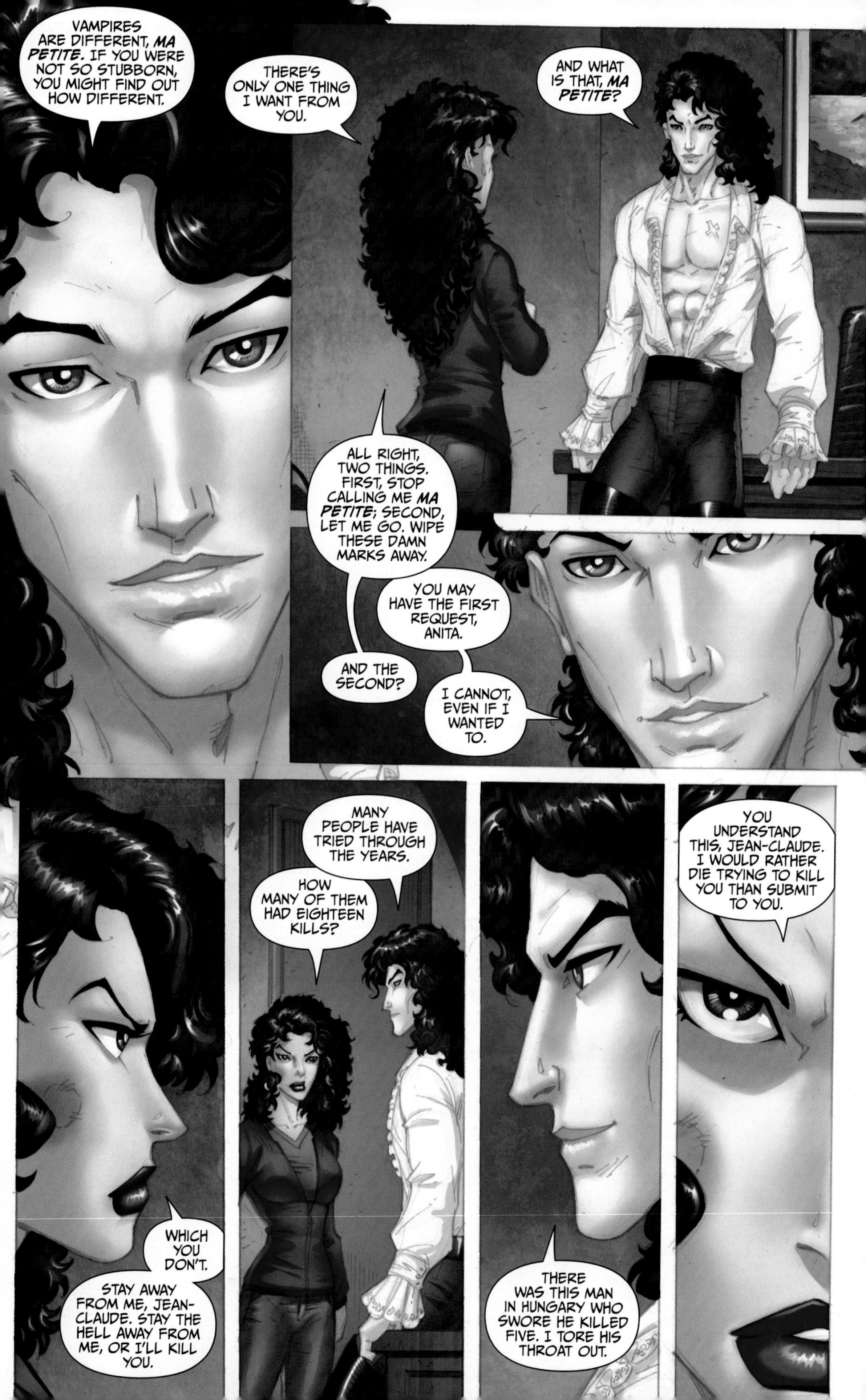

VAMPIRES ARE DIFFERENT, *MA PETITE.* IF YOU WERE NOT SO STUBBORN, YOU MIGHT FIND OUT HOW DIFFERENT.
THERE'S ONLY ONE THING I WANT FROM YOU.
AND WHAT IS THAT, *MA PETITE?*
ALL RIGHT, TWO THINGS. FIRST, STOP CALLING ME *MA PETITE;* SECOND, LET ME GO. WIPE THESE DAMN MARKS AWAY.
YOU MAY HAVE THE FIRST REQUEST, ANITA.
AND THE SECOND?
I CANNOT, EVEN IF I WANTED TO.
WHICH YOU DON'T.
STAY AWAY FROM ME, JEAN-CLAUDE. STAY THE HELL AWAY FROM ME, OR I'LL KILL YOU.
MANY PEOPLE HAVE TRIED THROUGH THE YEARS.
HOW MANY OF THEM HAD EIGHTEEN KILLS?
THERE WAS THIS MAN IN HUNGARY WHO SWORE HE KILLED FIVE. I TORE HIS THROAT OUT.
YOU UNDERSTAND THIS, JEAN-CLAUDE. I WOULD RATHER DIE TRYING TO KILL YOU THAN SUBMIT TO YOU.

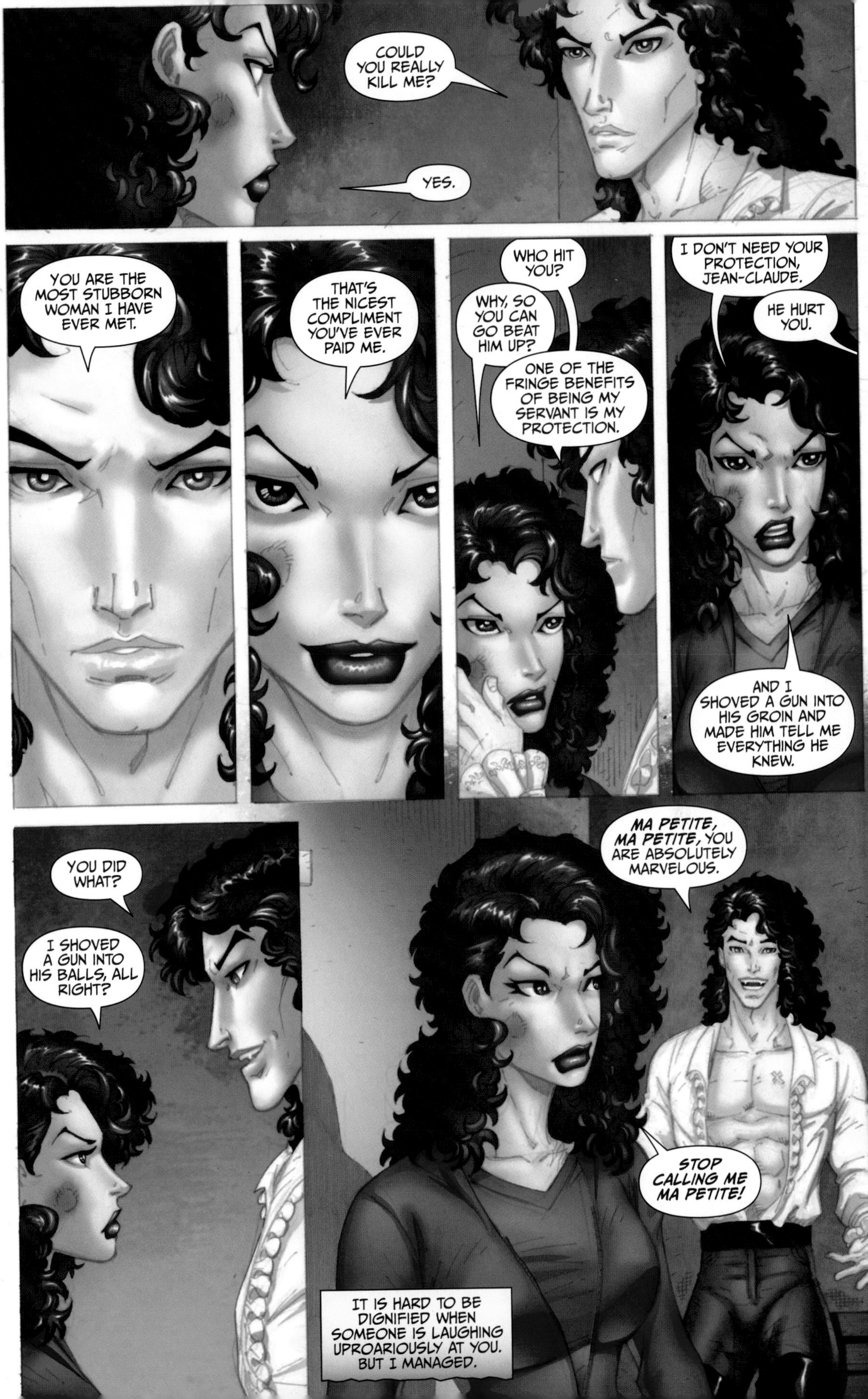

COULD YOU REALLY KILL ME?
YES.
YOU ARE THE MOST STUBBORN WOMAN I HAVE EVER MET.
THAT'S THE NICEST COMPLIMENT YOU'VE EVER PAID ME.
WHO HIT YOU?
WHY, SO YOU CAN GO BEAT HIM UP?
ONE OF THE FRINGE BENEFITS OF BEING MY SERVANT IS MY PROTECTION.
I DON'T NEED YOUR PROTECTION, JEAN-CLAUDE.
HE HURT YOU.
AND I SHOVED A GUN INTO HIS GROIN AND MADE HIM TELL ME EVERYTHING HE KNEW.
YOU DID WHAT?
I SHOVED A GUN INTO HIS BALLS, ALL RIGHT?
MA PETITE, MA PETITE, YOU ARE ABSOLUTELY MARVELOUS.
STOP CALLING ME MA PETITE!
IT IS HARD TO BE DIGNIFIED WHEN SOMEONE IS LAUGHING UPROARIOUSLY AT YOU. BUT I MANAGED.

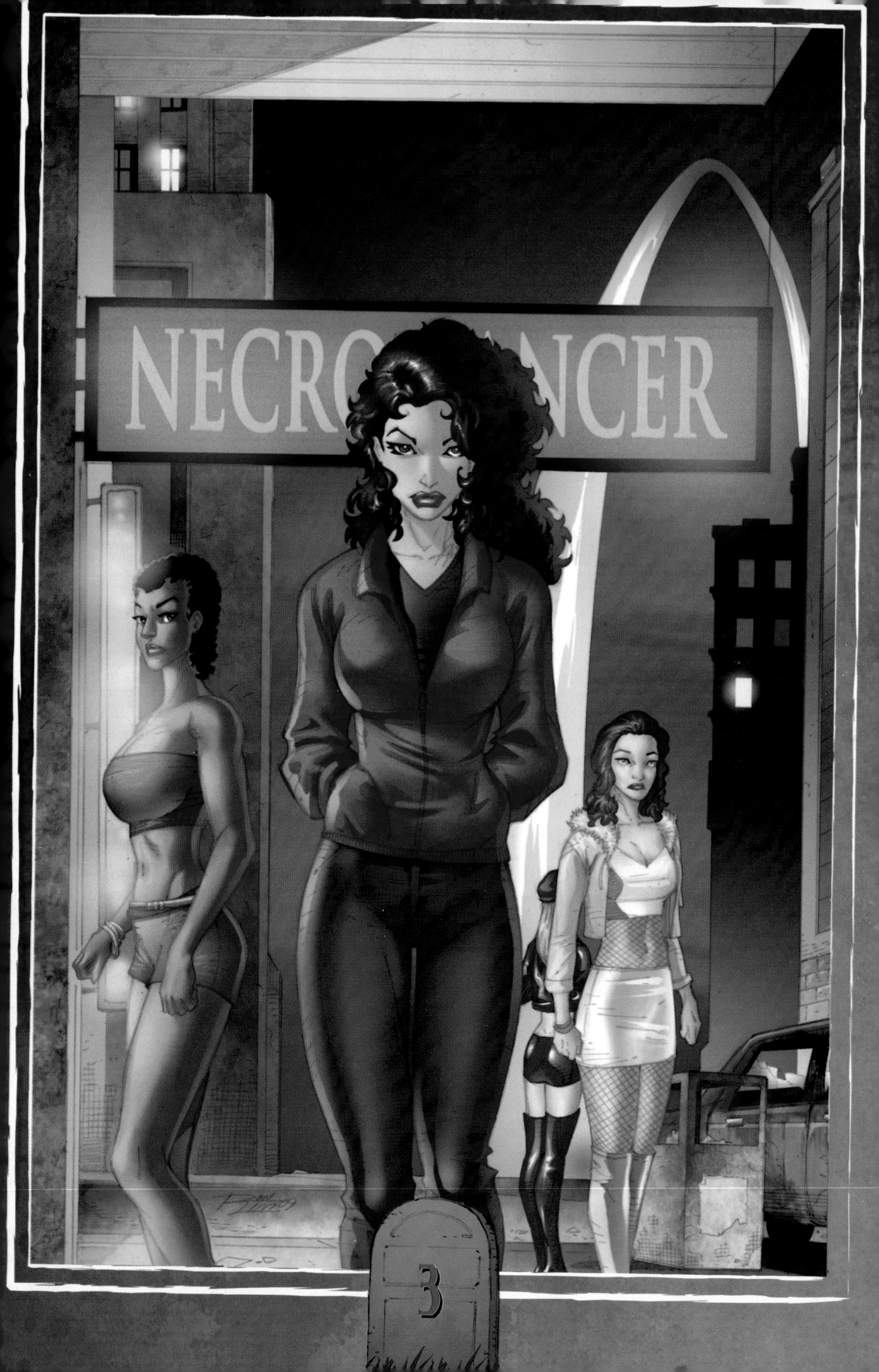
NECRO NCER
3

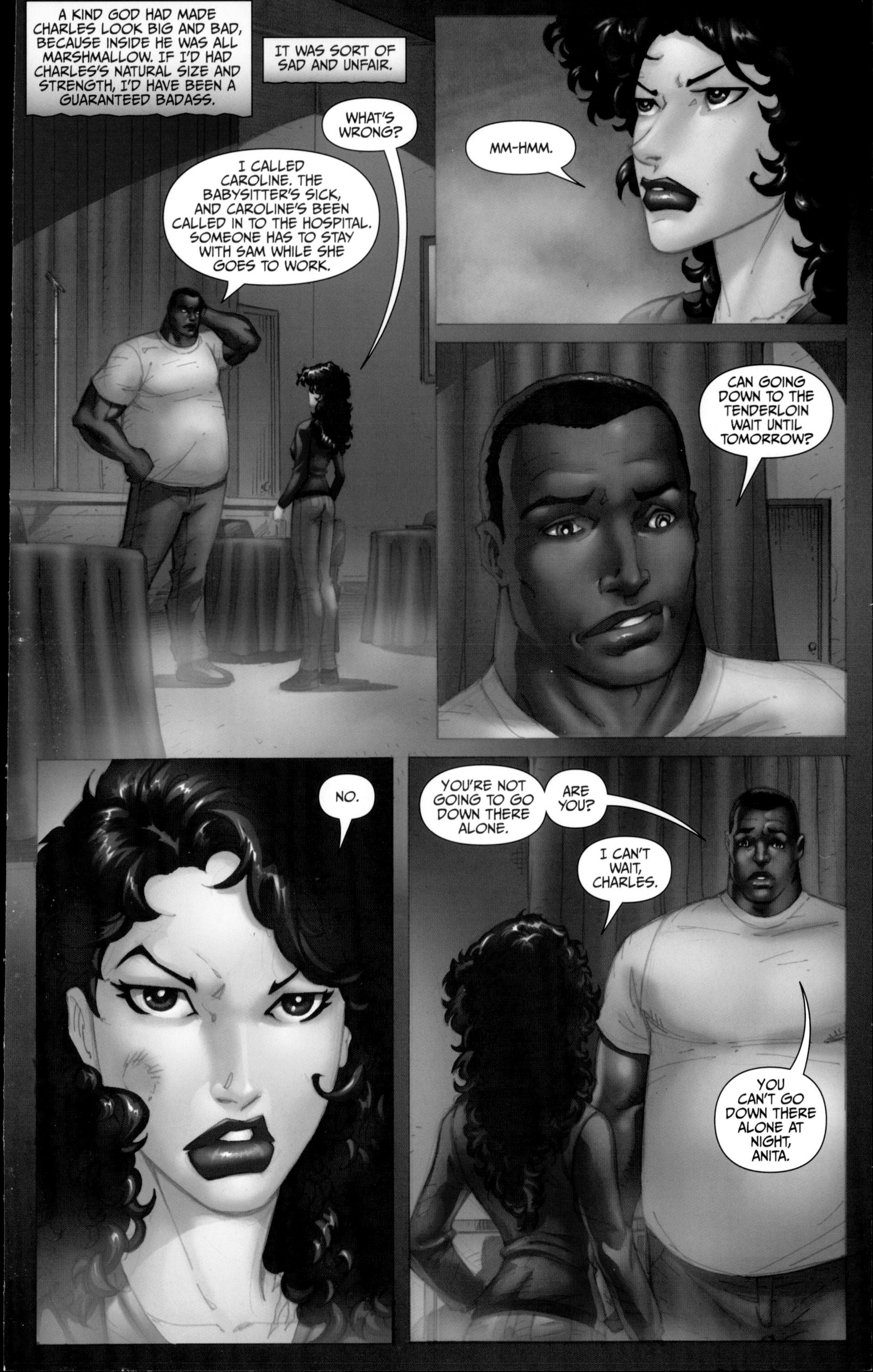
A KIND GOD HAD MADE CHARLES LOOK BIG AND BAD, BECAUSE INSIDE HE WAS ALL MARSHMALLOW. IF I'D HAD CHARLES'S NATURAL SIZE AND STRENGTH, I'D HAVE BEEN A GUARANTEED BADASS.
IT WAS SORT OF SAD AND UNFAIR.
WHAT'S WRONG?
I CALLED CAROLINE. THE BABYSITTER'S SICK, AND CAROLINE'S BEEN CALLED IN TO THE HOSPITAL. SOMEONE HAS TO STAY WITH SAM WHILE SHE GOES TO WORK.
MM-HMM.
CAN GOING DOWN TO THE TENDERLOIN WAIT UNTIL TOMORROW?
NO.
YOU'RE NOT GOING TO GO DOWN THERE ALONE.
ARE YOU?
I CAN'T WAIT, CHARLES.
YOU CAN'T GO DOWN THERE ALONE AT NIGHT, ANITA.

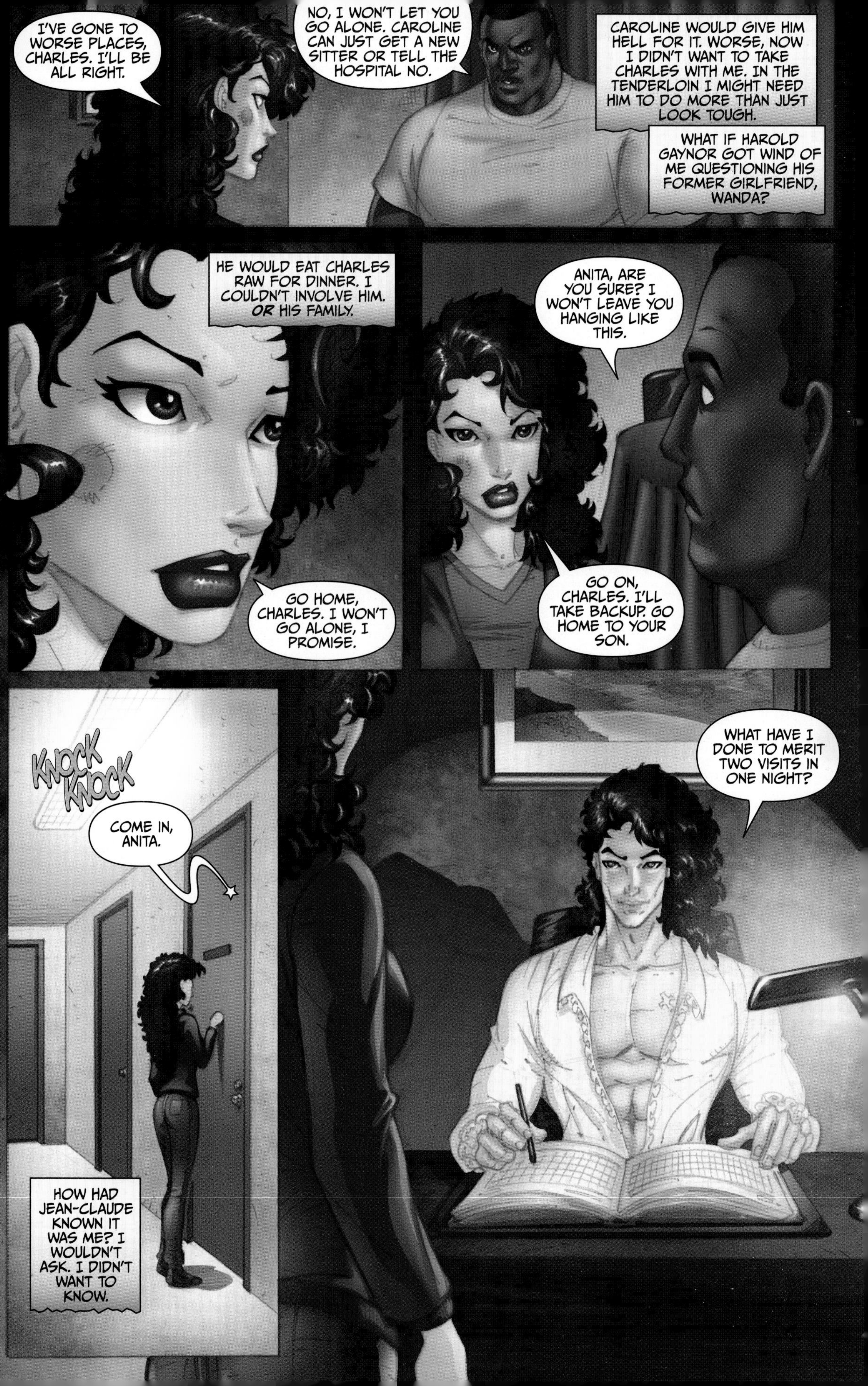
I'VE GONE TO WORSE PLACES, CHARLES. I'LL BE ALL RIGHT.
NO, I WON'T LET YOU GO ALONE. CAROLINE CAN JUST GET A NEW SITTER OR TELL THE HOSPITAL NO.
CAROLINE WOULD GIVE HIM HELL FOR IT. WORSE, NOW I DIDN'T WANT TO TAKE CHARLES WITH ME. IN THE TENDERLOIN I MIGHT NEED HIM TO DO MORE THAN JUST LOOK TOUGH.
WHAT IF HAROLD GAYNOR GOT WIND OF ME QUESTIONING HIS FORMER GIRLFRIEND, WANDA?
HE WOULD EAT CHARLES RAW FOR DINNER. I COULDN'T INVOLVE HIM. OR HIS FAMILY.
GO HOME, CHARLES. I WON'T GO ALONE, I PROMISE.
ANITA, ARE YOU SURE? I WON'T LEAVE YOU HANGING LIKE THIS.
GO ON, CHARLES. I'LL TAKE BACKUP. GO HOME TO YOUR SON.
KNOCK KNOCK
COME IN, ANITA.
HOW HAD JEAN-CLAUDE KNOWN IT WAS ME? I WOULDN'T ASK. I DIDN'T WANT TO KNOW.
WHAT HAVE I DONE TO MERIT TWO VISITS IN ONE NIGHT?

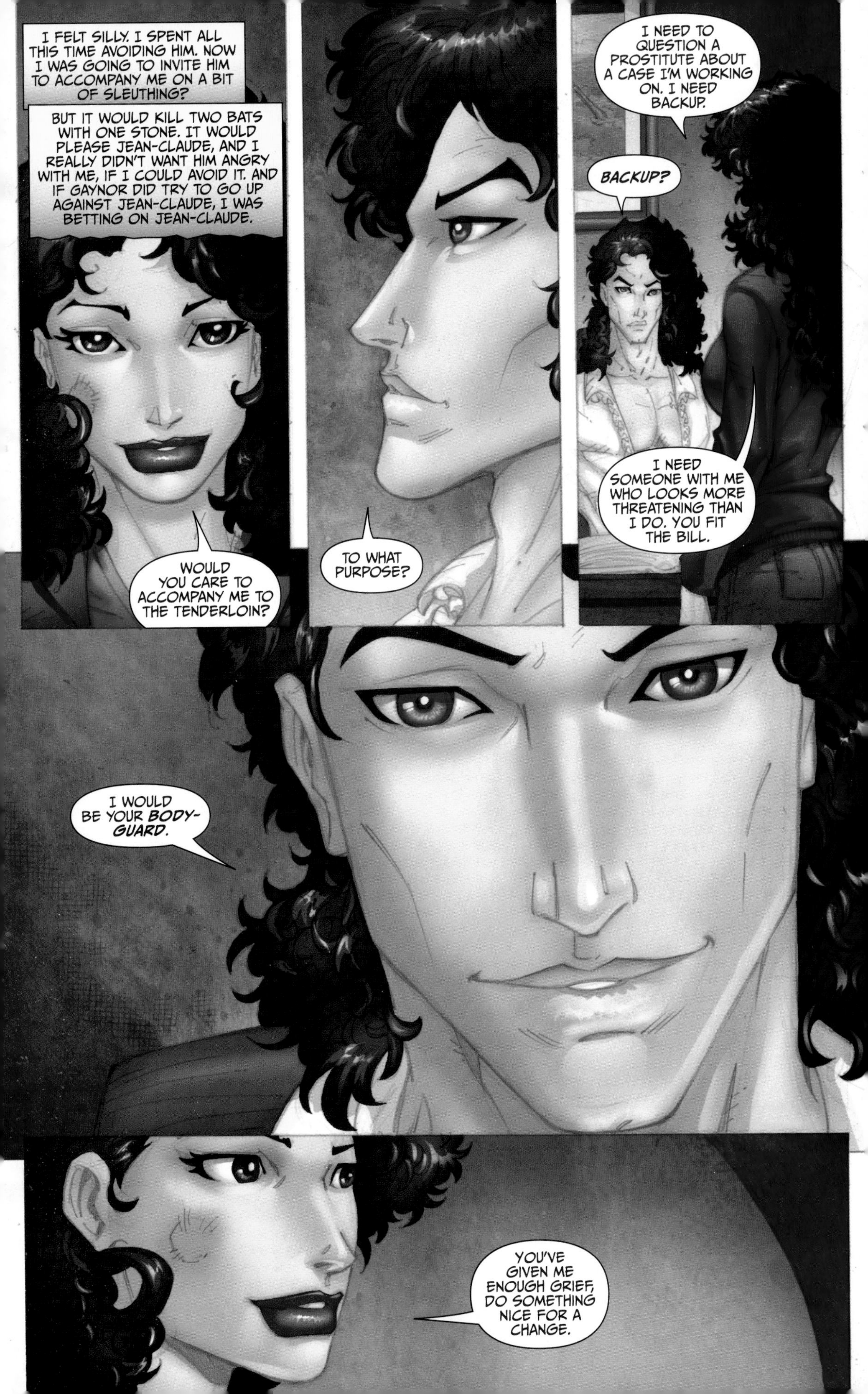
I FELT SILLY. I SPENT ALL THIS TIME AVOIDING HIM. NOW I WAS GOING TO INVITE HIM TO ACCOMPANY ME ON A BIT OF SLEUTHING?
BUT IT WOULD KILL TWO BATS WITH ONE STONE. IT WOULD PLEASE JEAN-CLAUDE, AND I REALLY DIDN'T WANT HIM ANGRY WITH ME, IF I COULD AVOID IT. AND IF GAYNOR DID TRY TO GO UP AGAINST JEAN-CLAUDE, I WAS BETTING ON JEAN-CLAUDE.
WOULD YOU CARE TO ACCOMPANY ME TO THE TENDERLOIN?
TO WHAT PURPOSE?
I NEED TO QUESTION A PROSTITUTE ABOUT A CASE I'M WORKING ON. I NEED BACKUP.
BACKUP?
I NEED SOMEONE WITH ME WHO LOOKS MORE THREATENING THAN I DO. YOU FIT THE BILL.
I WOULD BE YOUR BODY-GUARD.
YOU'VE GIVEN ME ENOUGH GRIEF, DO SOMETHING NICE FOR A CHANGE.

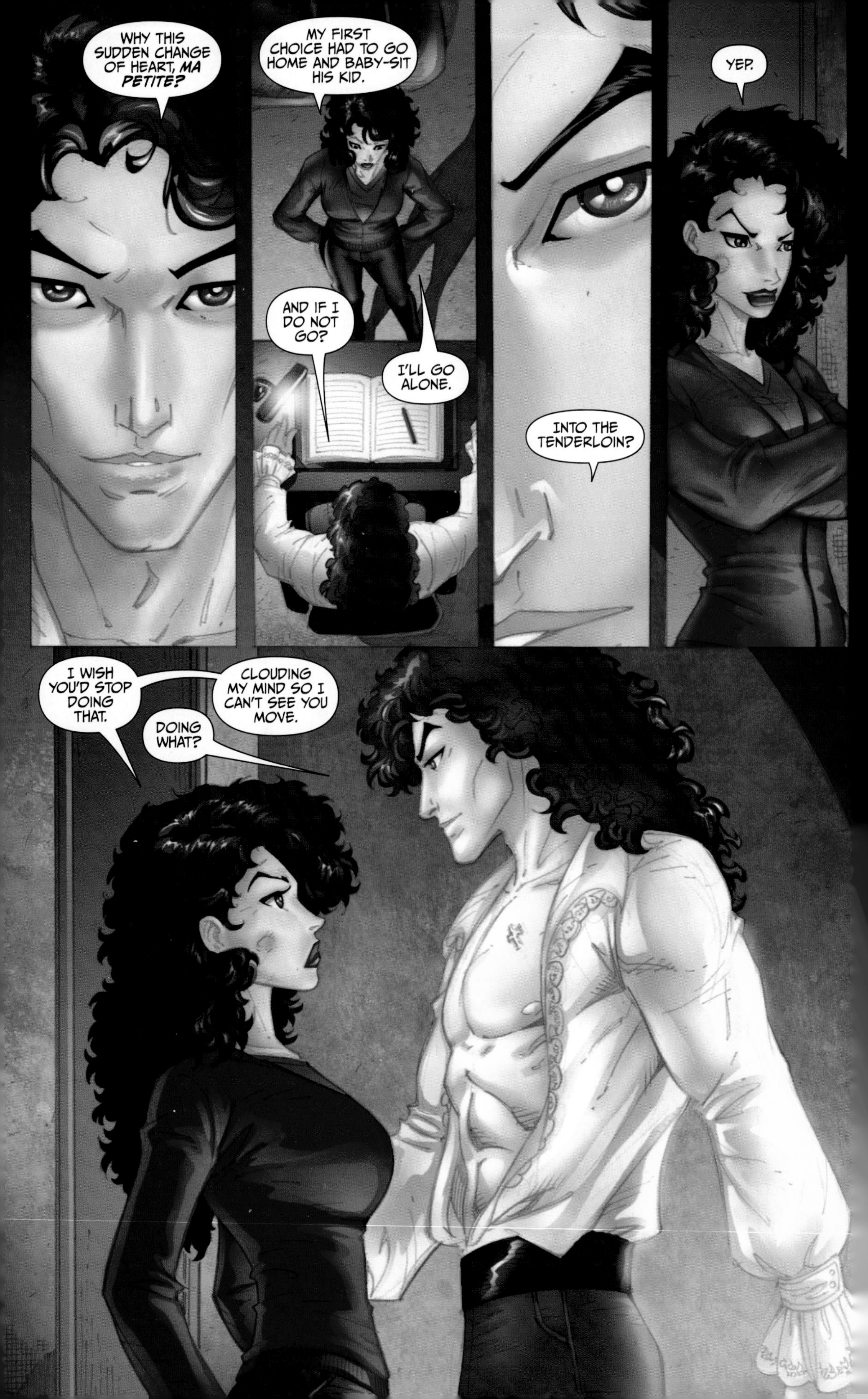
WHY THIS SUDDEN CHANGE OF HEART, *MA PETITE?*
MY FIRST CHOICE HAD TO GO HOME AND BABY-SIT HIS KID.
AND IF I DO NOT GO?
I'LL GO ALONE.
INTO THE TENDERLOIN?
YEP.
I WISH YOU'D STOP DOING THAT.
DOING WHAT?
CLOUDING MY MIND SO I CAN'T SEE YOU MOVE.

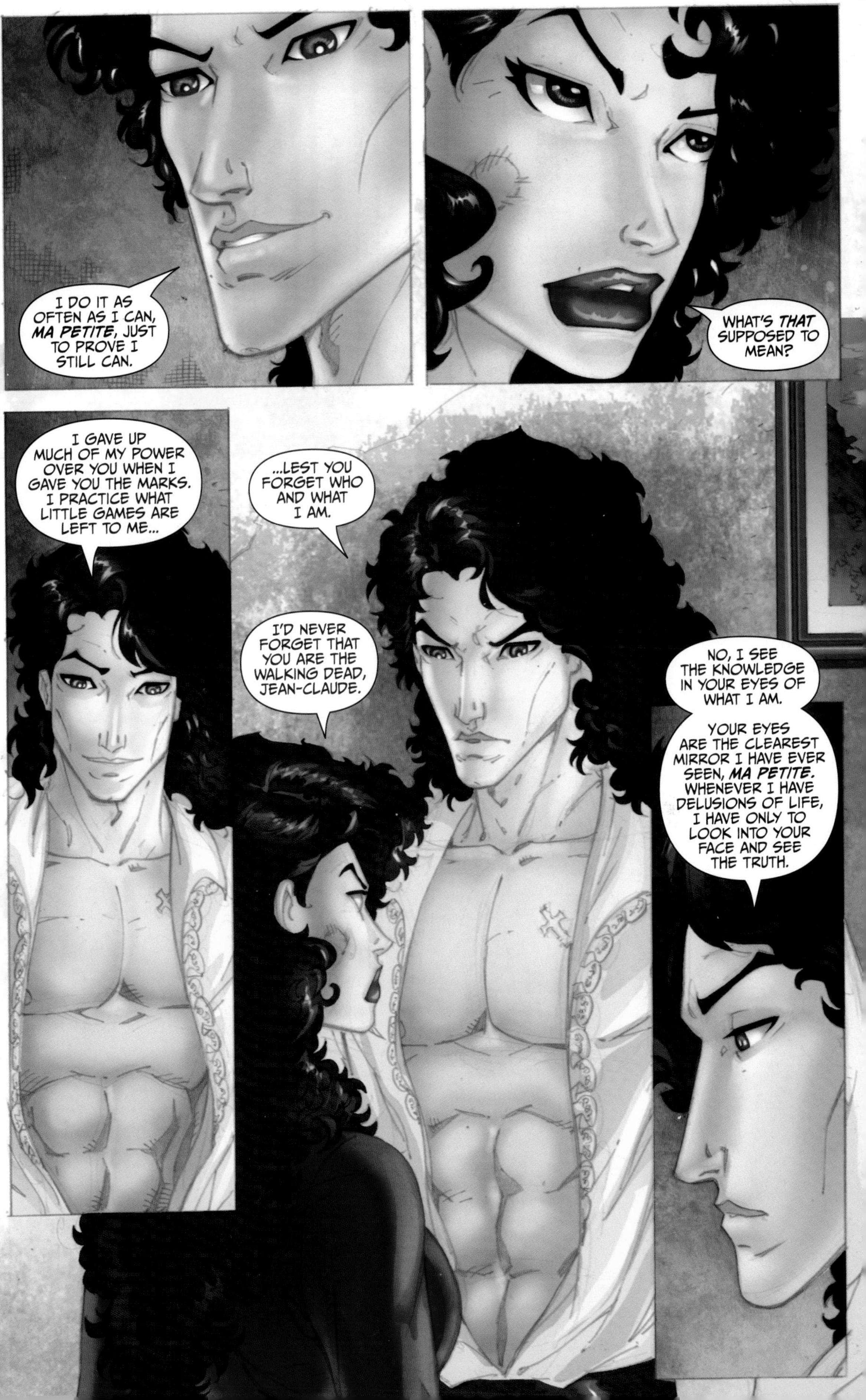
I DO IT AS OFTEN AS I CAN, *MA PETITE*, JUST TO PROVE I STILL CAN.
WHAT'S *THAT* SUPPOSED TO MEAN?
I GAVE UP MUCH OF MY POWER OVER YOU WHEN I GAVE YOU THE MARKS. I PRACTICE WHAT LITTLE GAMES ARE LEFT TO ME...
...LEST YOU FORGET WHO AND WHAT I AM.
I'D NEVER FORGET THAT YOU ARE THE WALKING DEAD, JEAN-CLAUDE.
NO, I SEE THE KNOWLEDGE IN YOUR EYES OF WHAT I AM.
YOUR EYES ARE THE CLEAREST MIRROR I HAVE EVER SEEN, *MA PETITE.* WHENEVER I HAVE DELUSIONS OF LIFE, I HAVE ONLY TO LOOK INTO YOUR FACE AND SEE THE TRUTH.

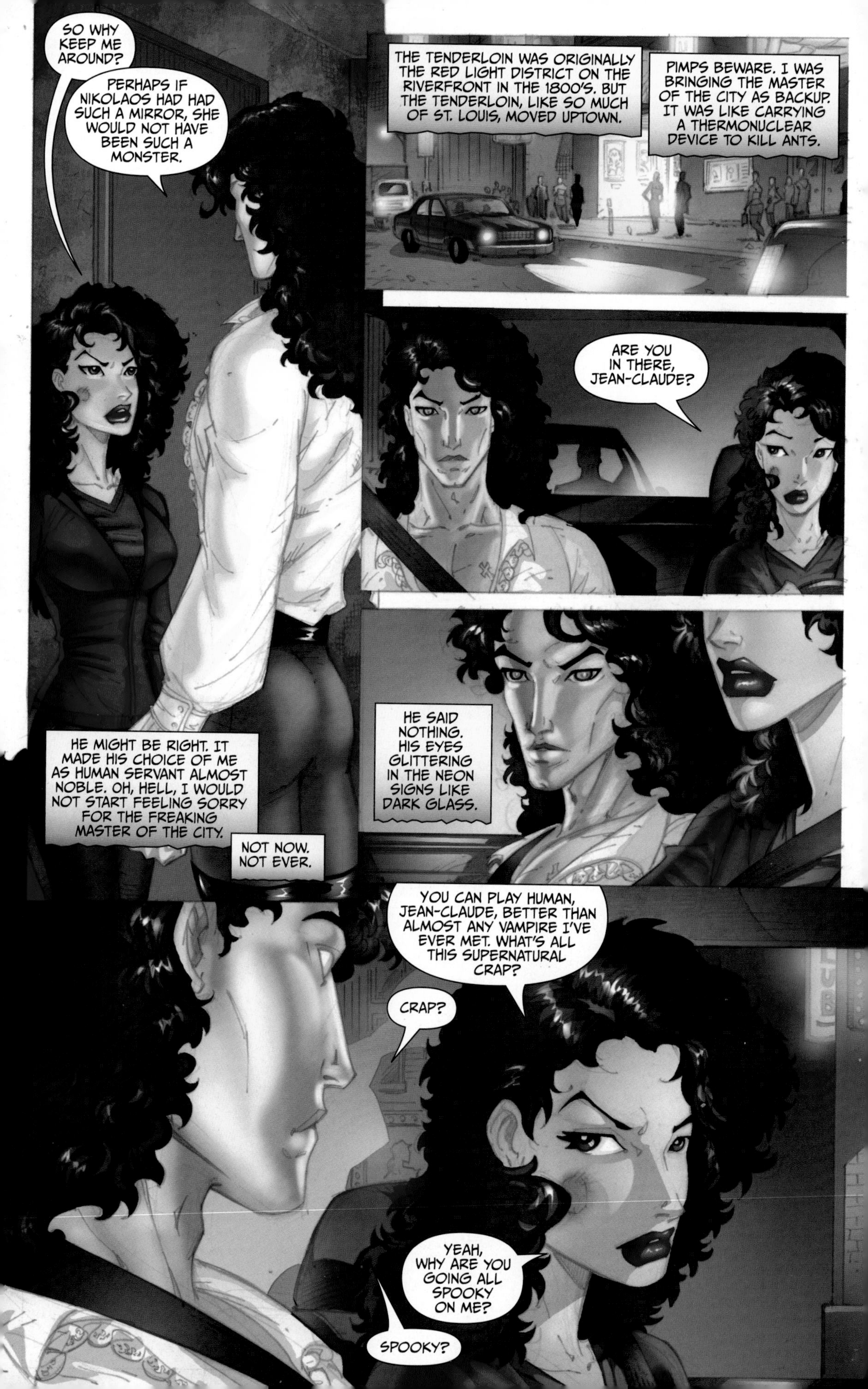
SO WHY KEEP ME AROUND?
PERHAPS IF NIKOLAOS HAD HAD SUCH A MIRROR, SHE WOULD NOT HAVE BEEN SUCH A MONSTER.
HE MIGHT BE RIGHT. IT MADE HIS CHOICE OF ME AS HUMAN SERVANT ALMOST NOBLE. OH, HELL, I WOULD NOT START FEELING SORRY FOR THE FREAKING MASTER OF THE CITY.
NOT NOW. NOT EVER.
THE TENDERLOIN WAS ORIGINALLY THE RED LIGHT DISTRICT ON THE RIVERFRONT IN THE 1800'S. BUT THE TENDERLOIN, LIKE SO MUCH OF ST. LOUIS, MOVED UPTOWN.
PIMPS BEWARE. I WAS BRINGING THE MASTER OF THE CITY AS BACKUP. IT WAS LIKE CARRYING A THERMONUCLEAR DEVICE TO KILL ANTS.
ARE YOU IN THERE, JEAN-CLAUDE?
HE SAID NOTHING. HIS EYES GLITTERING IN THE NEON SIGNS LIKE DARK GLASS.
YOU CAN PLAY HUMAN, JEAN-CLAUDE, BETTER THAN ALMOST ANY VAMPIRE I'VE EVER MET. WHAT'S ALL THIS SUPERNATURAL CRAP?
CRAP?
YEAH, WHY ARE YOU GOING ALL SPOOKY ON ME?
SPOOKY?

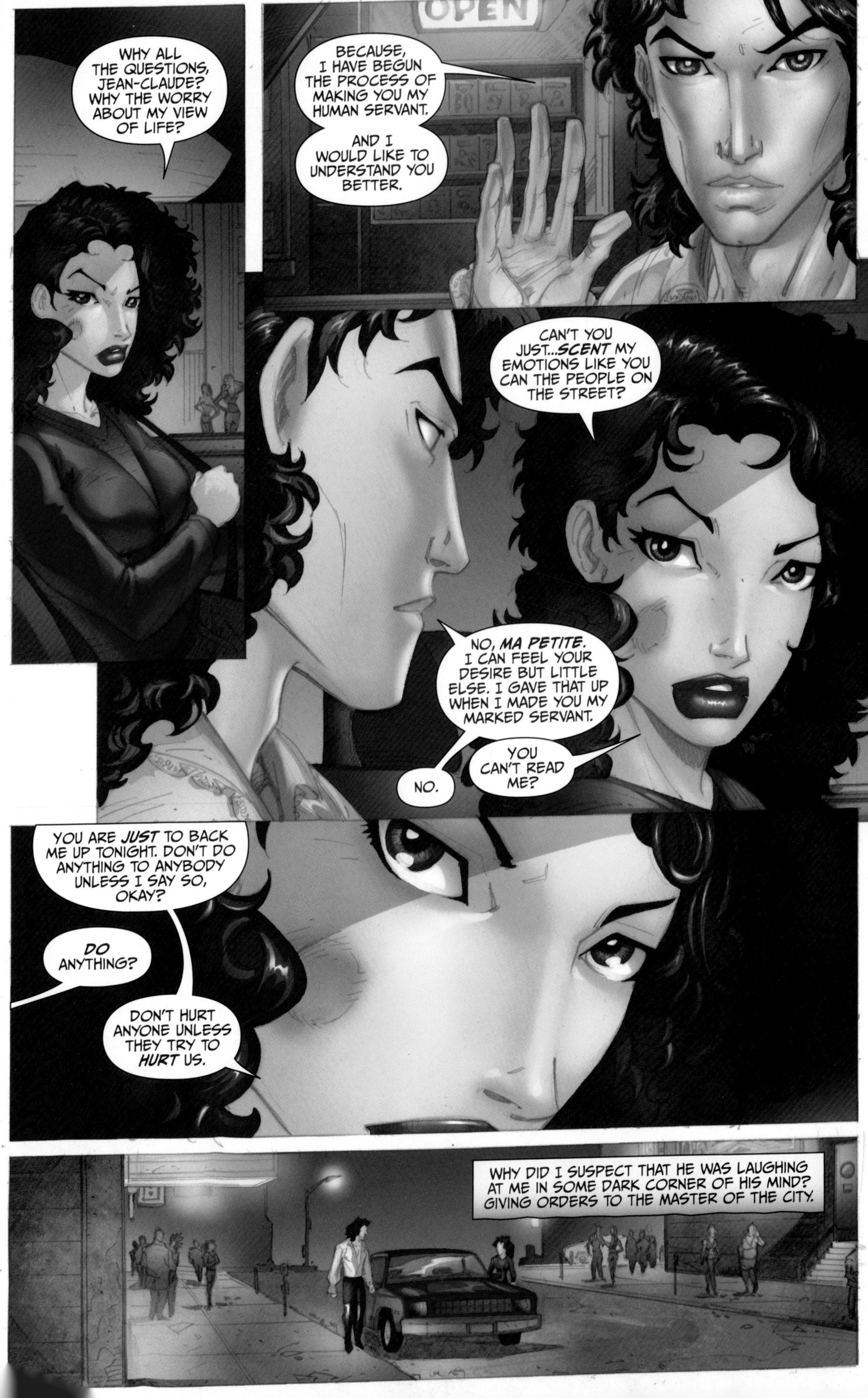
WHY ALL THE QUESTIONS, JEAN-CLAUDE? WHY THE WORRY ABOUT MY VIEW OF LIFE?
OPEN
BECAUSE, I HAVE BEGUN THE PROCESS OF MAKING YOU MY HUMAN SERVANT.
AND I WOULD LIKE TO UNDERSTAND YOU BETTER.
CAN'T YOU JUST...SCENT MY EMOTIONS LIKE YOU CAN THE PEOPLE ON THE STREET?
NO, MA PETITE. I CAN FEEL YOUR DESIRE BUT LITTLE ELSE. I GAVE THAT UP WHEN I MADE YOU MY MARKED SERVANT.
YOU CAN'T READ ME?
NO.
YOU ARE JUST TO BACK ME UP TONIGHT. DON'T DO ANYTHING TO ANYBODY UNLESS I SAY SO, OKAY?
DO ANYTHING?
DON'T HURT ANYONE UNLESS THEY TRY TO HURT US.
WHY DID I SUSPECT THAT HE WAS LAUGHING AT ME IN SOME DARK CORNER OF HIS MIND? GIVING ORDERS TO THE MASTER OF THE CITY.

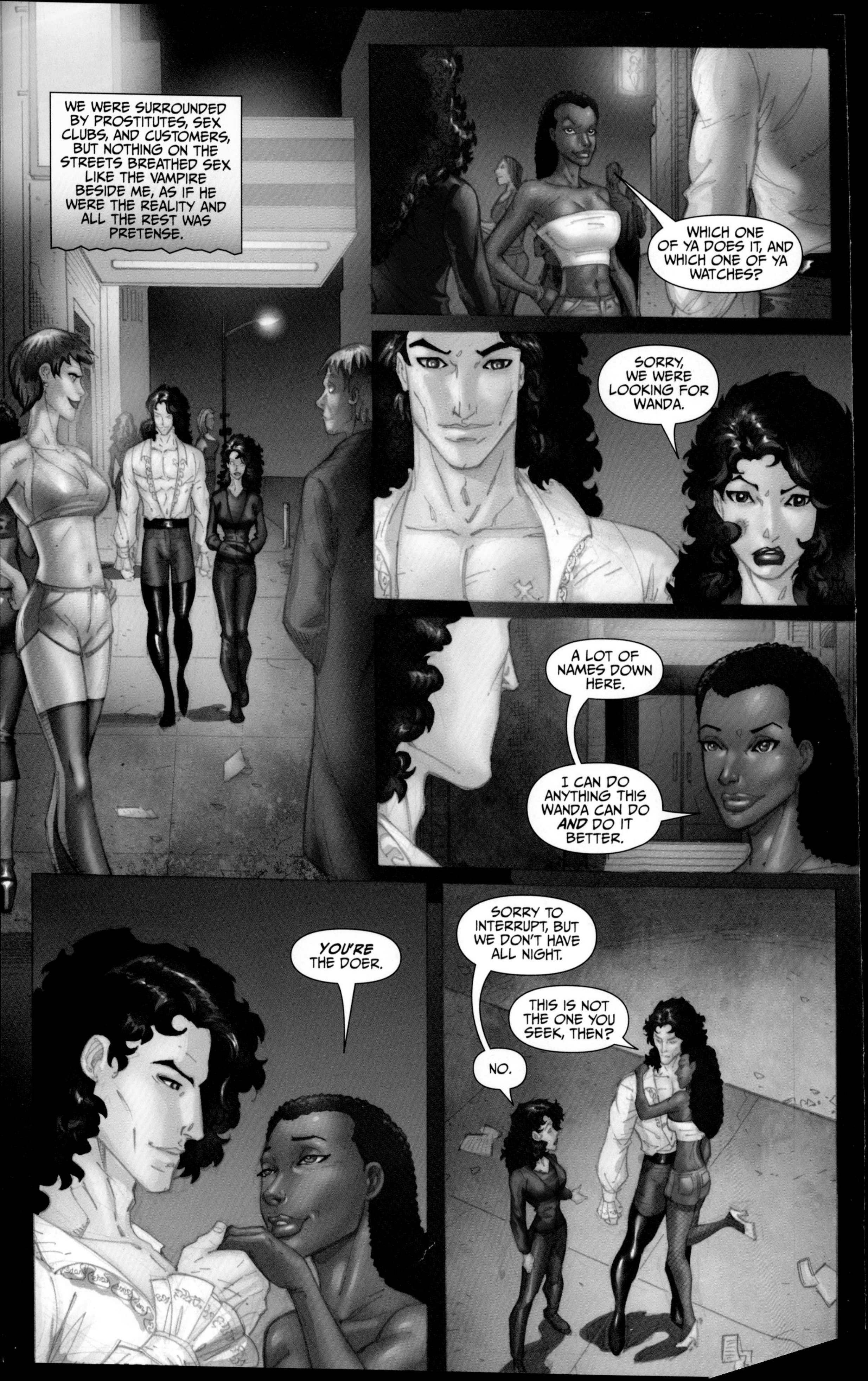
WE WERE SURROUNDED BY PROSTITUTES, SEX CLUBS, AND CUSTOMERS, BUT NOTHING ON THE STREETS BREATHED SEX LIKE THE VAMPIRE BESIDE ME, AS IF HE WERE THE REALITY AND ALL THE REST WAS PRETENSE.
WHICH ONE OF YA DOES IT, AND WHICH ONE OF YA WATCHES?
SORRY, WE WERE LOOKING FOR WANDA.
A LOT OF NAMES DOWN HERE.
I CAN DO ANYTHING THIS WANDA CAN DO *AND* DO IT BETTER.
YOU'RE THE DOER.
SORRY TO INTERRUPT, BUT WE DON'T HAVE ALL NIGHT.
THIS IS NOT THE ONE YOU SEEK, THEN?
NO.

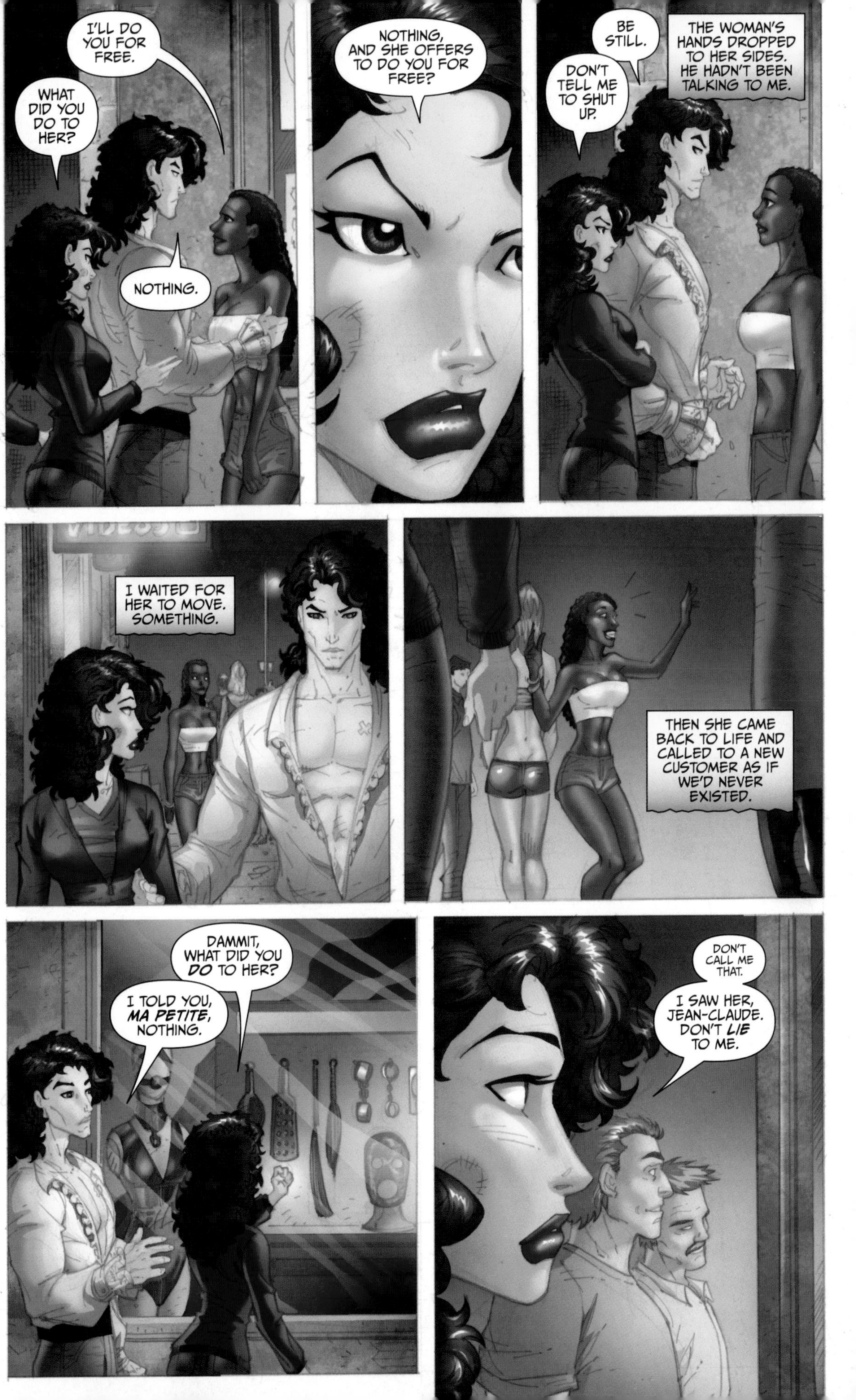
I'LL DO YOU FOR FREE.
WHAT DID YOU DO TO HER?
NOTHING.
NOTHING, AND SHE OFFERS TO DO YOU FOR FREE?
BE STILL.
DON'T TELL ME TO SHUT UP.
THE WOMAN'S HANDS DROPPED TO HER SIDES. HE HADN'T BEEN TALKING TO ME.
I WAITED FOR HER TO MOVE. SOMETHING.
THEN SHE CAME BACK TO LIFE AND CALLED TO A NEW CUSTOMER AS IF WE'D NEVER EXISTED.
DAMMIT, WHAT DID YOU *DO* TO HER?
I TOLD YOU, ***MA PETITE***, NOTHING.
DON'T CALL ME THAT.
I SAW HER, JEAN-CLAUDE. DON'T ***LIE*** TO ME.

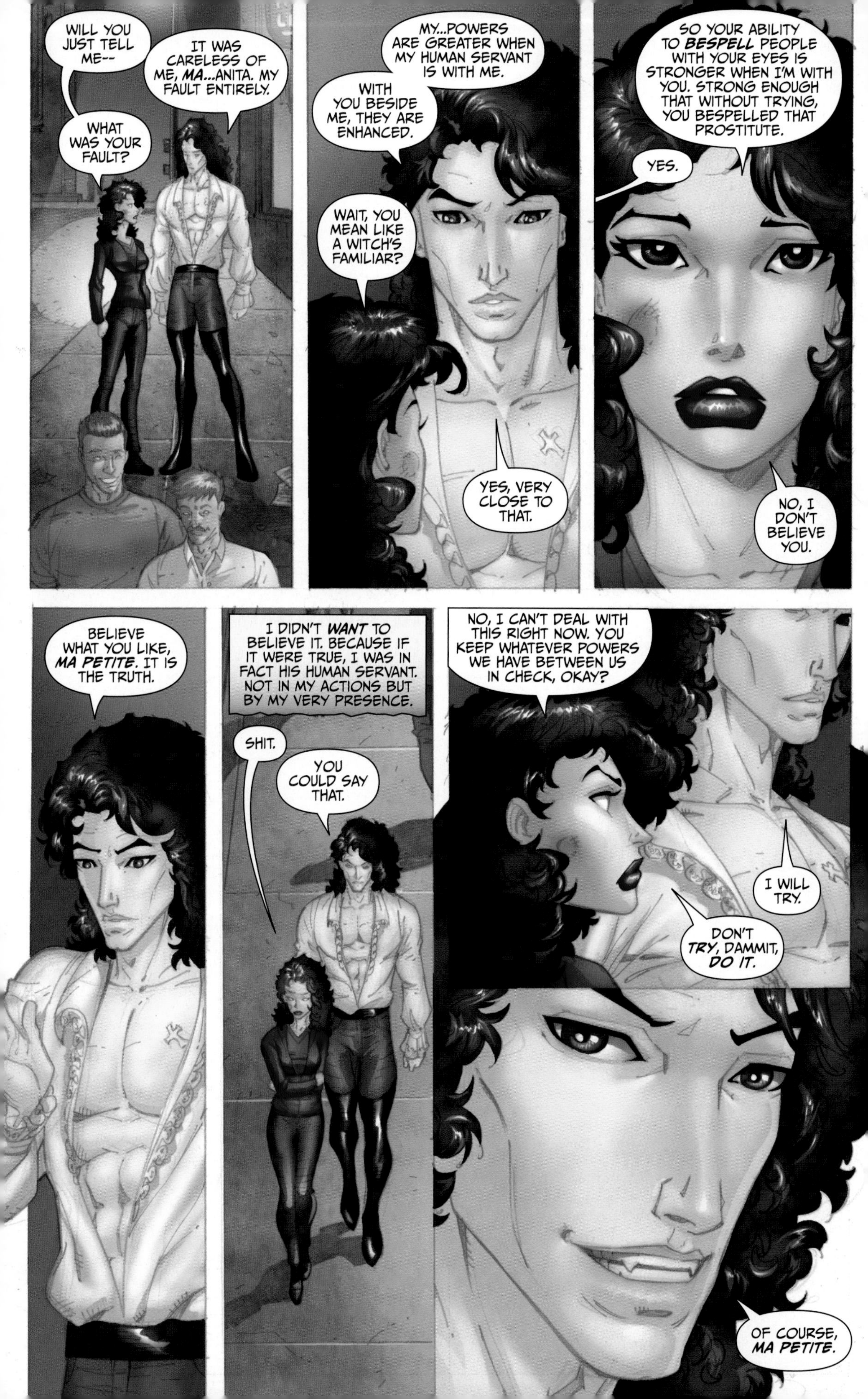
WILL YOU JUST TELL ME--
IT WAS CARELESS OF ME, MA...ANITA. MY FAULT ENTIRELY.
WHAT WAS YOUR FAULT?
MY...POWERS ARE GREATER WHEN MY HUMAN SERVANT IS WITH ME.
WITH YOU BESIDE ME, THEY ARE ENHANCED.
WAIT, YOU MEAN LIKE A WITCH'S FAMILIAR?
YES, VERY CLOSE TO THAT.
SO YOUR ABILITY TO BESPELL PEOPLE WITH YOUR EYES IS STRONGER WHEN I'M WITH YOU. STRONG ENOUGH THAT WITHOUT TRYING, YOU BESPELLED THAT PROSTITUTE.
YES.
NO, I DON'T BELIEVE YOU.
BELIEVE WHAT YOU LIKE, MA PETITE. IT IS THE TRUTH.
I DIDN'T WANT TO BELIEVE IT. BECAUSE IF IT WERE TRUE, I WAS IN FACT HIS HUMAN SERVANT. NOT IN MY ACTIONS BUT BY MY VERY PRESENCE.
SHIT.
YOU COULD SAY THAT.
NO, I CAN'T DEAL WITH THIS RIGHT NOW. YOU KEEP WHATEVER POWERS WE HAVE BETWEEN US IN CHECK, OKAY?
I WILL TRY.
DON'T TRY, DAMMIT, DO IT.
OF COURSE, MA PETITE.

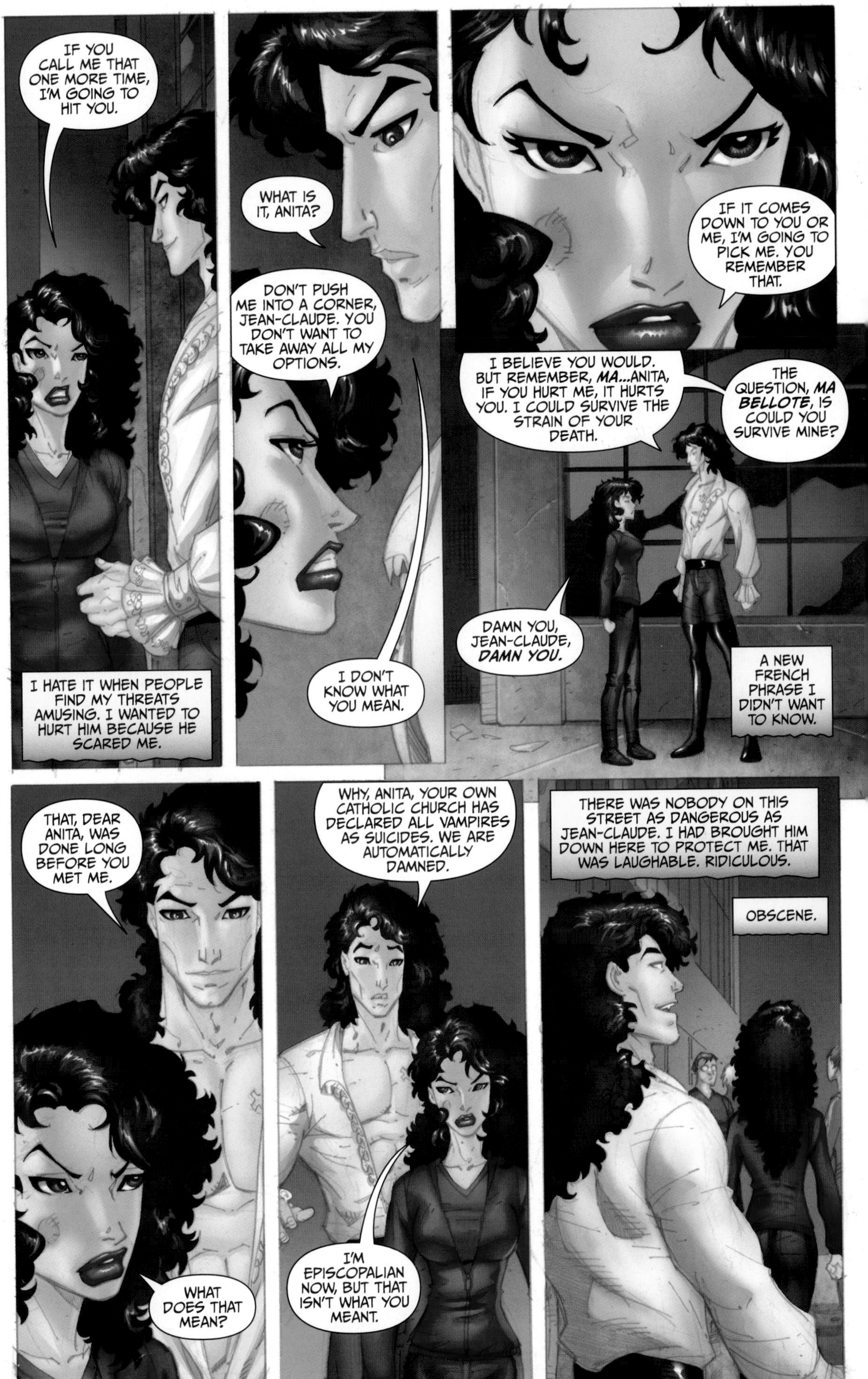

IF YOU CALL ME THAT ONE MORE TIME, I'M GOING TO HIT YOU.
I HATE IT WHEN PEOPLE FIND MY THREATS AMUSING. I WANTED TO HURT HIM BECAUSE HE SCARED ME.
WHAT IS IT, ANITA?
DON'T PUSH ME INTO A CORNER, JEAN-CLAUDE. YOU DON'T WANT TO TAKE AWAY ALL MY OPTIONS.
I DON'T KNOW WHAT YOU MEAN.
IF IT COMES DOWN TO YOU OR ME, I'M GOING TO PICK ME. YOU REMEMBER THAT.
I BELIEVE YOU WOULD. BUT REMEMBER, MA...ANITA, IF YOU HURT ME, IT HURTS YOU. I COULD SURVIVE THE STRAIN OF YOUR DEATH.
THE QUESTION, MA BELLOTE, IS COULD YOU SURVIVE MINE?
DAMN YOU, JEAN-CLAUDE, DAMN YOU.
A NEW FRENCH PHRASE I DIDN'T WANT TO KNOW.
THAT, DEAR ANITA, WAS DONE LONG BEFORE YOU MET ME.
WHAT DOES THAT MEAN?
WHY, ANITA, YOUR OWN CATHOLIC CHURCH HAS DECLARED ALL VAMPIRES AS SUICIDES. WE ARE AUTOMATICALLY DAMNED.
I'M EPISCOPALIAN NOW, BUT THAT ISN'T WHAT YOU MEANT.
THERE WAS NOBODY ON THIS STREET AS DANGEROUS AS JEAN-CLAUDE. I HAD BROUGHT HIM DOWN HERE TO PROTECT ME. THAT WAS LAUGHABLE. RIDICULOUS.
OBSCENE.

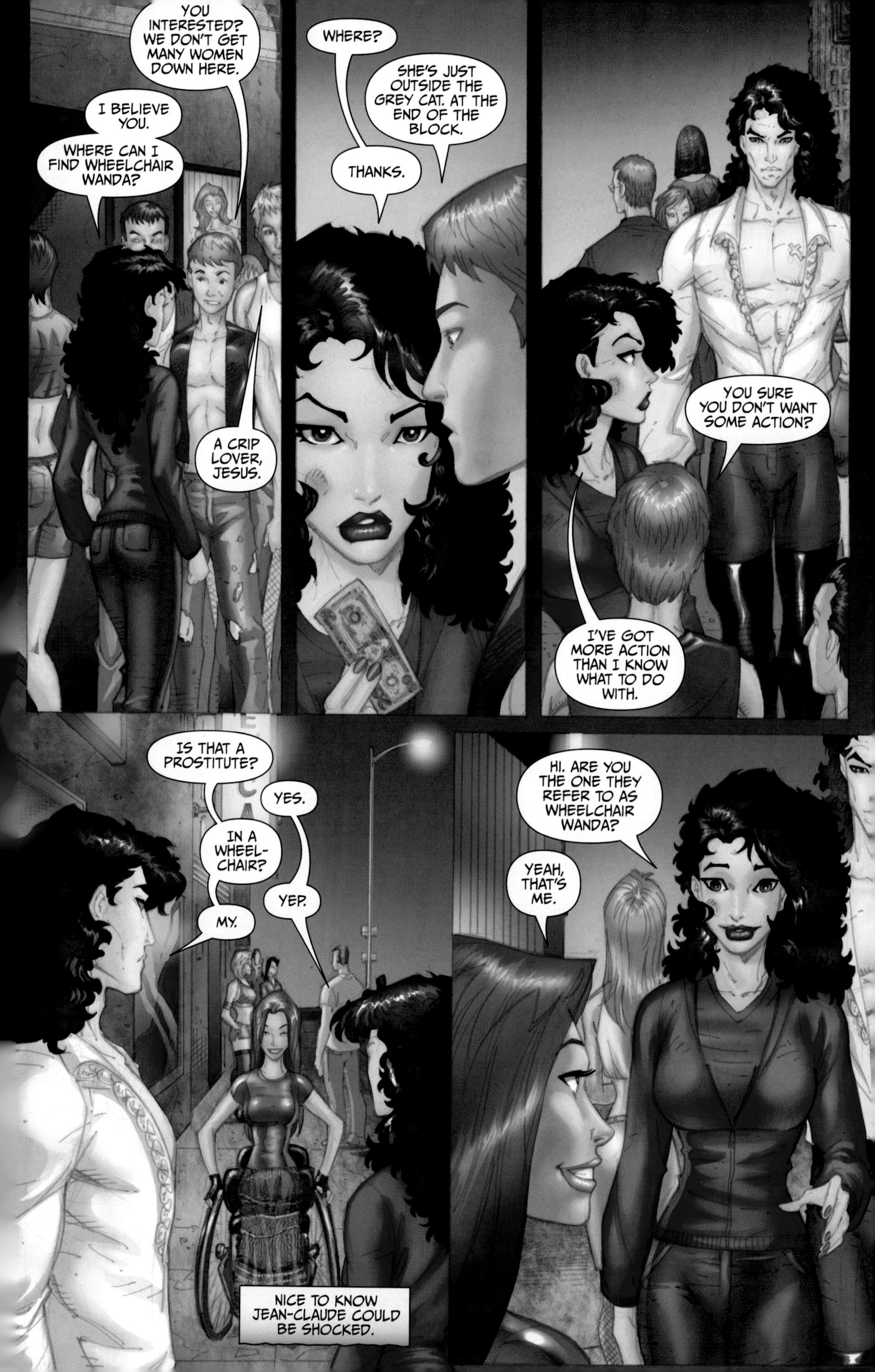
YOU INTERESTED? WE DON'T GET MANY WOMEN DOWN HERE.
I BELIEVE YOU.
WHERE CAN I FIND WHEELCHAIR WANDA?
A CRIP LOVER, JESUS.
WHERE?
SHE'S JUST OUTSIDE THE GREY CAT. AT THE END OF THE BLOCK.
THANKS.
YOU SURE YOU DON'T WANT SOME ACTION?
I'VE GOT MORE ACTION THAN I KNOW WHAT TO DO WITH.
IS THAT A PROSTITUTE?
YES.
IN A WHEEL-CHAIR?
YEP.
MY.
NICE TO KNOW JEAN-CLAUDE COULD BE SHOCKED.
HI. ARE YOU THE ONE THEY REFER TO AS WHEELCHAIR WANDA?
YEAH, THAT'S ME.

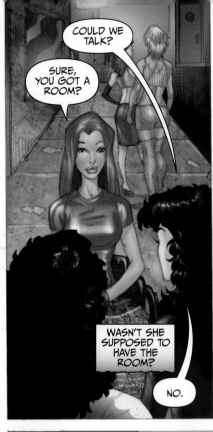

COULD WE TALK?

SURE, YOU GOT A ROOM?

WASN'T SHE SUPPOSED TO HAVE THE ROOM?

NO.

SHE JUST LOOKED AT ME LIKE I WAS SUPPOSED TO DO SOMETHING.

WE JUST WANT TO TALK TO YOU FOR AN HOUR, OR TWO. WE'LL PAY WHATEVER THE GOING RATE IS.

THREE-FIFTY.

JESUS, THAT'S A LITTLE STEEP.

SUPPLY AND DEMAND. YOU CAN'T GET A TASTE OF WHAT I HAVE ANYWHERE ELSE.

OKAY, YOU GOT A DEAL.

THERE ARE NO ELEVATORS IN MY APARTMENT BUILDING. THE ONLY CONSOLATION WAS THAT I GOT TO WATCH JEAN-CLAUDE CLIMB TWO FLIGHT OF STAIRS. SO SUE ME.

IT WAS A BUSINESS EXPENSE. COMPUTER PAPER, INK PENS, ONE PROSTITUTE, MANILA FOLDERS. SEE, IT FIT RIGHT IN.

BERT WAS GOING TO LOVE THIS ONE.

HE HAD A VERY NICE BACKSIDE FOR A VAMPIRE. BUT I WAS CAREFUL HE DIDN'T CATCH ME LOOKING.

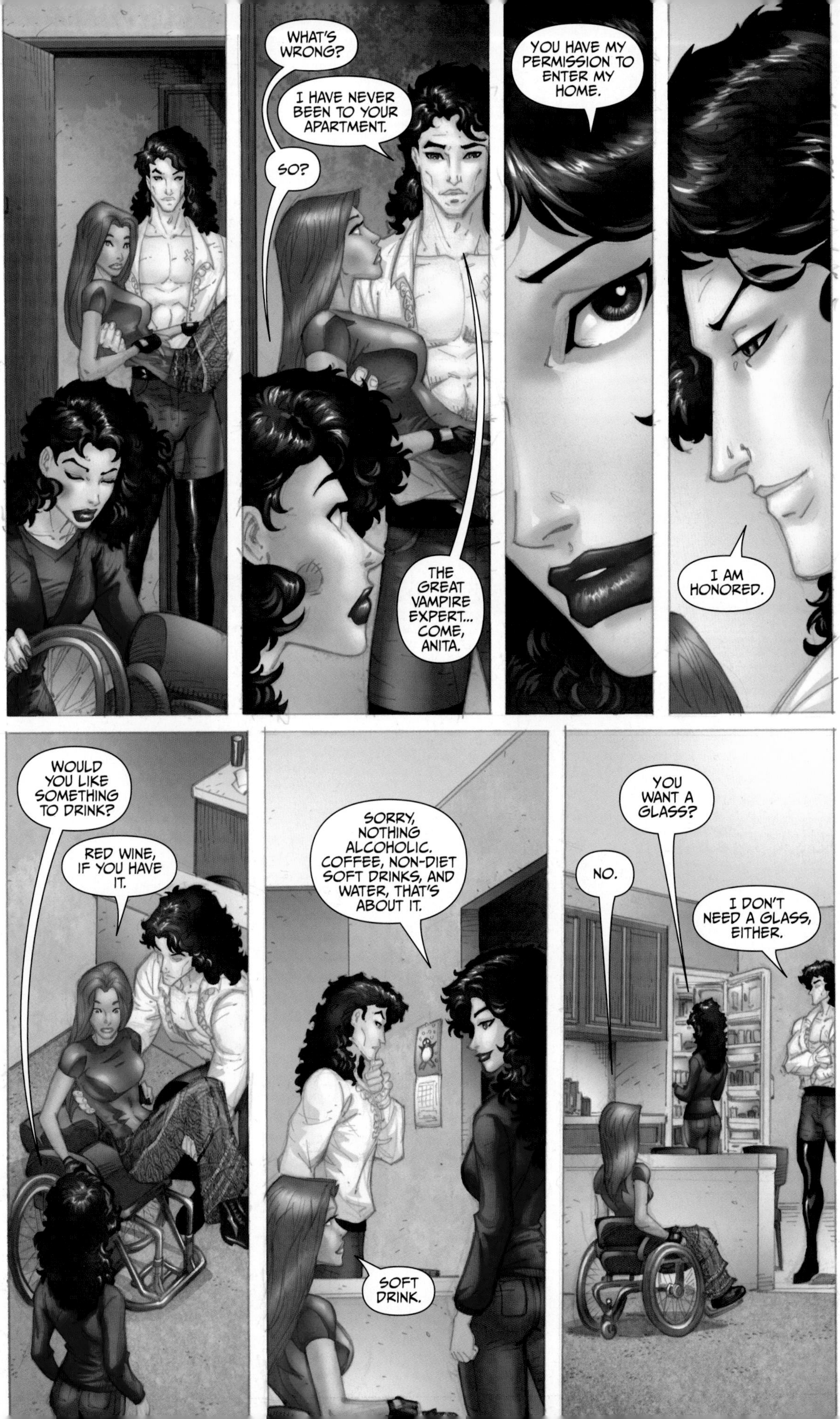
WHAT'S WRONG?
I HAVE NEVER BEEN TO YOUR APARTMENT.
SO?
THE GREAT VAMPIRE EXPERT... COME, ANITA.
YOU HAVE MY PERMISSION TO ENTER MY HOME.
I AM HONORED.
WOULD YOU LIKE SOMETHING TO DRINK?
RED WINE, IF YOU HAVE IT.
SORRY, NOTHING ALCOHOLIC. COFFEE, NON-DIET SOFT DRINKS, AND WATER, THAT'S ABOUT IT.
SOFT DRINK.
YOU WANT A GLASS?
NO.
I DON'T NEED A GLASS, EITHER.

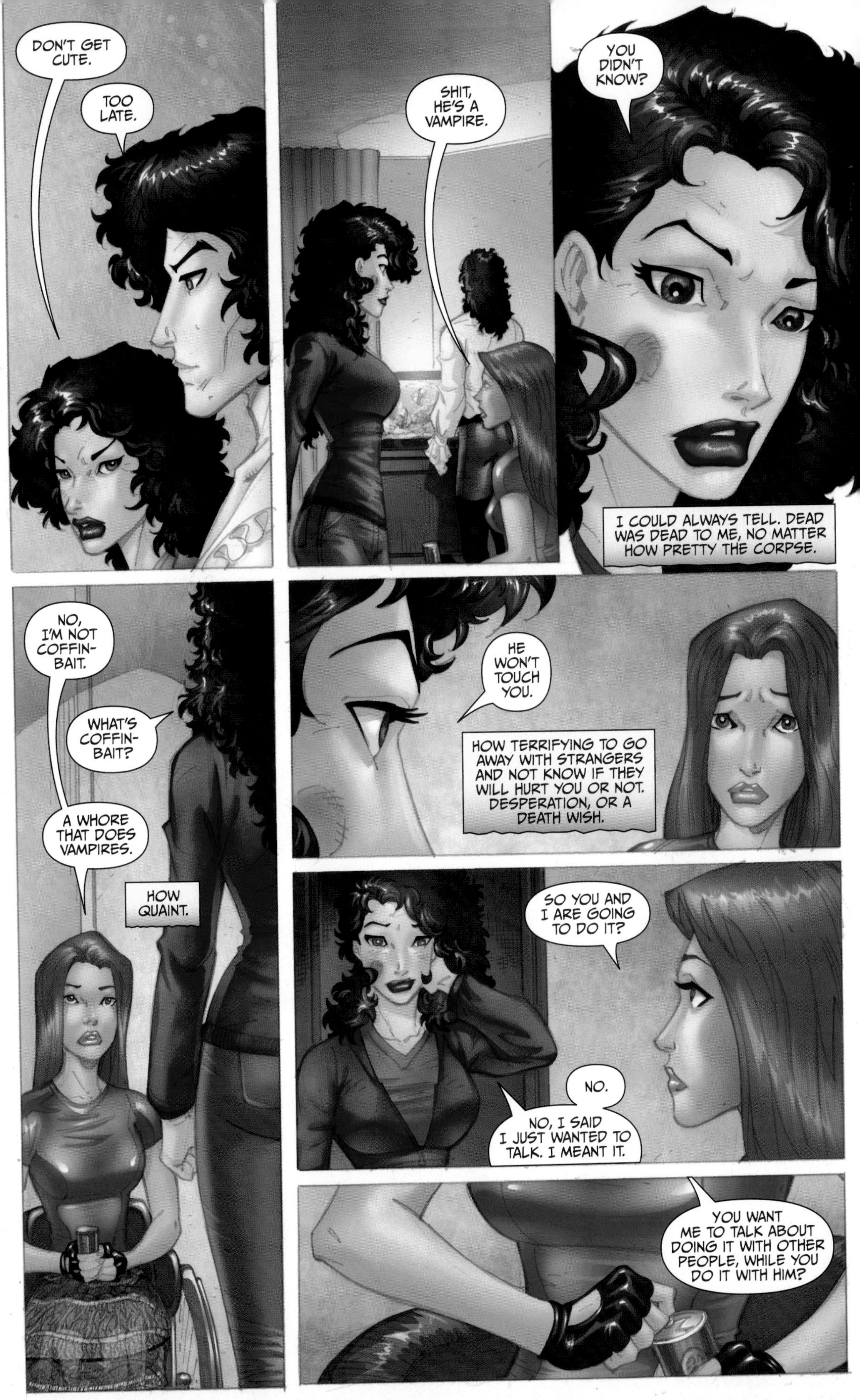
DON'T GET CUTE.
TOO LATE.
SHIT, HE'S A VAMPIRE.
YOU DIDN'T KNOW?
I COULD ALWAYS TELL. DEAD WAS DEAD TO ME, NO MATTER HOW PRETTY THE CORPSE.
NO, I'M NOT COFFIN-BAIT.
WHAT'S COFFIN-BAIT?
A WHORE THAT DOES VAMPIRES.
HOW QUAINT.
HE WON'T TOUCH YOU.
HOW TERRIFYING TO GO AWAY WITH STRANGERS AND NOT KNOW IF THEY WILL HURT YOU OR NOT. DESPERATION, OR A DEATH WISH.
SO YOU AND I ARE GOING TO DO IT?
NO.
NO, I SAID I JUST WANTED TO TALK. I MEANT IT.
YOU WANT ME TO TALK ABOUT DOING IT WITH OTHER PEOPLE, WHILE YOU DO IT WITH HIM?

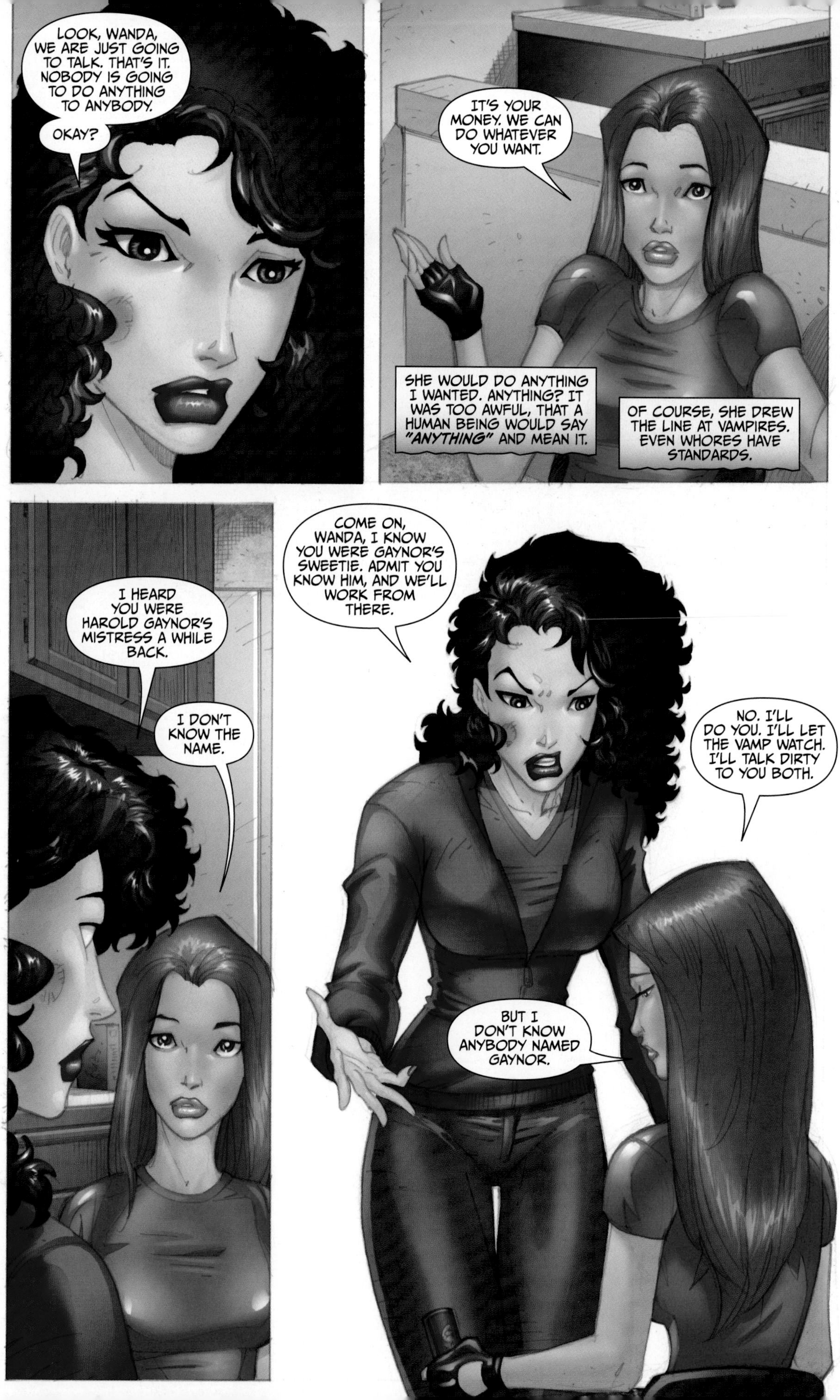
LOOK, WANDA, WE ARE JUST GOING TO TALK. THAT'S IT. NOBODY IS GOING TO DO ANYTHING TO ANYBODY.
OKAY?
IT'S YOUR MONEY. WE CAN DO WHATEVER YOU WANT.
SHE WOULD DO ANYTHING I WANTED. ANYTHING? IT WAS TOO AWFUL, THAT A HUMAN BEING WOULD SAY "ANYTHING" AND MEAN IT.
OF COURSE, SHE DREW THE LINE AT VAMPIRES. EVEN WHORES HAVE STANDARDS.
I HEARD YOU WERE HAROLD GAYNOR'S MISTRESS A WHILE BACK.
I DON'T KNOW THE NAME.
COME ON, WANDA, I KNOW YOU WERE GAYNOR'S SWEETIE. ADMIT YOU KNOW HIM, AND WE'LL WORK FROM THERE.
BUT I DON'T KNOW ANYBODY NAMED GAYNOR.
NO. I'LL DO YOU. I'LL LET THE VAMP WATCH. I'LL TALK DIRTY TO YOU BOTH.

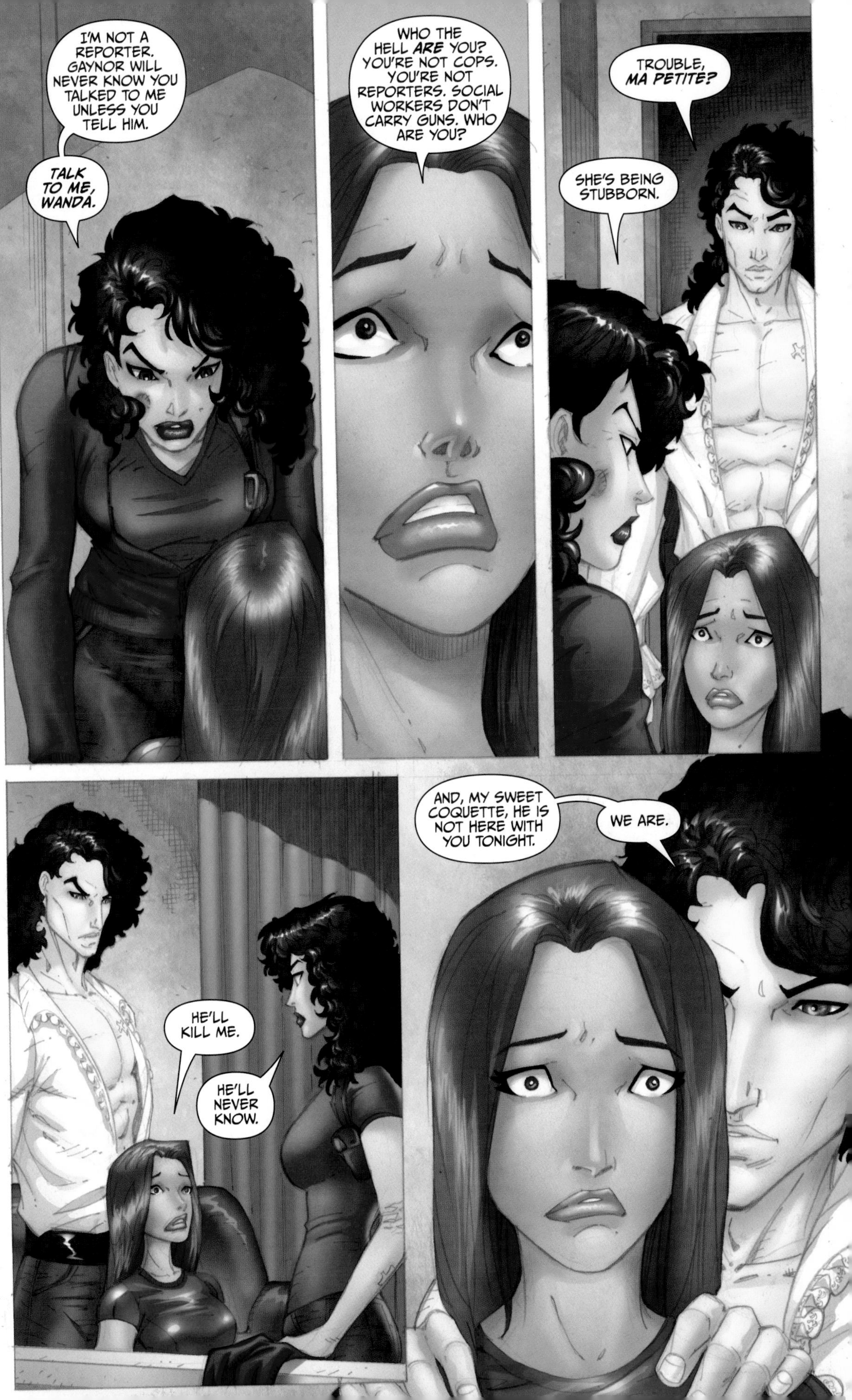
I'M NOT A REPORTER. GAYNOR WILL NEVER KNOW YOU TALKED TO ME UNLESS YOU TELL HIM.
TALK TO ME, WANDA.
WHO THE HELL ARE YOU? YOU'RE NOT COPS. YOU'RE NOT REPORTERS. SOCIAL WORKERS DON'T CARRY GUNS. WHO ARE YOU?
TROUBLE, MA PETITE?
SHE'S BEING STUBBORN.
HE'LL KILL ME.
HE'LL NEVER KNOW.
AND, MY SWEET COQUETTE, HE IS NOT HERE WITH YOU TONIGHT.
WE ARE.

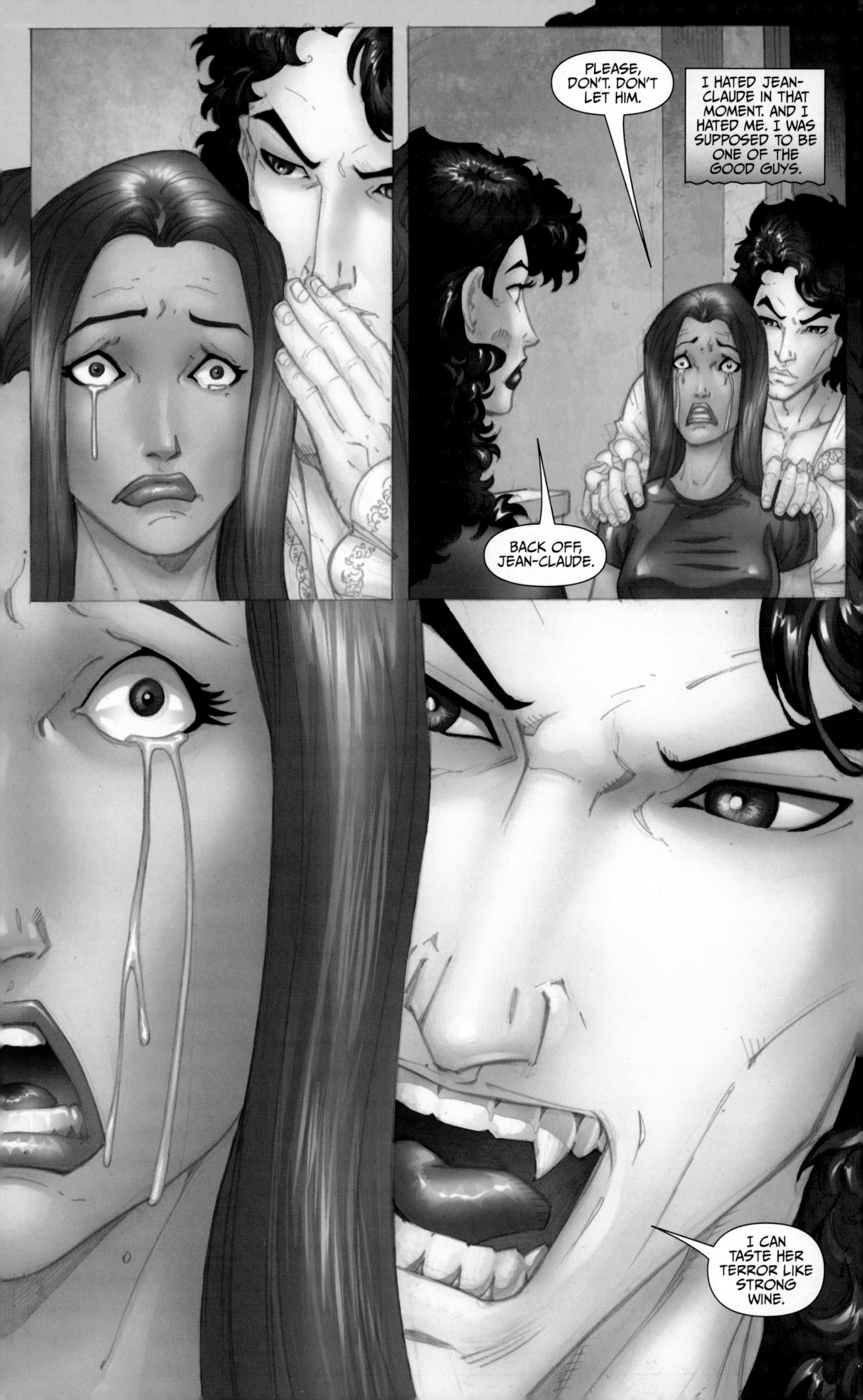
PLEASE, DON'T. DON'T LET HIM.
I HATED JEAN-CLAUDE IN THAT MOMENT. AND I HATED ME. I WAS SUPPOSED TO BE ONE OF THE GOOD GUYS.
BACK OFF, JEAN-CLAUDE.
I CAN TASTE HER TERROR LIKE STRONG WINE.

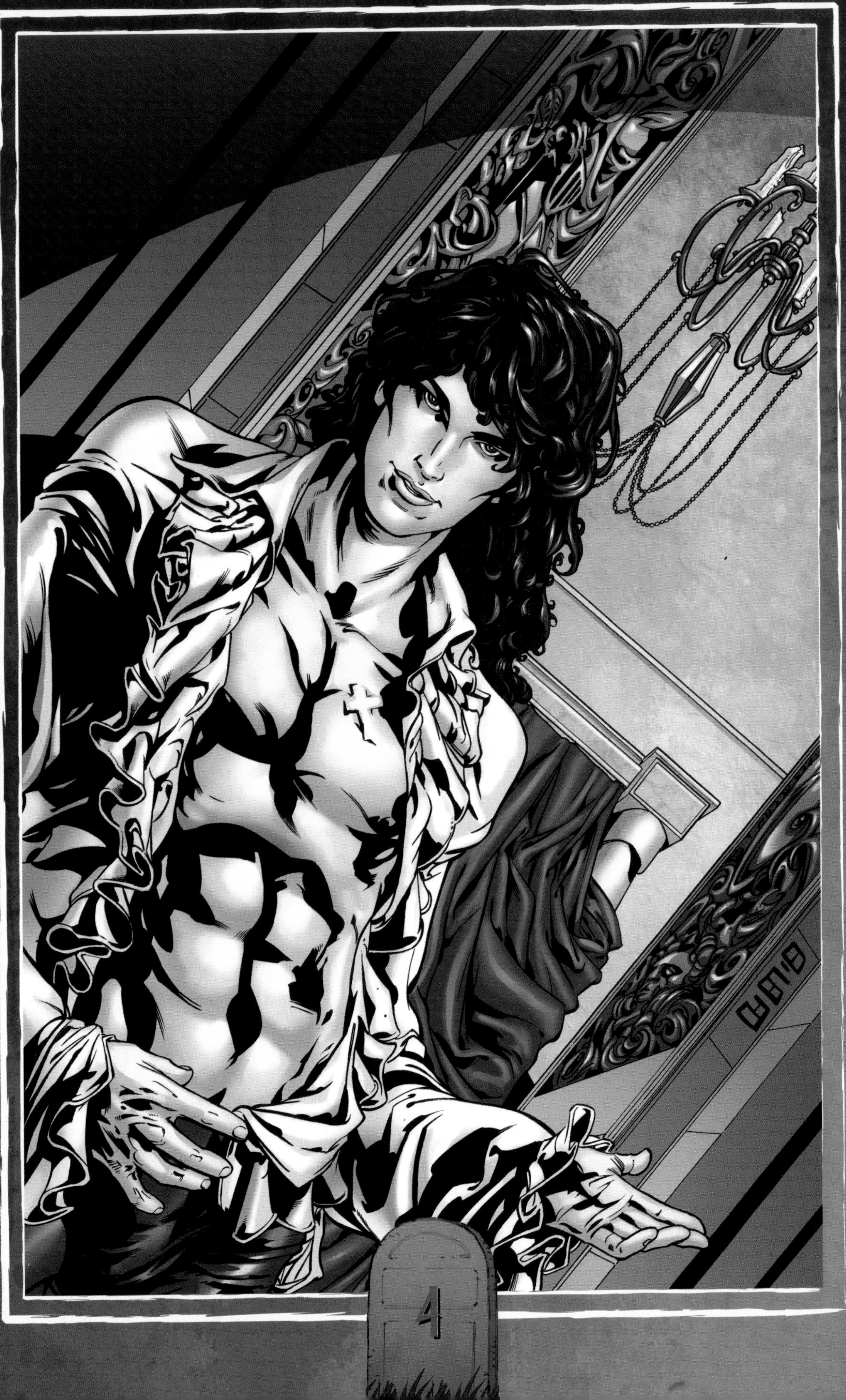
4

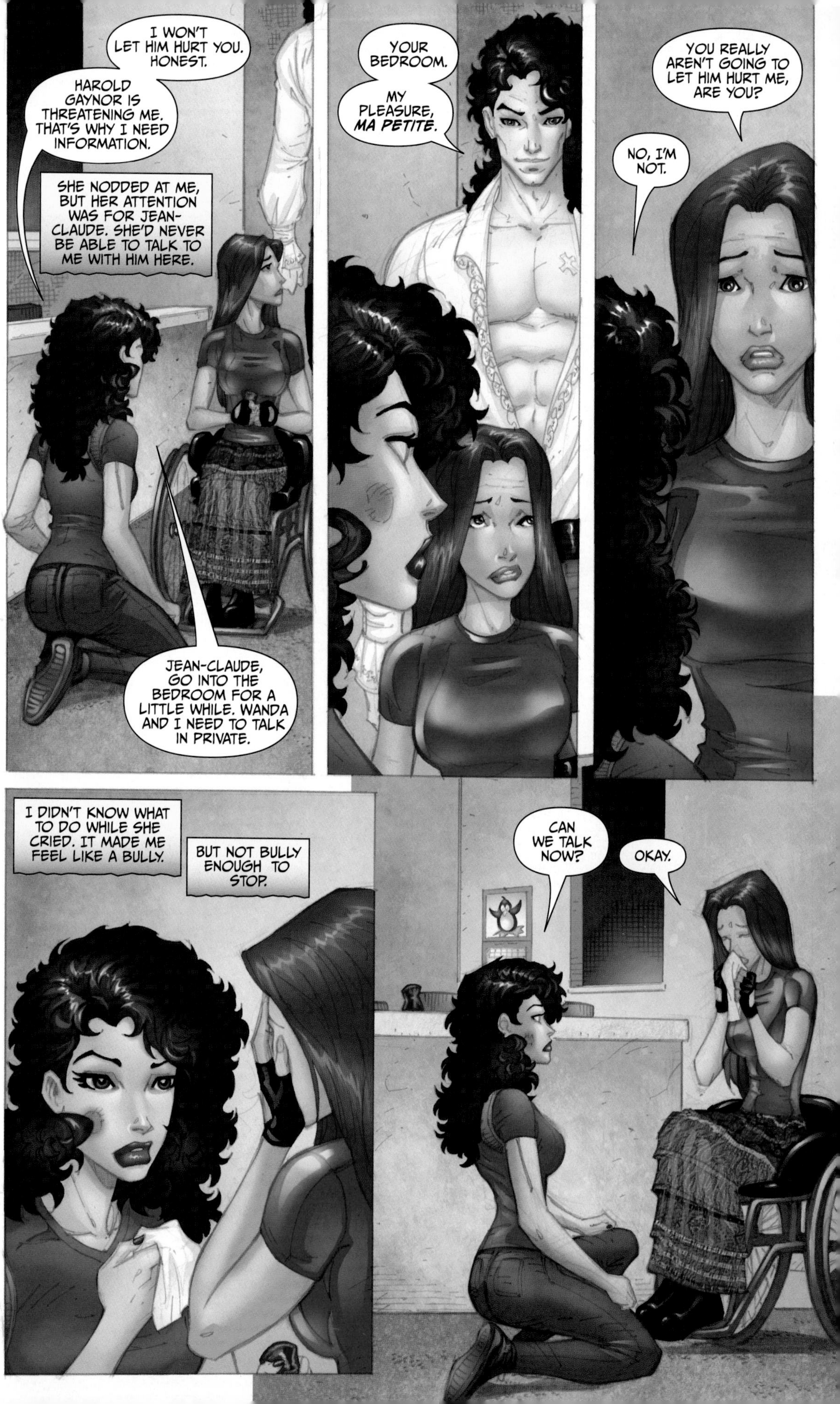

I WON'T LET HIM HURT YOU. HONEST.
HAROLD GAYNOR IS THREATENING ME. THAT'S WHY I NEED INFORMATION.
SHE NODDED AT ME, BUT HER ATTENTION WAS FOR JEAN-CLAUDE. SHE'D NEVER BE ABLE TO TALK TO ME WITH HIM HERE.
JEAN-CLAUDE, GO INTO THE BEDROOM FOR A LITTLE WHILE. WANDA AND I NEED TO TALK IN PRIVATE.
YOUR BEDROOM.
MY PLEASURE, *MA PETITE*.
YOU REALLY AREN'T GOING TO LET HIM HURT ME, ARE YOU?
NO, I'M NOT.
I DIDN'T KNOW WHAT TO DO WHILE SHE CRIED. IT MADE ME FEEL LIKE A BULLY.
BUT NOT BULLY ENOUGH TO STOP.
CAN WE TALK NOW?
OKAY.

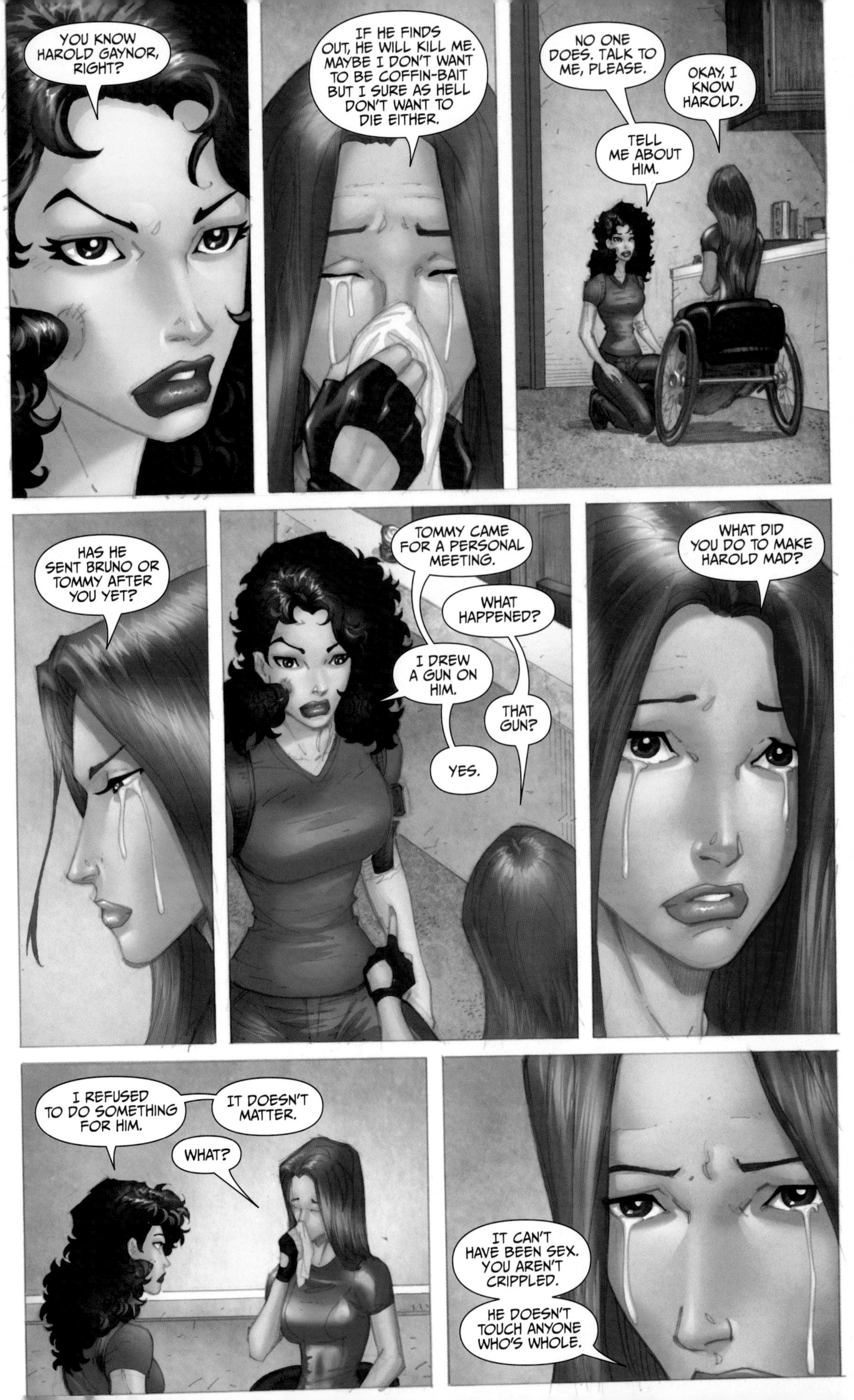
YOU KNOW HAROLD GAYNOR, RIGHT?
IF HE FINDS OUT, HE WILL KILL ME. MAYBE I DON'T WANT TO BE COFFIN-BAIT BUT I SURE AS HELL DON'T WANT TO DIE EITHER.
NO ONE DOES. TALK TO ME, PLEASE.
OKAY, I KNOW HAROLD.
TELL ME ABOUT HIM.
HAS HE SENT BRUNO OR TOMMY AFTER YOU YET?
TOMMY CAME FOR A PERSONAL MEETING.
WHAT HAPPENED?
I DREW A GUN ON HIM.
THAT GUN?
YES.
WHAT DID YOU DO TO MAKE HAROLD MAD?
I REFUSED TO DO SOMETHING FOR HIM.
IT DOESN'T MATTER.
WHAT?
IT CAN'T HAVE BEEN SEX. YOU AREN'T CRIPPLED.
HE DOESN'T TOUCH ANYONE WHO'S WHOLE.

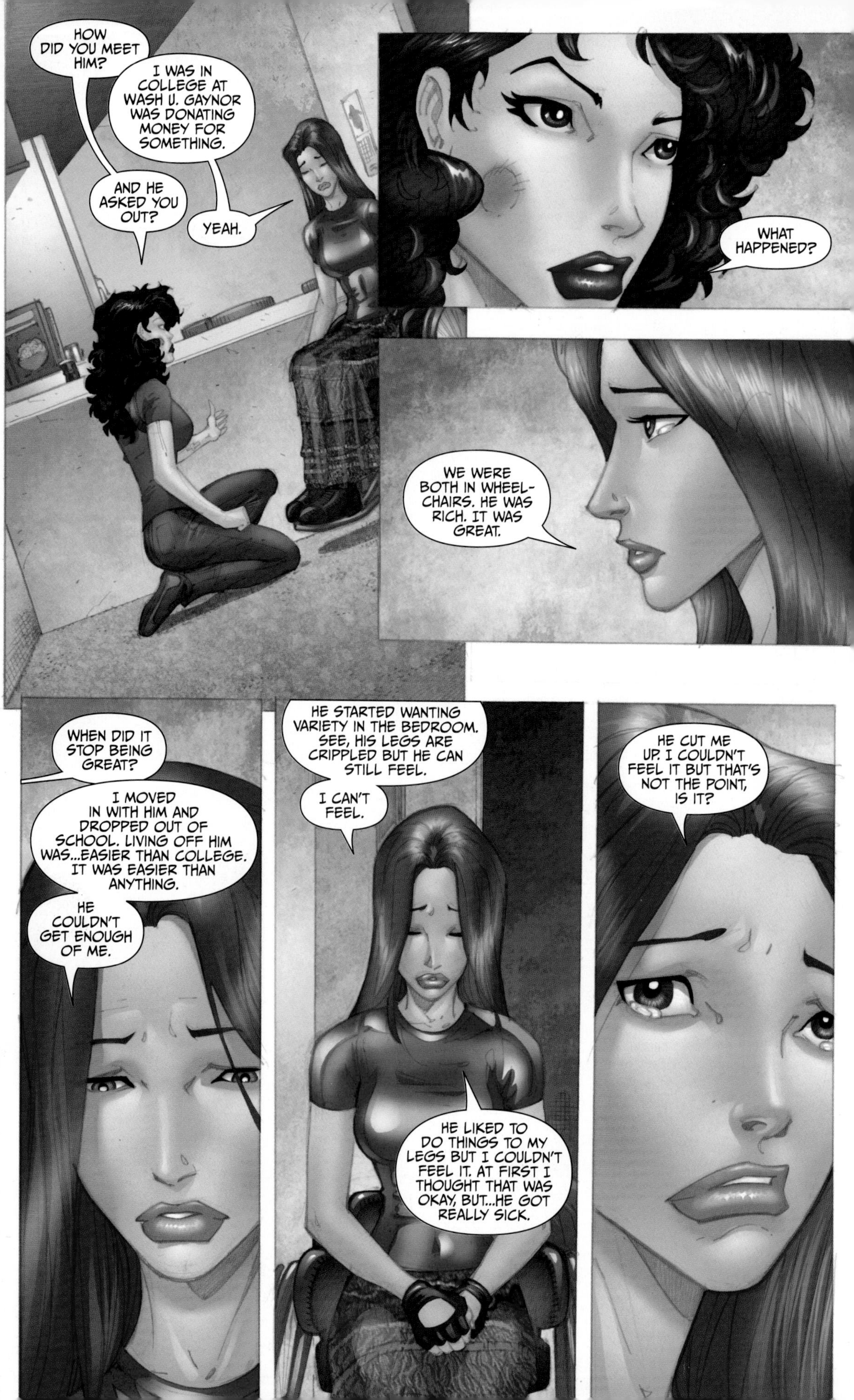
HOW DID YOU MEET HIM?
I WAS IN COLLEGE AT WASH U. GAYNOR WAS DONATING MONEY FOR SOMETHING.
AND HE ASKED YOU OUT?
YEAH.
WHAT HAPPENED?
WE WERE BOTH IN WHEEL-CHAIRS. HE WAS RICH. IT WAS GREAT.
WHEN DID IT STOP BEING GREAT?
I MOVED IN WITH HIM AND DROPPED OUT OF SCHOOL. LIVING OFF HIM WAS...EASIER THAN COLLEGE. IT WAS EASIER THAN ANYTHING.
HE COULDN'T GET ENOUGH OF ME.
HE STARTED WANTING VARIETY IN THE BEDROOM. SEE, HIS LEGS ARE CRIPPLED BUT HE CAN STILL FEEL.
I CAN'T FEEL.
HE LIKED TO DO THINGS TO MY LEGS BUT I COULDN'T FEEL IT. AT FIRST I THOUGHT THAT WAS OKAY, BUT...HE GOT REALLY SICK.
HE CUT ME UP. I COULDN'T FEEL IT BUT THAT'S NOT THE POINT, IS IT?

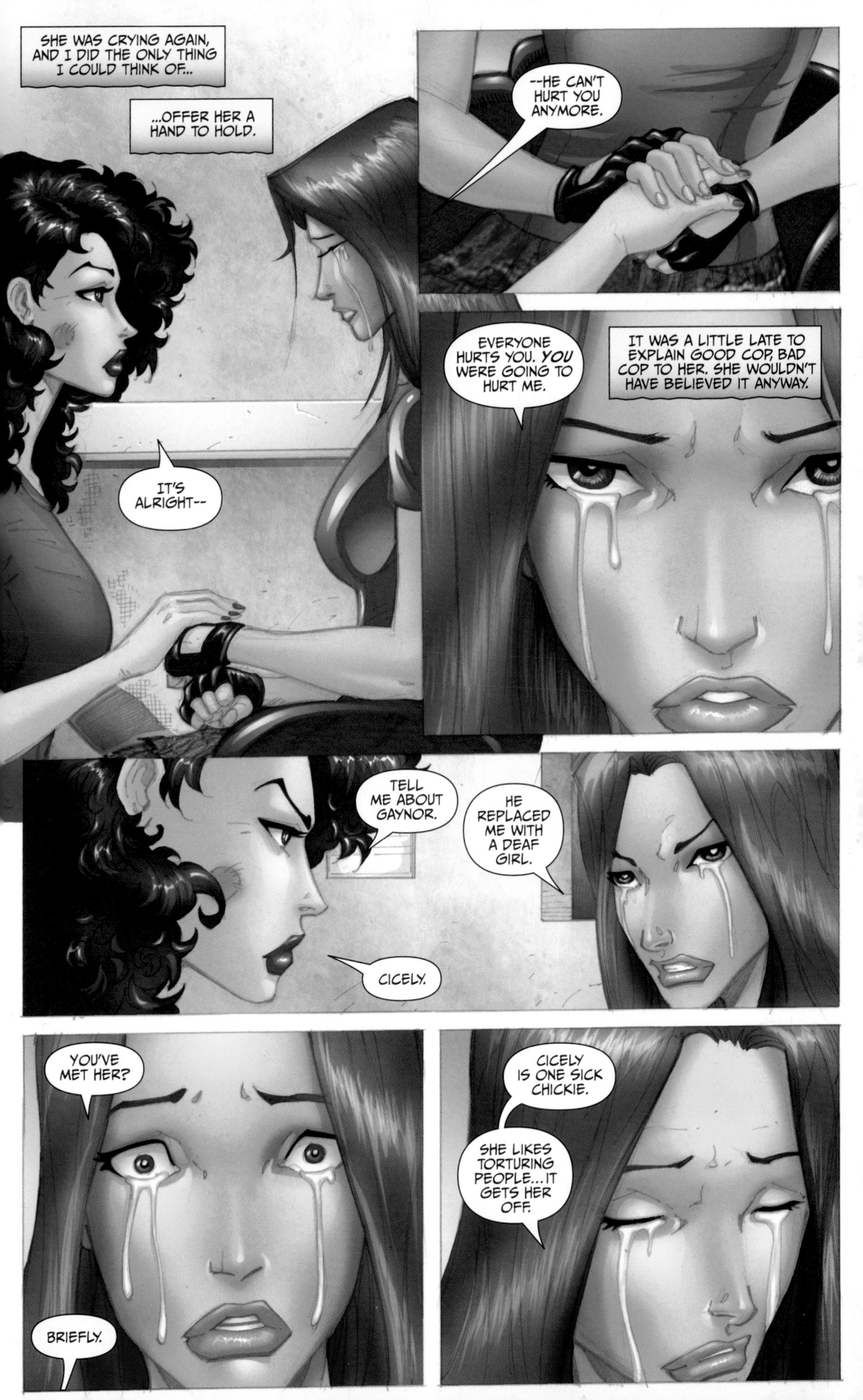
SHE WAS CRYING AGAIN, AND I DID THE ONLY THING I COULD THINK OF...
...OFFER HER A HAND TO HOLD.
IT'S ALRIGHT--
--HE CAN'T HURT YOU ANYMORE.
EVERYONE HURTS YOU. *YOU* WERE GOING TO HURT ME.
IT WAS A LITTLE LATE TO EXPLAIN GOOD COP, BAD COP TO HER. SHE WOULDN'T HAVE BELIEVED IT ANYWAY.
TELL ME ABOUT GAYNOR.
HE REPLACED ME WITH A DEAF GIRL.
CICELY.
YOU'VE MET HER?
BRIEFLY.
CICELY IS ONE SICK CHICKIE.
SHE LIKES TORTURING PEOPLE... IT GETS HER OFF.

HAROLD SLEPT WITH BOTH OF US AT THE SAME TIME, SOMETIMES. AT THE END IT WAS ALWAYS A THREESOME.

IT GOT REAL ROUGH.

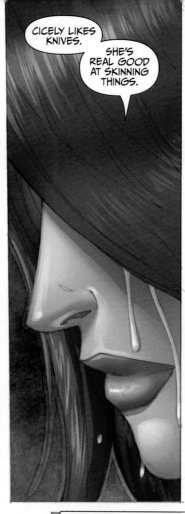

CICELY LIKES KNIVES.

SHE'S REAL GOOD AT SKINNING THINGS.

GAYNOR WOULD KILL ME JUST FOR TELLING YOU HIS BEDROOM SECRETS.

DO YOU KNOW ANY BUSINESS SECRETS?

NO, I SWEAR. HE WAS ALWAYS VERY CAREFUL TO KEEP ME OUT OF THAT.

I THOUGHT AT FIRST IT WAS SO IF THE POLICE CAME, I WOULDN'T BE ARRESTED.

LATER, I REALIZED IT WAS BECAUSE HE KNEW I WOULD BE REPLACED.

HE DIDN'T WANT ME TO KNOW ANYTHING THAT COULD HURT HIM AFTER HE THREW ME AWAY.

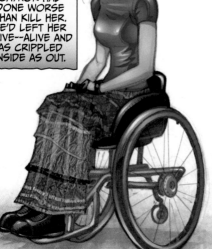

GAYNOR HAD DONE WORSE THAN KILL HER. HE'D LEFT HER ALIVE--ALIVE AND AS CRIPPLED INSIDE AS OUT.

I CAN'T TELL YOU ANYTHING BUT BEDROOM TALK. IT WON'T HELP YOU HURT HIM THOUGH.

WHAT DO YOU MEAN?

IS THERE ANY BEDROOM TALK THAT ISN'T ABOUT SEX?

PERSONAL SECRETS BUT NOT SEX. YOU WERE HIS SWEETIE FOR TWO YEARS. HE MUST HAVE TALKED ABOUT SOMETHING OTHER THAN SEX.

I...I GUESS HE TALKED ABOUT HIS FAMILY. HE WAS ILLEGITIMATE. HE WAS OBSESSED WITH HIS REAL FATHER'S FAMILY.

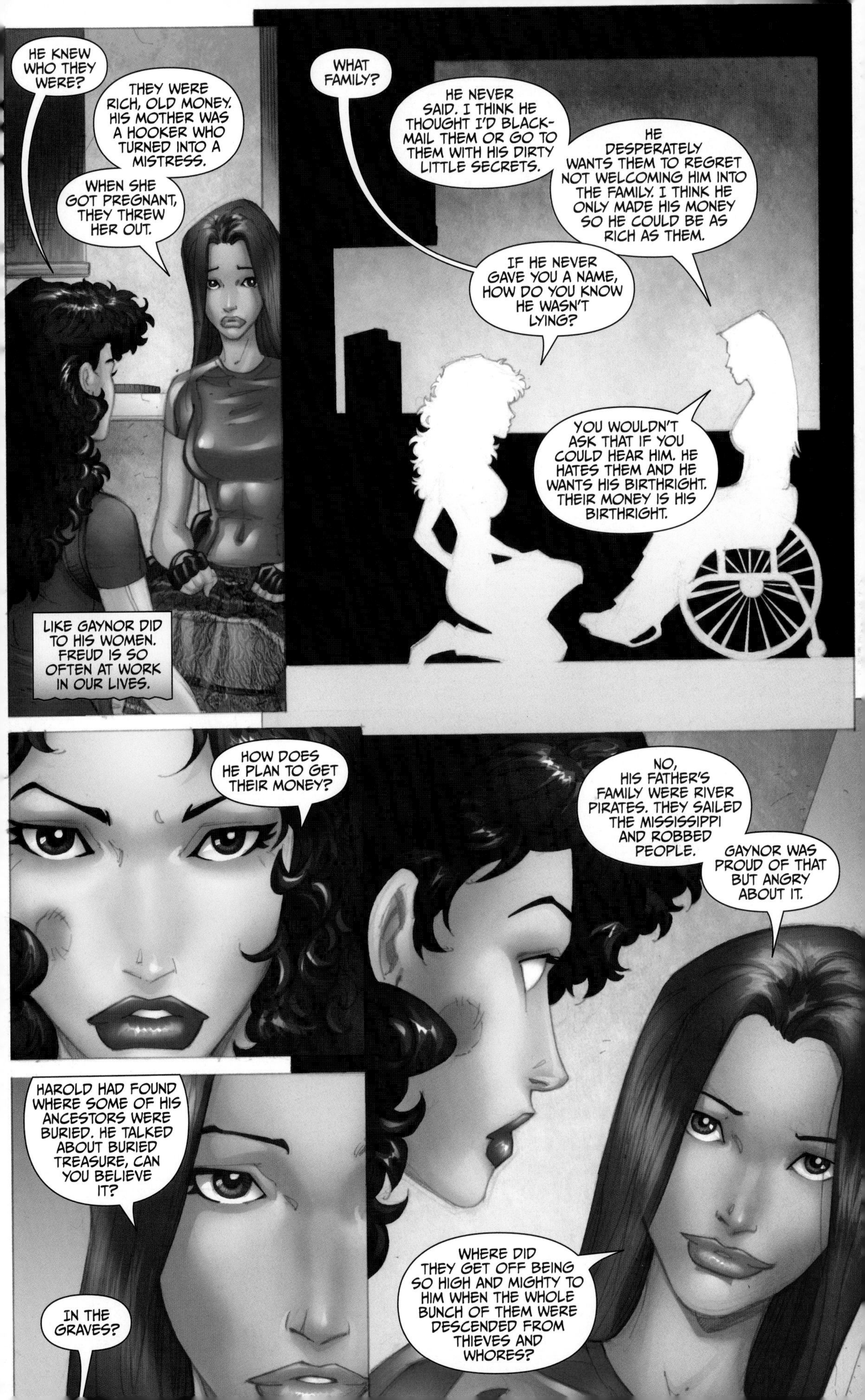
HE KNEW WHO THEY WERE?
THEY WERE RICH, OLD MONEY. HIS MOTHER WAS A HOOKER WHO TURNED INTO A MISTRESS.
WHEN SHE GOT PREGNANT, THEY THREW HER OUT.
LIKE GAYNOR DID TO HIS WOMEN. FREUD IS SO OFTEN AT WORK IN OUR LIVES.
WHAT FAMILY?
HE NEVER SAID. I THINK HE THOUGHT I'D BLACK-MAIL THEM OR GO TO THEM WITH HIS DIRTY LITTLE SECRETS.
HE DESPERATELY WANTS THEM TO REGRET NOT WELCOMING HIM INTO THE FAMILY. I THINK HE ONLY MADE HIS MONEY SO HE COULD BE AS RICH AS THEM.
IF HE NEVER GAVE YOU A NAME, HOW DO YOU KNOW HE WASN'T LYING?
YOU WOULDN'T ASK THAT IF YOU COULD HEAR HIM. HE HATES THEM AND HE WANTS HIS BIRTHRIGHT. THEIR MONEY IS HIS BIRTHRIGHT.
HOW DOES HE PLAN TO GET THEIR MONEY?
NO, HIS FATHER'S FAMILY WERE RIVER PIRATES. THEY SAILED THE MISSISSIPPI AND ROBBED PEOPLE.
GAYNOR WAS PROUD OF THAT BUT ANGRY ABOUT IT.
WHERE DID THEY GET OFF BEING SO HIGH AND MIGHTY TO HIM WHEN THE WHOLE BUNCH OF THEM WERE DESCENDED FROM THIEVES AND WHORES?
HAROLD HAD FOUND WHERE SOME OF HIS ANCESTORS WERE BURIED. HE TALKED ABOUT BURIED TREASURE, CAN YOU BELIEVE IT?
IN THE GRAVES?

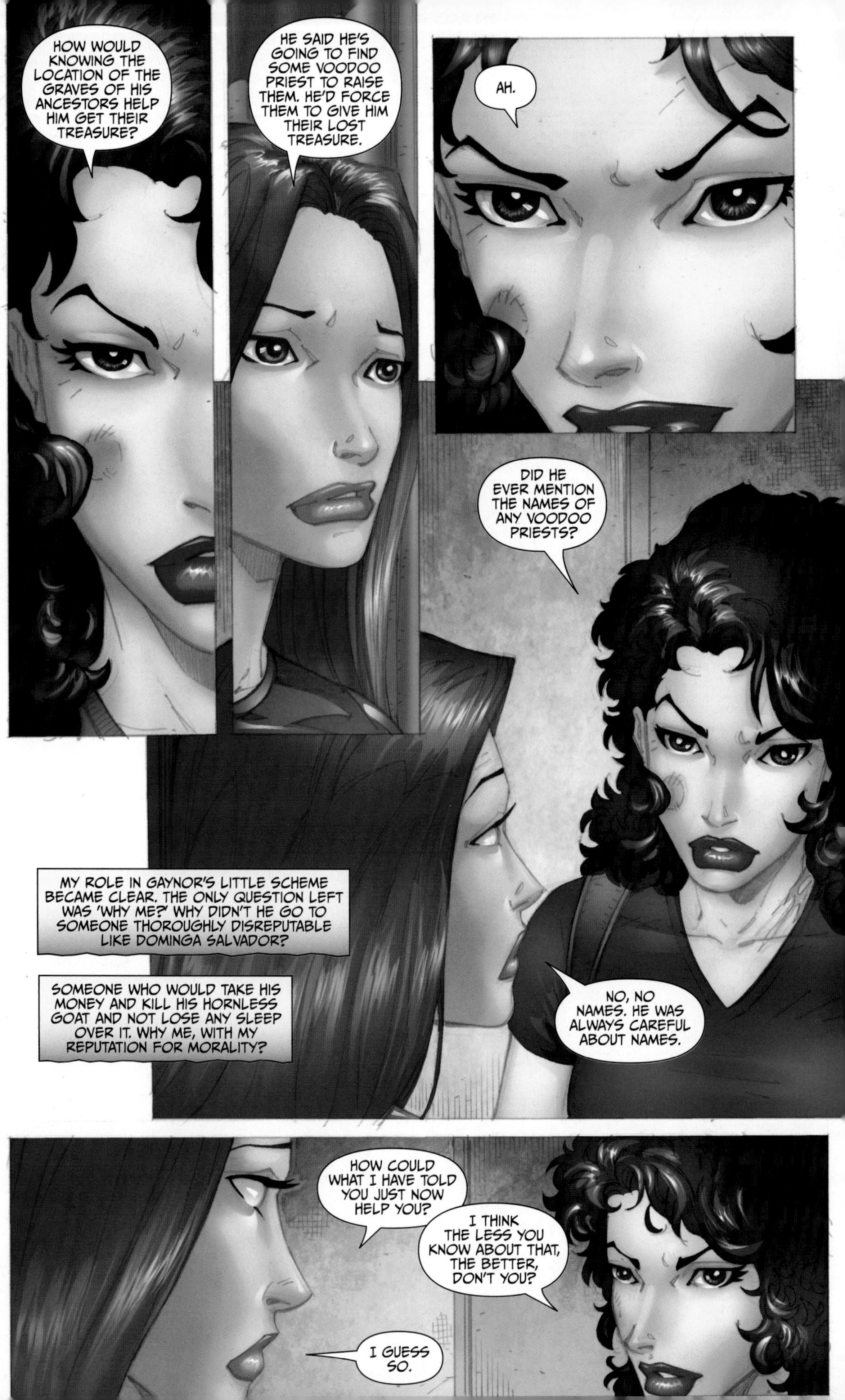
HOW WOULD KNOWING THE LOCATION OF THE GRAVES OF HIS ANCESTORS HELP HIM GET THEIR TREASURE?
HE SAID HE'S GOING TO FIND SOME VOODOO PRIEST TO RAISE THEM. HE'D FORCE THEM TO GIVE HIM THEIR LOST TREASURE.
AH.
DID HE EVER MENTION THE NAMES OF ANY VOODOO PRIESTS?
MY ROLE IN GAYNOR'S LITTLE SCHEME BECAME CLEAR. THE ONLY QUESTION LEFT WAS 'WHY ME?' WHY DIDN'T HE GO TO SOMEONE THOROUGHLY DISREPUTABLE LIKE DOMINGA SALVADOR?
SOMEONE WHO WOULD TAKE HIS MONEY AND KILL HIS HORNLESS GOAT AND NOT LOSE ANY SLEEP OVER IT. WHY ME, WITH MY REPUTATION FOR MORALITY?
NO, NO NAMES. HE WAS ALWAYS CAREFUL ABOUT NAMES.
HOW COULD WHAT I HAVE TOLD YOU JUST NOW HELP YOU?
I THINK THE LESS YOU KNOW ABOUT THAT, THE BETTER, DON'T YOU?
I GUESS SO.

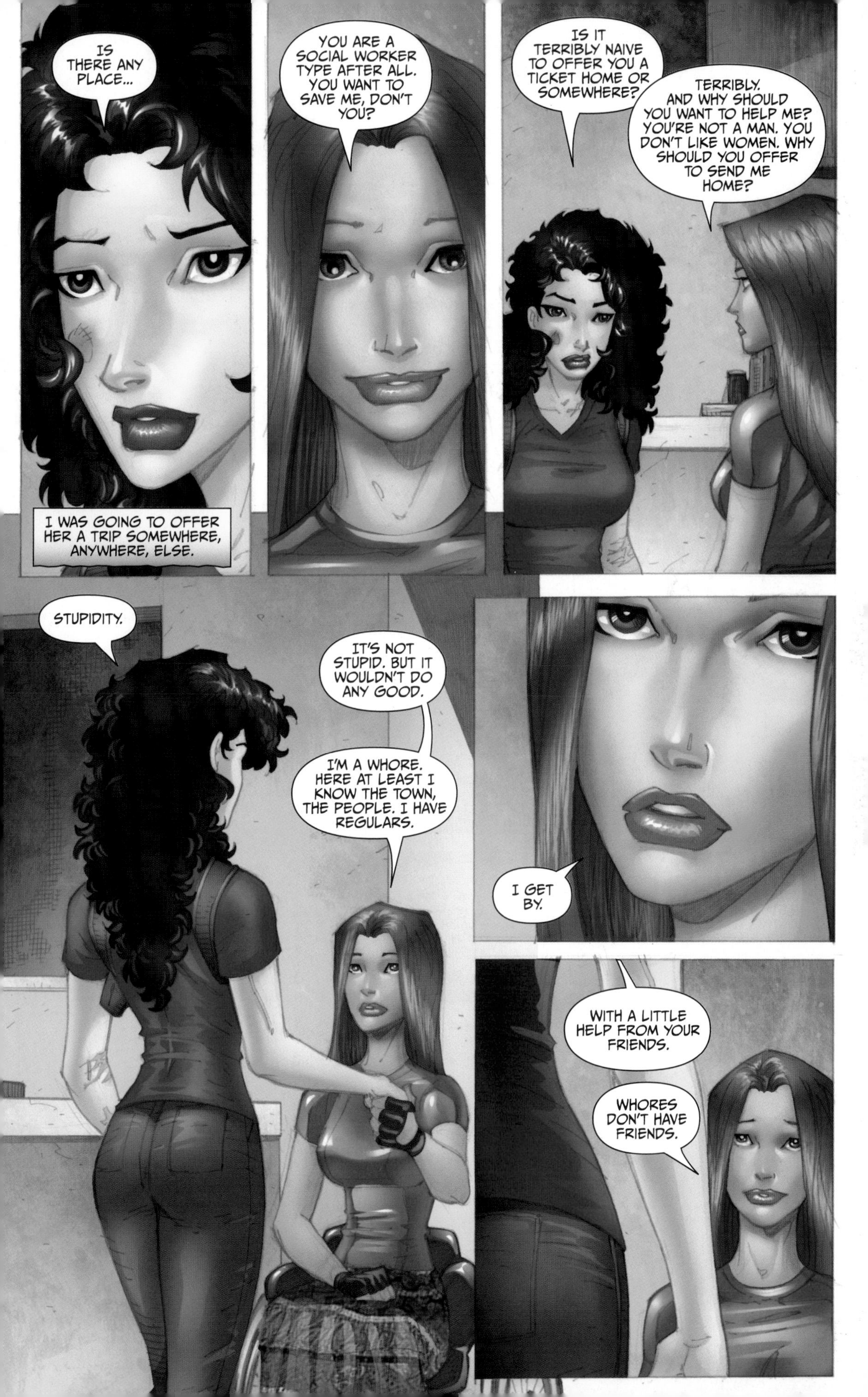
IS THERE ANY PLACE...
I WAS GOING TO OFFER HER A TRIP SOMEWHERE, ANYWHERE, ELSE.
YOU ARE A SOCIAL WORKER TYPE AFTER ALL. YOU WANT TO SAVE ME, DON'T YOU?
IS IT TERRIBLY NAIVE TO OFFER YOU A TICKET HOME OR SOMEWHERE?
TERRIBLY. AND WHY SHOULD YOU WANT TO HELP ME? YOU'RE NOT A MAN. YOU DON'T LIKE WOMEN. WHY SHOULD YOU OFFER TO SEND ME HOME?
STUPIDITY.
IT'S NOT STUPID. BUT IT WOULDN'T DO ANY GOOD.
I'M A WHORE. HERE AT LEAST I KNOW THE TOWN, THE PEOPLE. I HAVE REGULARS.
I GET BY.
WITH A LITTLE HELP FROM YOUR FRIENDS.
WHORES DON'T HAVE FRIENDS.

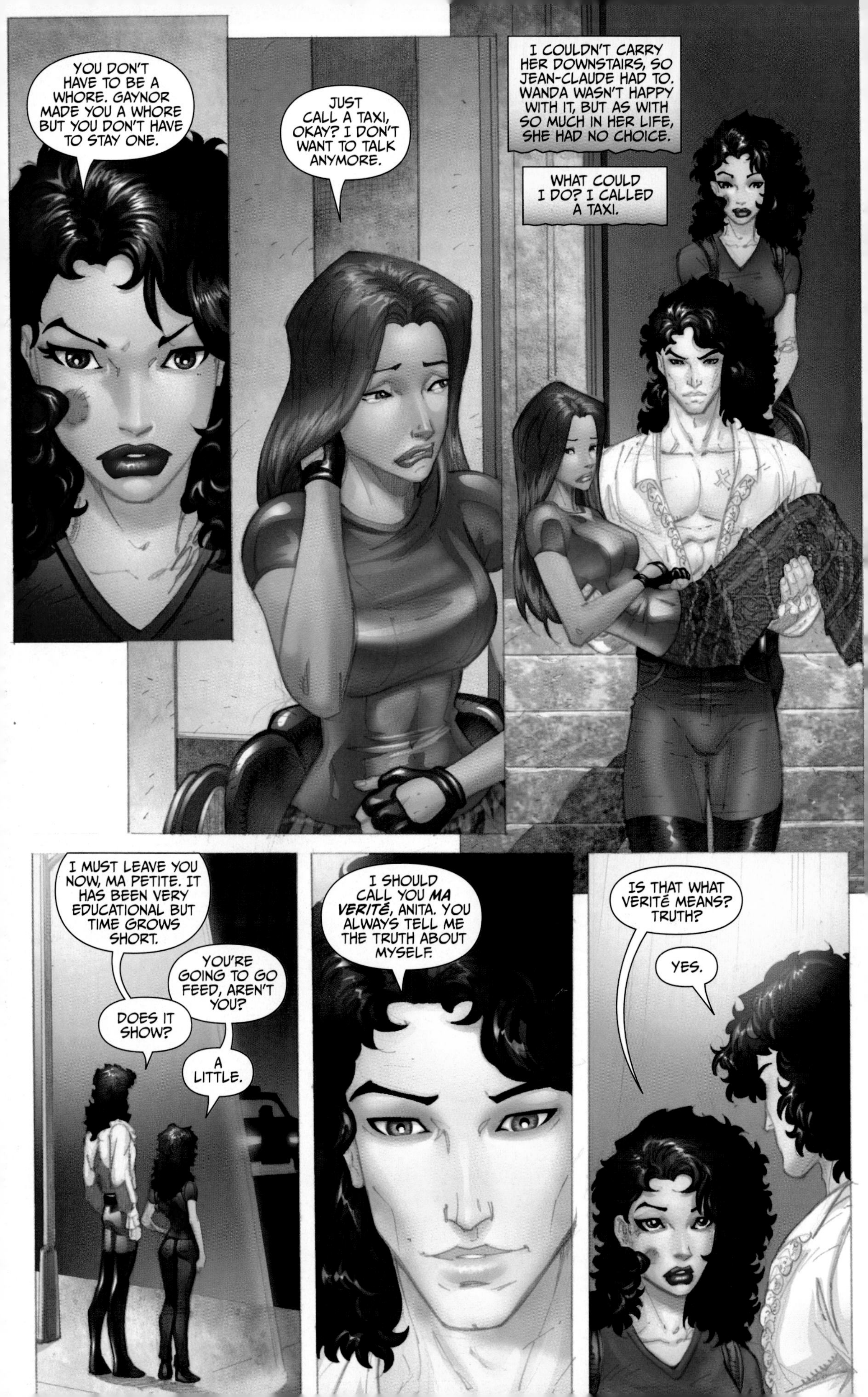
YOU DON'T HAVE TO BE A WHORE. GAYNOR MADE YOU A WHORE BUT YOU DON'T HAVE TO STAY ONE.
JUST CALL A TAXI, OKAY? I DON'T WANT TO TALK ANYMORE.
I COULDN'T CARRY HER DOWNSTAIRS, SO JEAN-CLAUDE HAD TO. WANDA WASN'T HAPPY WITH IT, BUT AS WITH SO MUCH IN HER LIFE, SHE HAD NO CHOICE.
WHAT COULD I DO? I CALLED A TAXI.
I MUST LEAVE YOU NOW, MA PETITE. IT HAS BEEN VERY EDUCATIONAL BUT TIME GROWS SHORT.
YOU'RE GOING TO GO FEED, AREN'T YOU?
DOES IT SHOW?
A LITTLE.
I SHOULD CALL YOU *MA VERITÉ*, ANITA. YOU ALWAYS TELL ME THE TRUTH ABOUT MYSELF.
IS THAT WHAT VERITÉ MEANS? TRUTH?
YES.

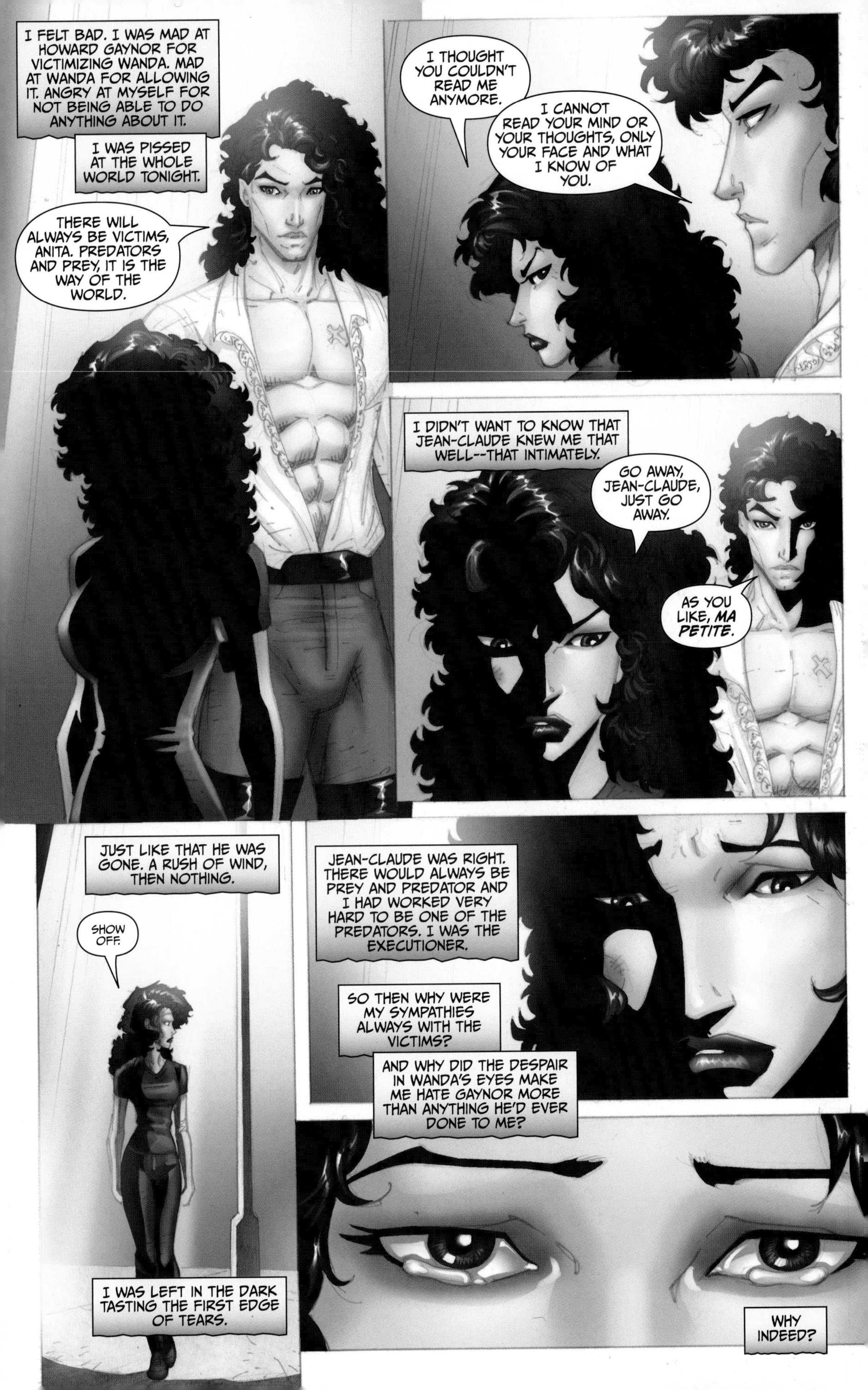
I FELT BAD. I WAS MAD AT HOWARD GAYNOR FOR VICTIMIZING WANDA. MAD AT WANDA FOR ALLOWING IT. ANGRY AT MYSELF FOR NOT BEING ABLE TO DO ANYTHING ABOUT IT.
I WAS PISSED AT THE WHOLE WORLD TONIGHT.
THERE WILL ALWAYS BE VICTIMS, ANITA. PREDATORS AND PREY, IT IS THE WAY OF THE WORLD.
I THOUGHT YOU COULDN'T READ ME ANYMORE.
I CANNOT READ YOUR MIND OR YOUR THOUGHTS, ONLY YOUR FACE AND WHAT I KNOW OF YOU.
I DIDN'T WANT TO KNOW THAT JEAN-CLAUDE KNEW ME THAT WELL--THAT INTIMATELY.
GO AWAY, JEAN-CLAUDE, JUST GO AWAY.
AS YOU LIKE, *MA PETITE*.
JUST LIKE THAT HE WAS GONE. A RUSH OF WIND, THEN NOTHING.
SHOW OFF.
I WAS LEFT IN THE DARK TASTING THE FIRST EDGE OF TEARS.
JEAN-CLAUDE WAS RIGHT. THERE WOULD ALWAYS BE PREY AND PREDATOR AND I HAD WORKED VERY HARD TO BE ONE OF THE PREDATORS. I WAS THE EXECUTIONER.
SO THEN WHY WERE MY SYMPATHIES ALWAYS WITH THE VICTIMS?
AND WHY DID THE DESPAIR IN WANDA'S EYES MAKE ME HATE GAYNOR MORE THAN ANYTHING HE'D EVER DONE TO ME?
WHY INDEED?

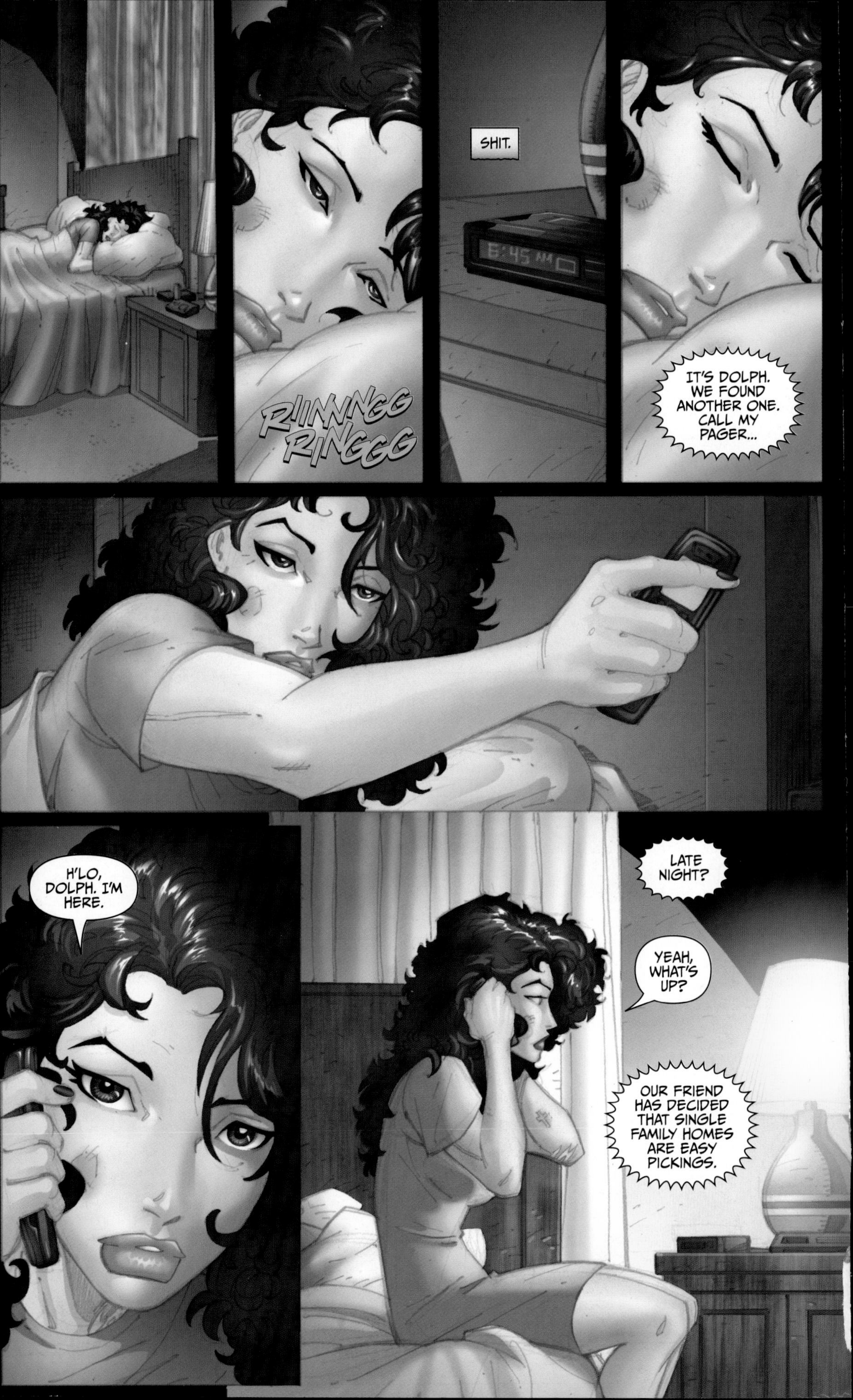
RIIINNNGG
RINGGG
SHIT.
6:45 AM
IT'S DOLPH. WE FOUND ANOTHER ONE. CALL MY PAGER...
H'LO, DOLPH. I'M HERE.
LATE NIGHT?
YEAH, WHAT'S UP?
OUR FRIEND HAS DECIDED THAT SINGLE FAMILY HOMES ARE EASY PICKINGS.

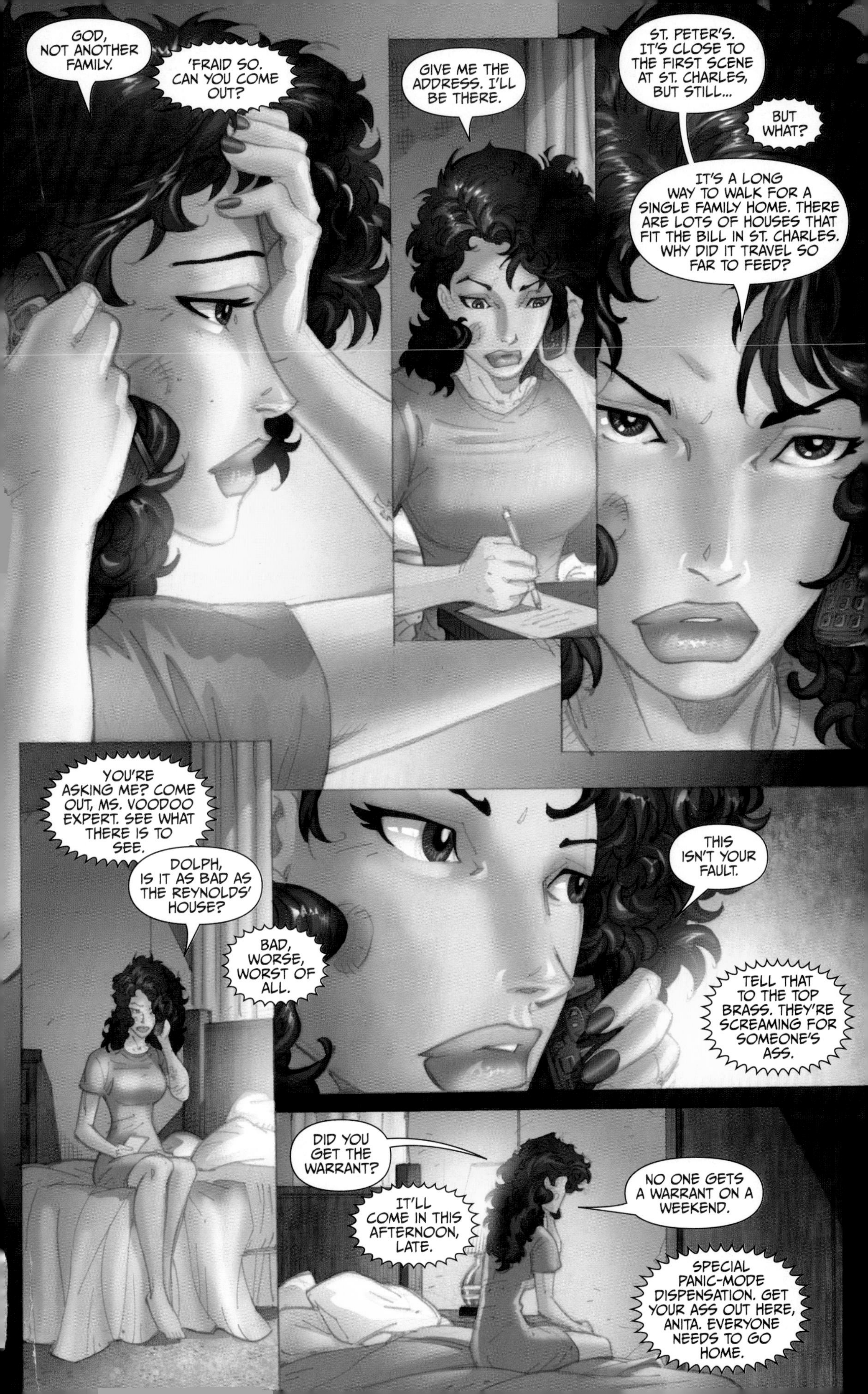
GOD, NOT ANOTHER FAMILY.
'FRAID SO. CAN YOU COME OUT?
GIVE ME THE ADDRESS. I'LL BE THERE.
ST. PETER'S. IT'S CLOSE TO THE FIRST SCENE AT ST. CHARLES, BUT STILL...
BUT WHAT?
IT'S A LONG WAY TO WALK FOR A SINGLE FAMILY HOME. THERE ARE LOTS OF HOUSES THAT FIT THE BILL IN ST. CHARLES. WHY DID IT TRAVEL SO FAR TO FEED?
YOU'RE ASKING ME? COME OUT, MS. VOODOO EXPERT. SEE WHAT THERE IS TO SEE.
DOLPH, IS IT AS BAD AS THE REYNOLDS' HOUSE?
BAD, WORSE, WORST OF ALL.
THIS ISN'T YOUR FAULT.
TELL THAT TO THE TOP BRASS. THEY'RE SCREAMING FOR SOMEONE'S ASS.
DID YOU GET THE WARRANT?
IT'LL COME IN THIS AFTERNOON, LATE.
NO ONE GETS A WARRANT ON A WEEKEND.
SPECIAL PANIC-MODE DISPENSATION. GET YOUR ASS OUT HERE, ANITA. EVERYONE NEEDS TO GO HOME.

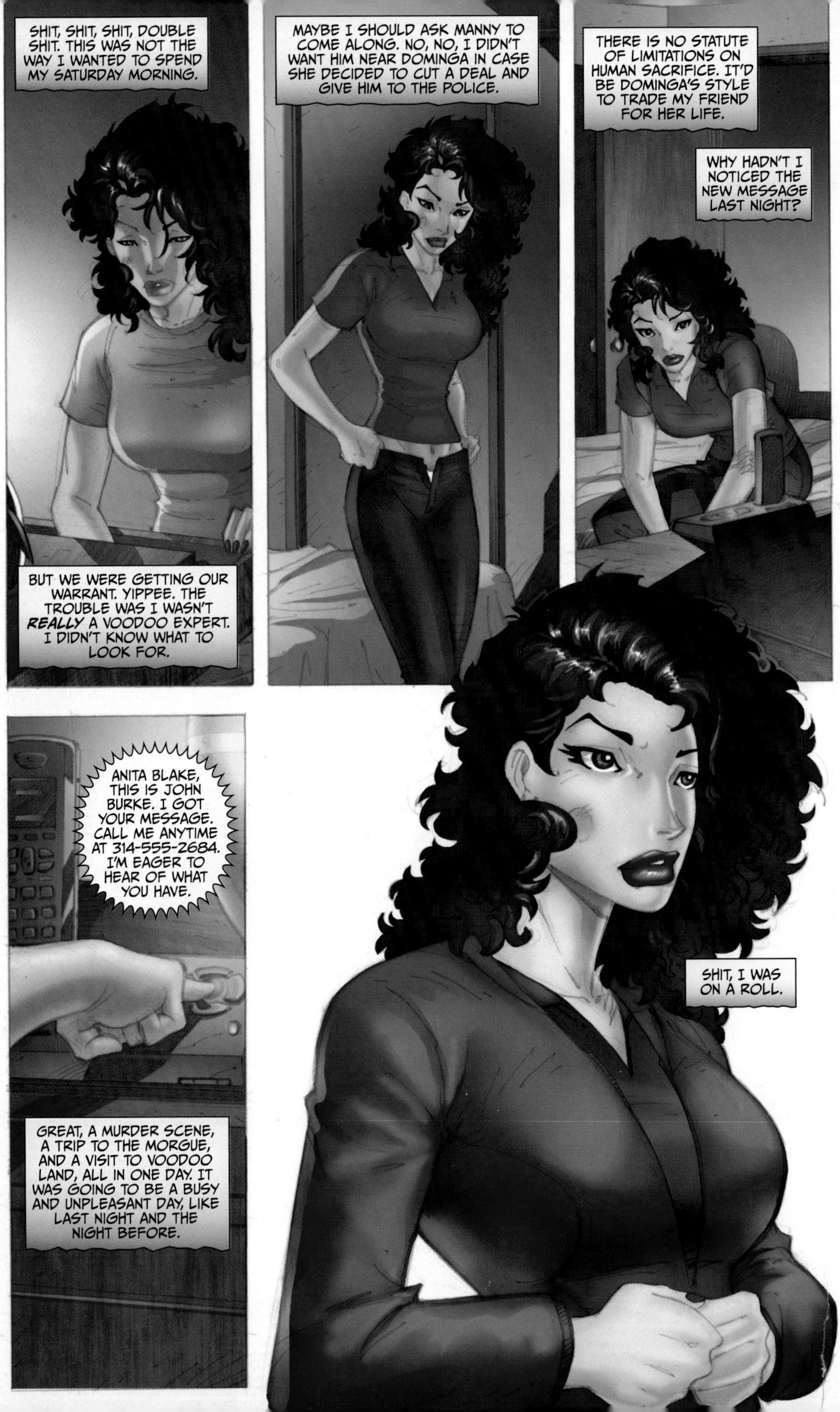

SHIT, SHIT, SHIT, DOUBLE SHIT. THIS WAS NOT THE WAY I WANTED TO SPEND MY SATURDAY MORNING.
BUT WE WERE GETTING OUR WARRANT. YIPPEE. THE TROUBLE WAS I WASN'T REALLY A VOODOO EXPERT. I DIDN'T KNOW WHAT TO LOOK FOR.
MAYBE I SHOULD ASK MANNY TO COME ALONG. NO, NO, I DIDN'T WANT HIM NEAR DOMINGA IN CASE SHE DECIDED TO CUT A DEAL AND GIVE HIM TO THE POLICE.
THERE IS NO STATUTE OF LIMITATIONS ON HUMAN SACRIFICE. IT'D BE DOMINGA'S STYLE TO TRADE MY FRIEND FOR HER LIFE.
WHY HADN'T I NOTICED THE NEW MESSAGE LAST NIGHT?
ANITA BLAKE, THIS IS JOHN BURKE. I GOT YOUR MESSAGE. CALL ME ANYTIME AT 314-555-2684. I'M EAGER TO HEAR OF WHAT YOU HAVE.
GREAT, A MURDER SCENE, A TRIP TO THE MORGUE, AND A VISIT TO VOODOO LAND, ALL IN ONE DAY. IT WAS GOING TO BE A BUSY AND UNPLEASANT DAY, LIKE LAST NIGHT AND THE NIGHT BEFORE.
SHIT, I WAS ON A ROLL.

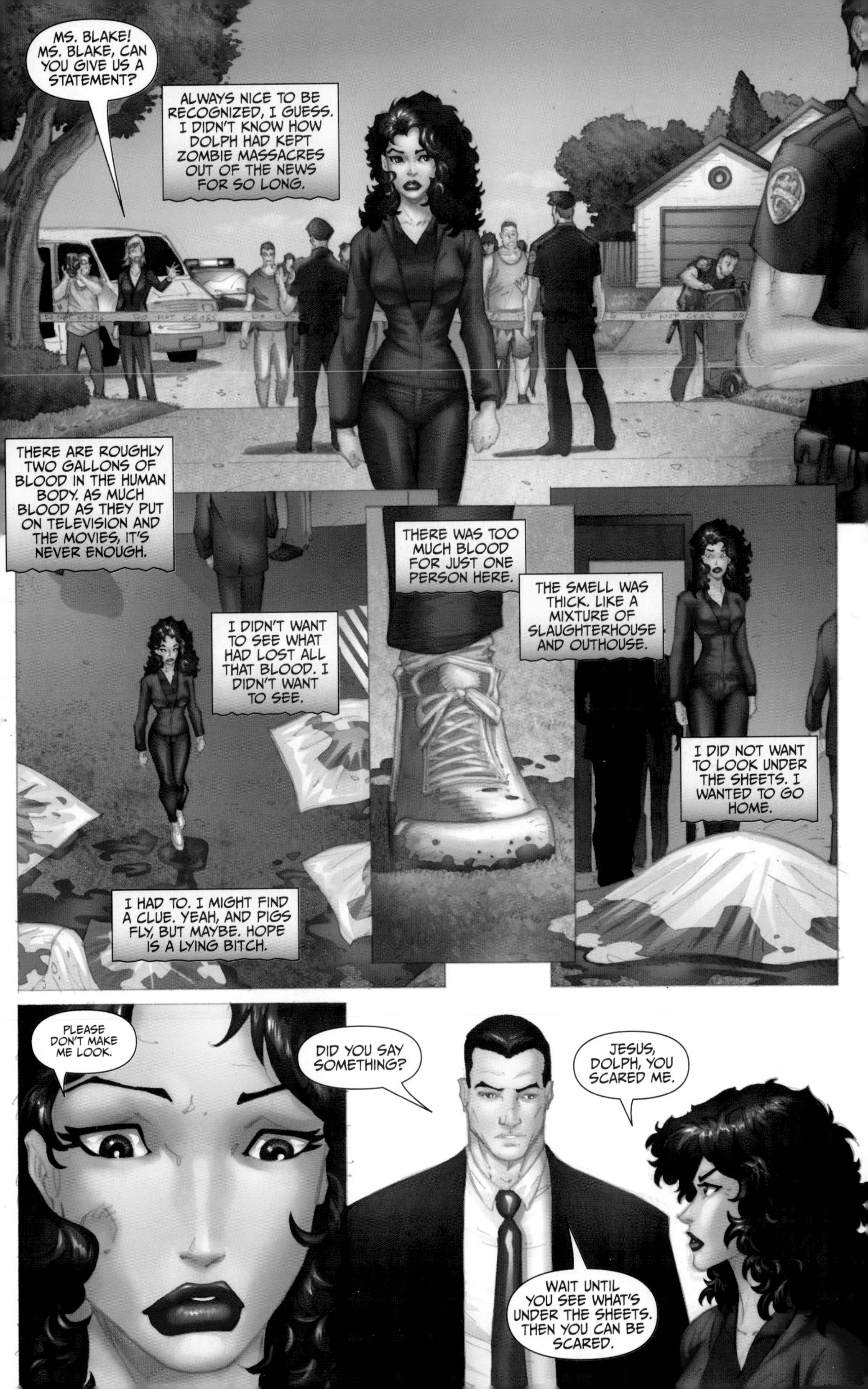
MS. BLAKE! MS. BLAKE, CAN YOU GIVE US A STATEMENT?
ALWAYS NICE TO BE RECOGNIZED, I GUESS. I DIDN'T KNOW HOW DOLPH HAD KEPT ZOMBIE MASSACRES OUT OF THE NEWS FOR SO LONG.
DO NOT CROSS
THERE ARE ROUGHLY TWO GALLONS OF BLOOD IN THE HUMAN BODY. AS MUCH BLOOD AS THEY PUT ON TELEVISION AND THE MOVIES, IT'S NEVER ENOUGH.
I DIDN'T WANT TO SEE WHAT HAD LOST ALL THAT BLOOD. I DIDN'T WANT TO SEE.
I HAD TO. I MIGHT FIND A CLUE. YEAH, AND PIGS FLY, BUT MAYBE. HOPE IS A LYING BITCH.
THERE WAS TOO MUCH BLOOD FOR JUST ONE PERSON HERE.
THE SMELL WAS THICK. LIKE A MIXTURE OF SLAUGHTERHOUSE AND OUTHOUSE.
I DID NOT WANT TO LOOK UNDER THE SHEETS. I WANTED TO GO HOME.
PLEASE DON'T MAKE ME LOOK.
DID YOU SAY SOMETHING?
JESUS, DOLPH, YOU SCARED ME.
WAIT UNTIL YOU SEE WHAT'S UNDER THE SHEETS. THEN YOU CAN BE SCARED.

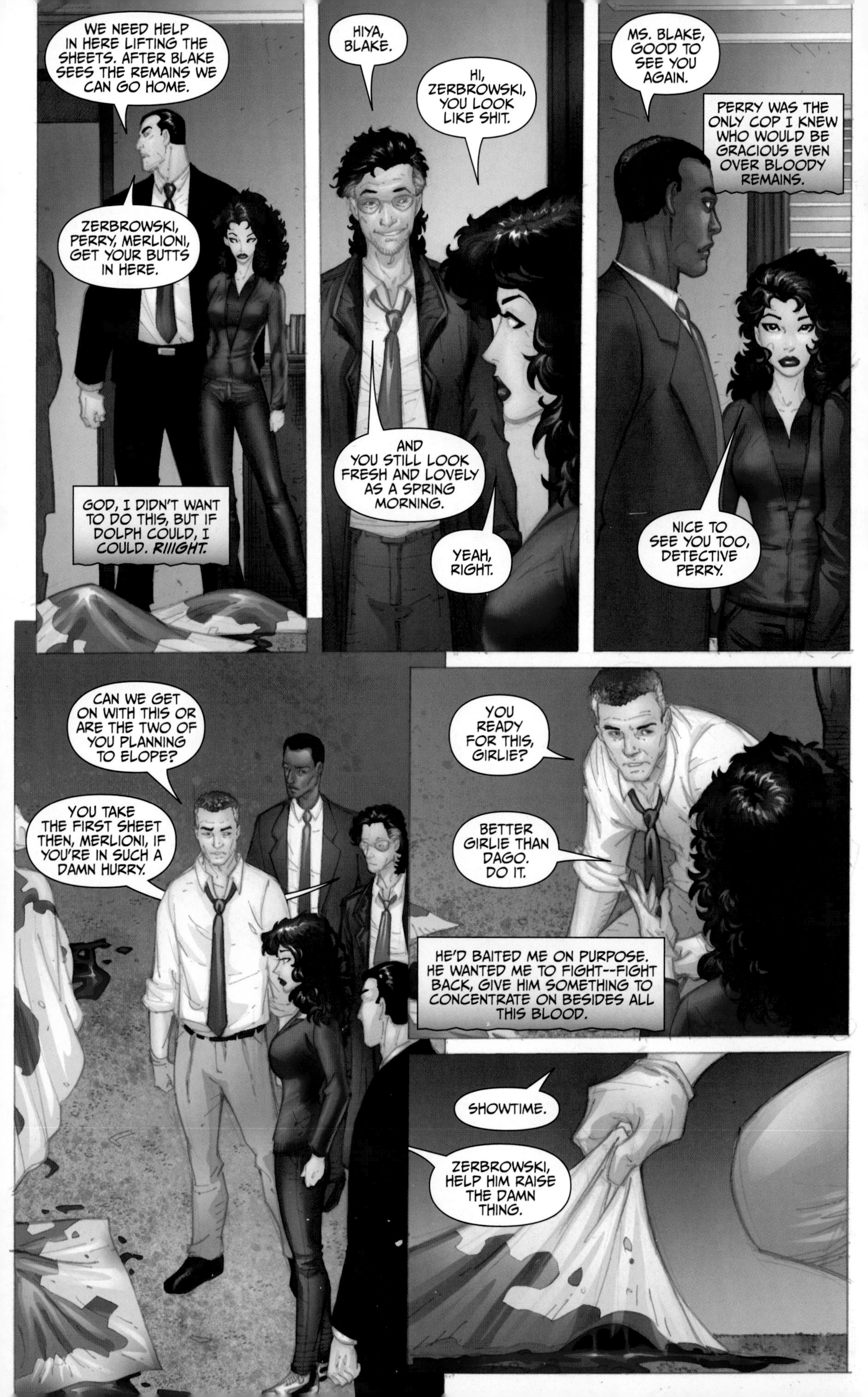
WE NEED HELP IN HERE LIFTING THE SHEETS. AFTER BLAKE SEES THE REMAINS WE CAN GO HOME.
ZERBROWSKI, PERRY, MERLIONI, GET YOUR BUTTS IN HERE.
GOD, I DIDN'T WANT TO DO THIS, BUT IF DOLPH COULD, I COULD. RIIIGHT.
HIYA, BLAKE.
HI, ZERBROWSKI, YOU LOOK LIKE SHIT.
AND YOU STILL LOOK FRESH AND LOVELY AS A SPRING MORNING.
YEAH, RIGHT.
MS. BLAKE, GOOD TO SEE YOU AGAIN.
PERRY WAS THE ONLY COP I KNEW WHO WOULD BE GRACIOUS EVEN OVER BLOODY REMAINS.
NICE TO SEE YOU TOO, DETECTIVE PERRY.
CAN WE GET ON WITH THIS OR ARE THE TWO OF YOU PLANNING TO ELOPE?
YOU TAKE THE FIRST SHEET THEN, MERLIONI, IF YOU'RE IN SUCH A DAMN HURRY.
YOU READY FOR THIS, GIRLIE?
BETTER GIRLIE THAN DAGO. DO IT.
HE'D BAITED ME ON PURPOSE. HE WANTED ME TO FIGHT--FIGHT BACK, GIVE HIM SOMETHING TO CONCENTRATE ON BESIDES ALL THIS BLOOD.
SHOWTIME.
ZERBROWSKI, HELP HIM RAISE THE DAMN THING.

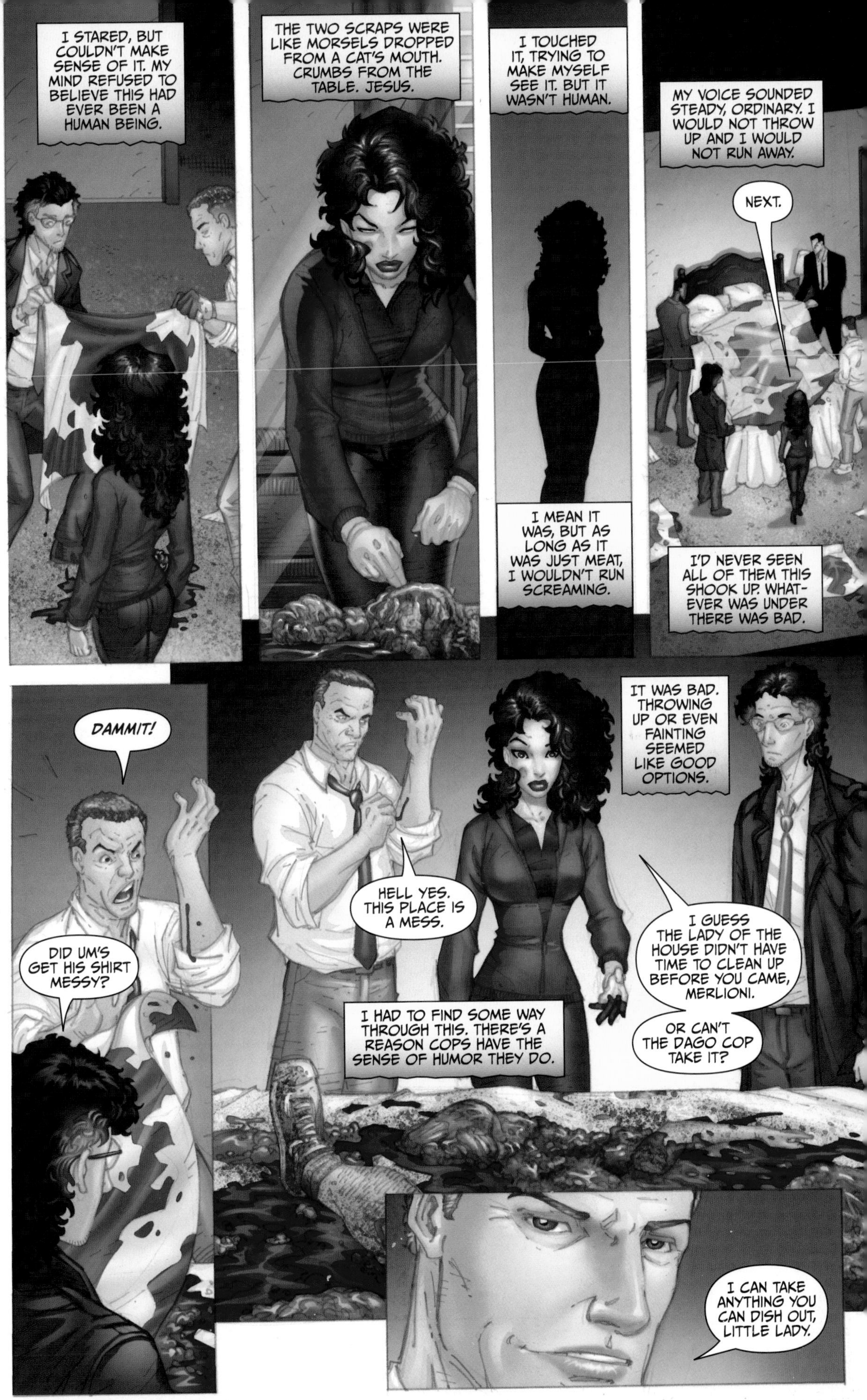
I STARED, BUT COULDN'T MAKE SENSE OF IT. MY MIND REFUSED TO BELIEVE THIS HAD EVER BEEN A HUMAN BEING.
THE TWO SCRAPS WERE LIKE MORSELS DROPPED FROM A CAT'S MOUTH. CRUMBS FROM THE TABLE. JESUS.
I TOUCHED IT, TRYING TO MAKE MYSELF SEE IT. BUT IT WASN'T HUMAN.
I MEAN IT WAS, BUT AS LONG AS IT WAS JUST MEAT, I WOULDN'T RUN SCREAMING.
MY VOICE SOUNDED STEADY, ORDINARY. I WOULD NOT THROW UP AND I WOULD NOT RUN AWAY.
NEXT.
I'D NEVER SEEN ALL OF THEM THIS SHOOK UP. WHATEVER WAS UNDER THERE WAS BAD.
DAMMIT!
DID UM'S GET HIS SHIRT MESSY?
HELL YES. THIS PLACE IS A MESS.
IT WAS BAD. THROWING UP OR EVEN FAINTING SEEMED LIKE GOOD OPTIONS.
I HAD TO FIND SOME WAY THROUGH THIS. THERE'S A REASON COPS HAVE THE SENSE OF HUMOR THEY DO.
I GUESS THE LADY OF THE HOUSE DIDN'T HAVE TIME TO CLEAN UP BEFORE YOU CAME, MERLIONI.
OR CAN'T THE DAGO COP TAKE IT?
I CAN TAKE ANYTHING YOU CAN DISH OUT, LITTLE LADY.

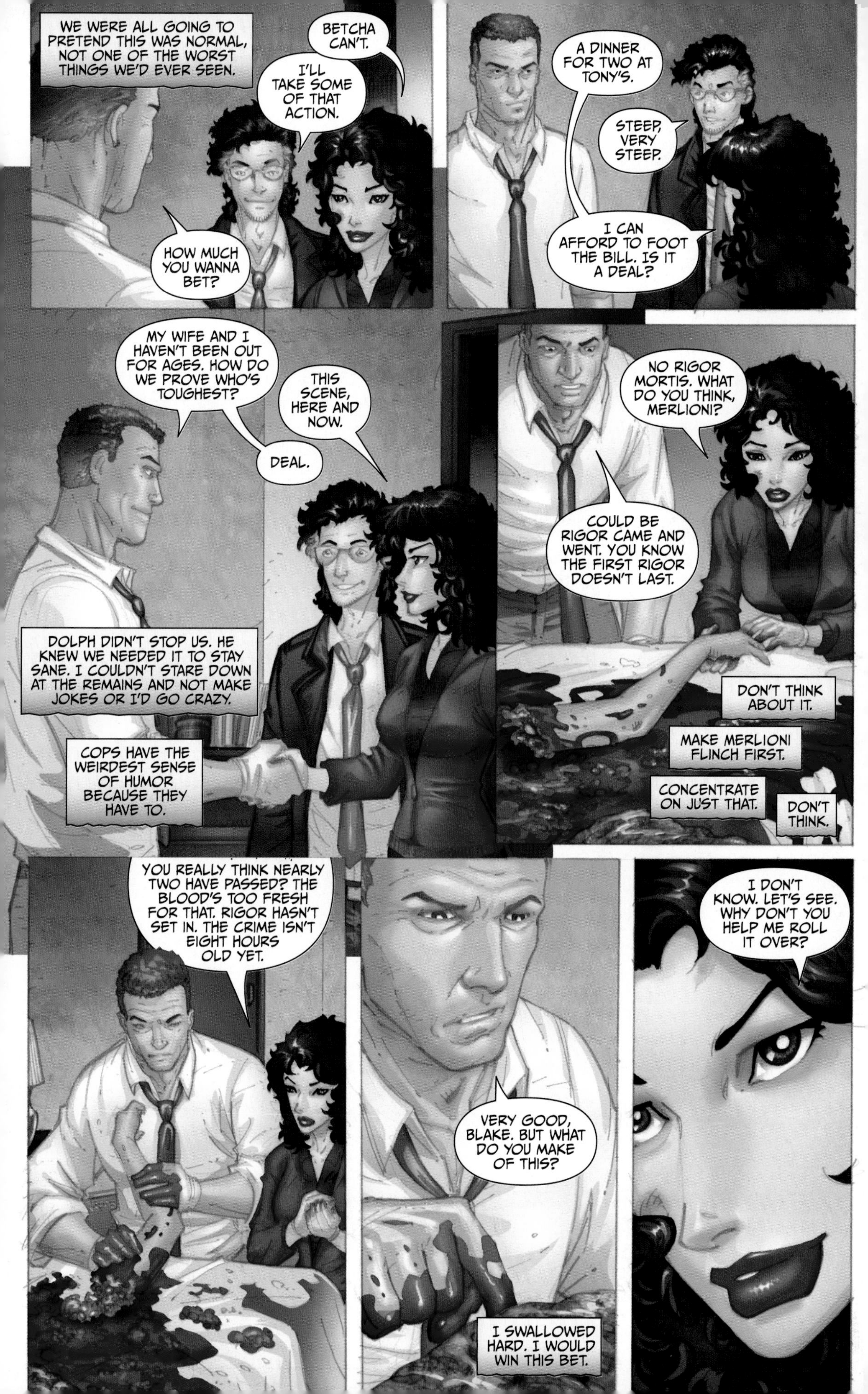
WE WERE ALL GOING TO PRETEND THIS WAS NORMAL, NOT ONE OF THE WORST THINGS WE'D EVER SEEN.
BETCHA CAN'T.
I'LL TAKE SOME OF THAT ACTION.
HOW MUCH YOU WANNA BET?
A DINNER FOR TWO AT TONY'S.
STEEP, VERY STEEP.
I CAN AFFORD TO FOOT THE BILL. IS IT A DEAL?
MY WIFE AND I HAVEN'T BEEN OUT FOR AGES. HOW DO WE PROVE WHO'S TOUGHEST?
THIS SCENE, HERE AND NOW.
DEAL.
DOLPH DIDN'T STOP US. HE KNEW WE NEEDED IT TO STAY SANE. I COULDN'T STARE DOWN AT THE REMAINS AND NOT MAKE JOKES OR I'D GO CRAZY.
COPS HAVE THE WEIRDEST SENSE OF HUMOR BECAUSE THEY HAVE TO.
NO RIGOR MORTIS. WHAT DO YOU THINK, MERLIONI?
COULD BE RIGOR CAME AND WENT. YOU KNOW THE FIRST RIGOR DOESN'T LAST.
DON'T THINK ABOUT IT.
MAKE MERLIONI FLINCH FIRST.
CONCENTRATE ON JUST THAT.
DON'T THINK.
YOU REALLY THINK NEARLY TWO HAVE PASSED? THE BLOOD'S TOO FRESH FOR THAT. RIGOR HASN'T SET IN. THE CRIME ISN'T EIGHT HOURS OLD YET.
VERY GOOD, BLAKE. BUT WHAT DO YOU MAKE OF THIS?
I SWALLOWED HARD. I WOULD WIN THIS BET.
I DON'T KNOW. LET'S SEE. WHY DON'T YOU HELP ME ROLL IT OVER?

MERLIONI PALED, I'D GOTTEN MY COLOR BACK. DON'T THINK ABOUT WHAT YOU'RE TOUCHING AT THE SAME TIME YOU'RE TRYING TO SEE ALL OF IT.

CLUES, WERE THERE ANY DAMN CLUES IN THIS PLACE?

ARE YOU ALRIGHT, MERLIONI? I WOULDN'T WANT TO CONTINUE IF IT'S UPSETTING YOU.

YOU AIN'T SEEN IT ALL, GIRLIE. I HAVE.

HE WAS GREEN AROUND THE EDGES, SO I PUSHED HIM.

AND ME.

BUT HAVE YOU TOUCHED IT ALL?

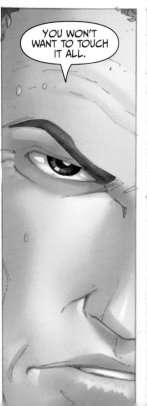

YOU WON'T WANT TO TOUCH IT ALL.

THAT MUST HAVE HURT LIKE A SON OF A BITCH.

YOU THINK HE WAS ALIVE WHEN THE LEG WAS PULLED OFF?

I REALLY WASN'T A HUNDRED PERCENT SURE. OH, WELL.

OH, YEAH.

BUT IT MADE MERLIONI GO PALER. HE'D FAINT FIRST.

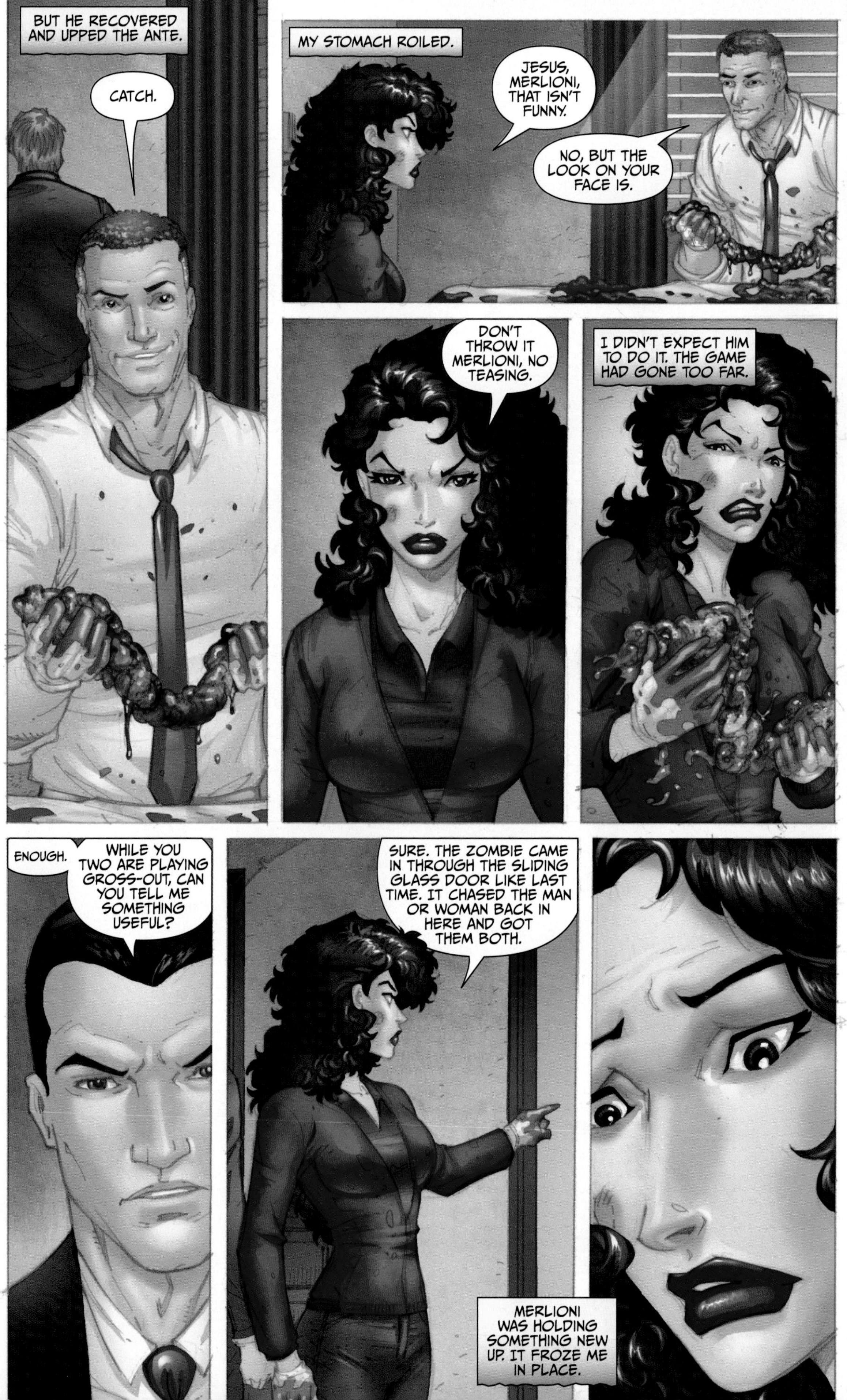

BUT HE RECOVERED AND UPPED THE ANTE.
CATCH.
MY STOMACH ROILED.
JESUS, MERLIONI, THAT ISN'T FUNNY.
NO, BUT THE LOOK ON YOUR FACE IS.
DON'T THROW IT MERLIONI, NO TEASING.
I DIDN'T EXPECT HIM TO DO IT. THE GAME HAD GONE TOO FAR.
ENOUGH.
WHILE YOU TWO ARE PLAYING GROSS-OUT, CAN YOU TELL ME SOMETHING USEFUL?
SURE. THE ZOMBIE CAME IN THROUGH THE SLIDING GLASS DOOR LIKE LAST TIME. IT CHASED THE MAN OR WOMAN BACK IN HERE AND GOT THEM BOTH.
MERLIONI WAS HOLDING SOMETHING NEW UP. IT FROZE ME IN PLACE.

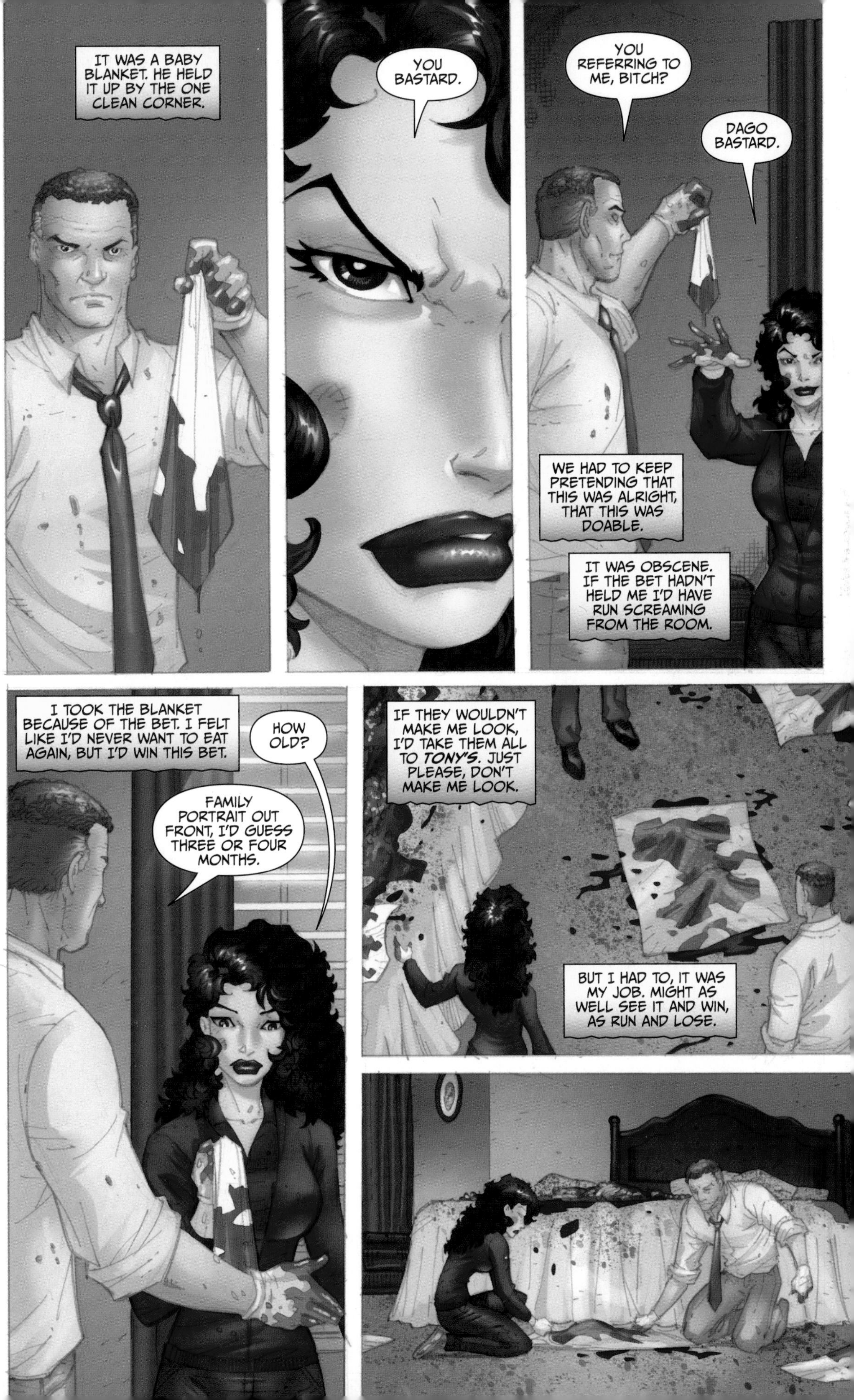
IT WAS A BABY BLANKET. HE HELD IT UP BY THE ONE CLEAN CORNER.
YOU BASTARD.
YOU REFERRING TO ME, BITCH?
DAGO BASTARD.
WE HAD TO KEEP PRETENDING THAT THIS WAS ALRIGHT, THAT THIS WAS DOABLE.
IT WAS OBSCENE. IF THE BET HADN'T HELD ME I'D HAVE RUN SCREAMING FROM THE ROOM.
I TOOK THE BLANKET BECAUSE OF THE BET. I FELT LIKE I'D NEVER WANT TO EAT AGAIN, BUT I'D WIN THIS BET.
HOW OLD?
FAMILY PORTRAIT OUT FRONT, I'D GUESS THREE OR FOUR MONTHS.
IF THEY WOULDN'T MAKE ME LOOK, I'D TAKE THEM ALL TO TONY'S. JUST PLEASE, DON'T MAKE ME LOOK.
BUT I HAD TO, IT WAS MY JOB. MIGHT AS WELL SEE IT AND WIN, AS RUN AND LOSE.

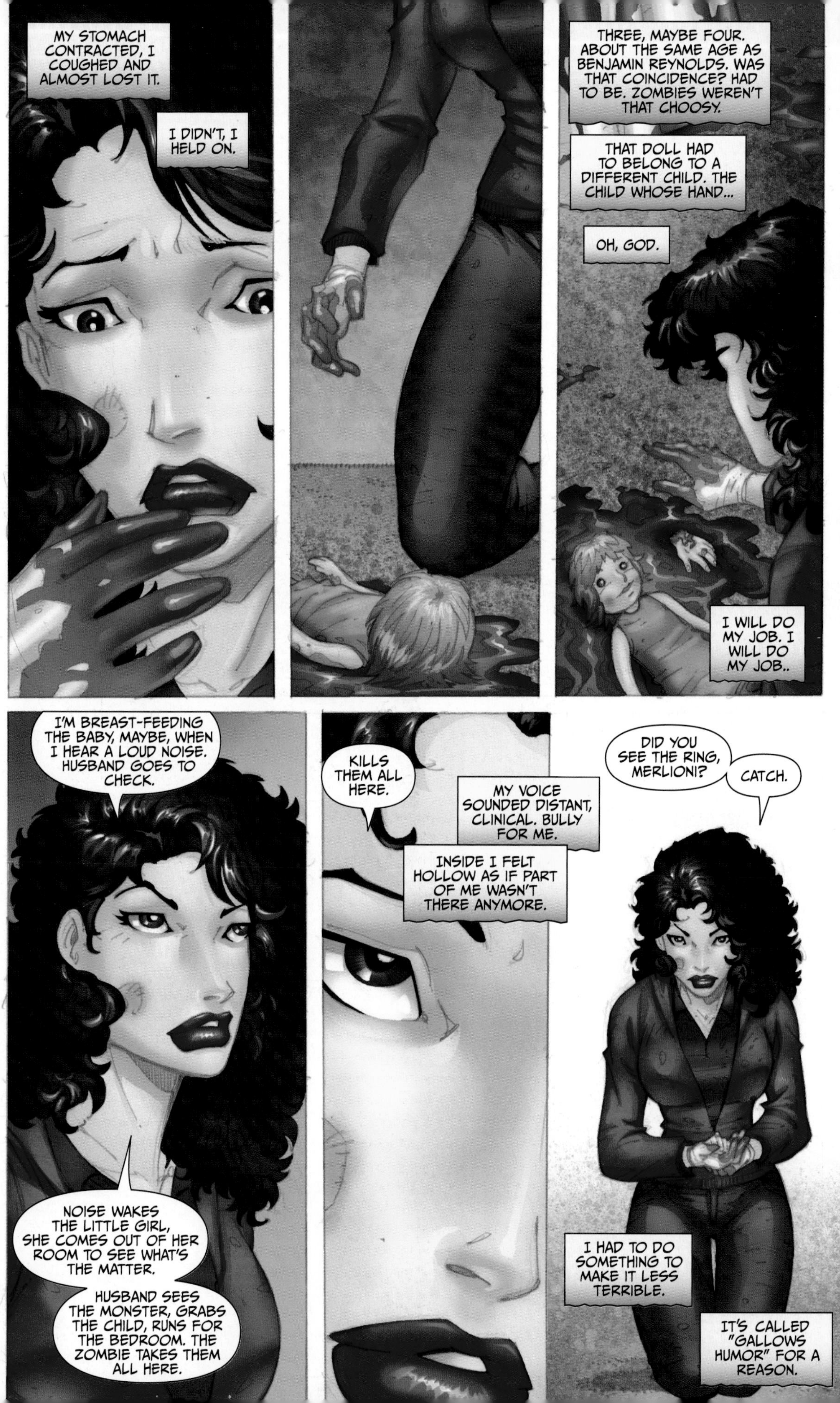

MY STOMACH CONTRACTED, I COUGHED AND ALMOST LOST IT.
I DIDN'T, I HELD ON.
THREE, MAYBE FOUR. ABOUT THE SAME AGE AS BENJAMIN REYNOLDS. WAS THAT COINCIDENCE? HAD TO BE. ZOMBIES WEREN'T THAT CHOOSY.
THAT DOLL HAD TO BELONG TO A DIFFERENT CHILD. THE CHILD WHOSE HAND...
OH, GOD.
I WILL DO MY JOB. I WILL DO MY JOB..
I'M BREAST-FEEDING THE BABY, MAYBE, WHEN I HEAR A LOUD NOISE. HUSBAND GOES TO CHECK.
NOISE WAKES THE LITTLE GIRL, SHE COMES OUT OF HER ROOM TO SEE WHAT'S THE MATTER.
HUSBAND SEES THE MONSTER, GRABS THE CHILD, RUNS FOR THE BEDROOM. THE ZOMBIE TAKES THEM ALL HERE.
KILLS THEM ALL HERE.
MY VOICE SOUNDED DISTANT, CLINICAL. BULLY FOR ME.
INSIDE I FELT HOLLOW AS IF PART OF ME WASN'T THERE ANYMORE.
DID YOU SEE THE RING, MERLIONI?
CATCH.
I HAD TO DO SOMETHING TO MAKE IT LESS TERRIBLE.
IT'S CALLED "GALLOWS HUMOR" FOR A REASON.

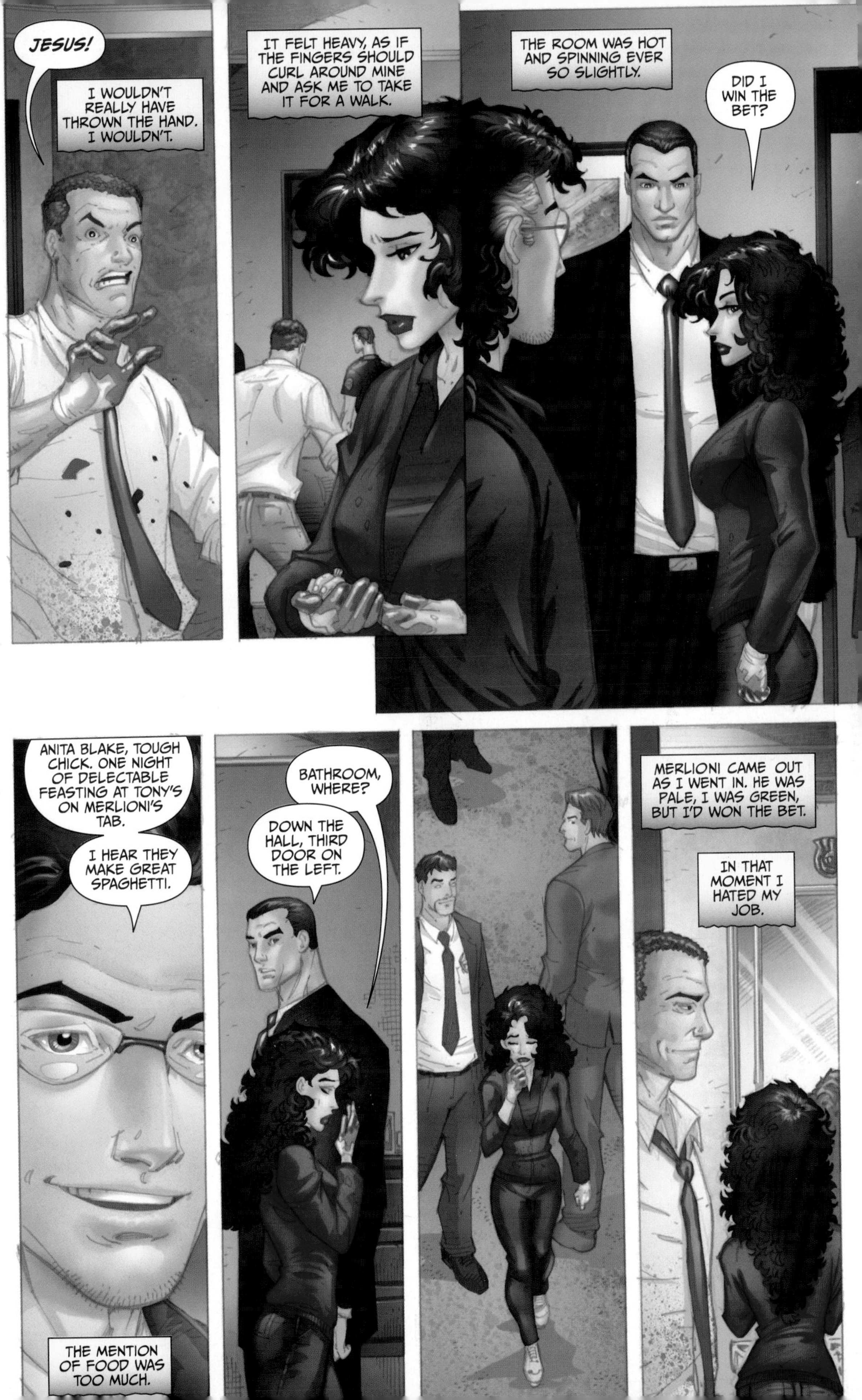
JESUS!
I WOULDN'T REALLY HAVE THROWN THE HAND. I WOULDN'T.
IT FELT HEAVY, AS IF THE FINGERS SHOULD CURL AROUND MINE AND ASK ME TO TAKE IT FOR A WALK.
THE ROOM WAS HOT AND SPINNING EVER SO SLIGHTLY.
DID I WIN THE BET?
ANITA BLAKE, TOUGH CHICK. ONE NIGHT OF DELECTABLE FEASTING AT TONY'S ON MERLIONI'S TAB.
I HEAR THEY MAKE GREAT SPAGHETTI.
THE MENTION OF FOOD WAS TOO MUCH.
BATHROOM, WHERE?
DOWN THE HALL, THIRD DOOR ON THE LEFT.
MERLIONI CAME OUT AS I WENT IN. HE WAS PALE, I WAS GREEN, BUT I'D WON THE BET.
IN THAT MOMENT I HATED MY JOB.

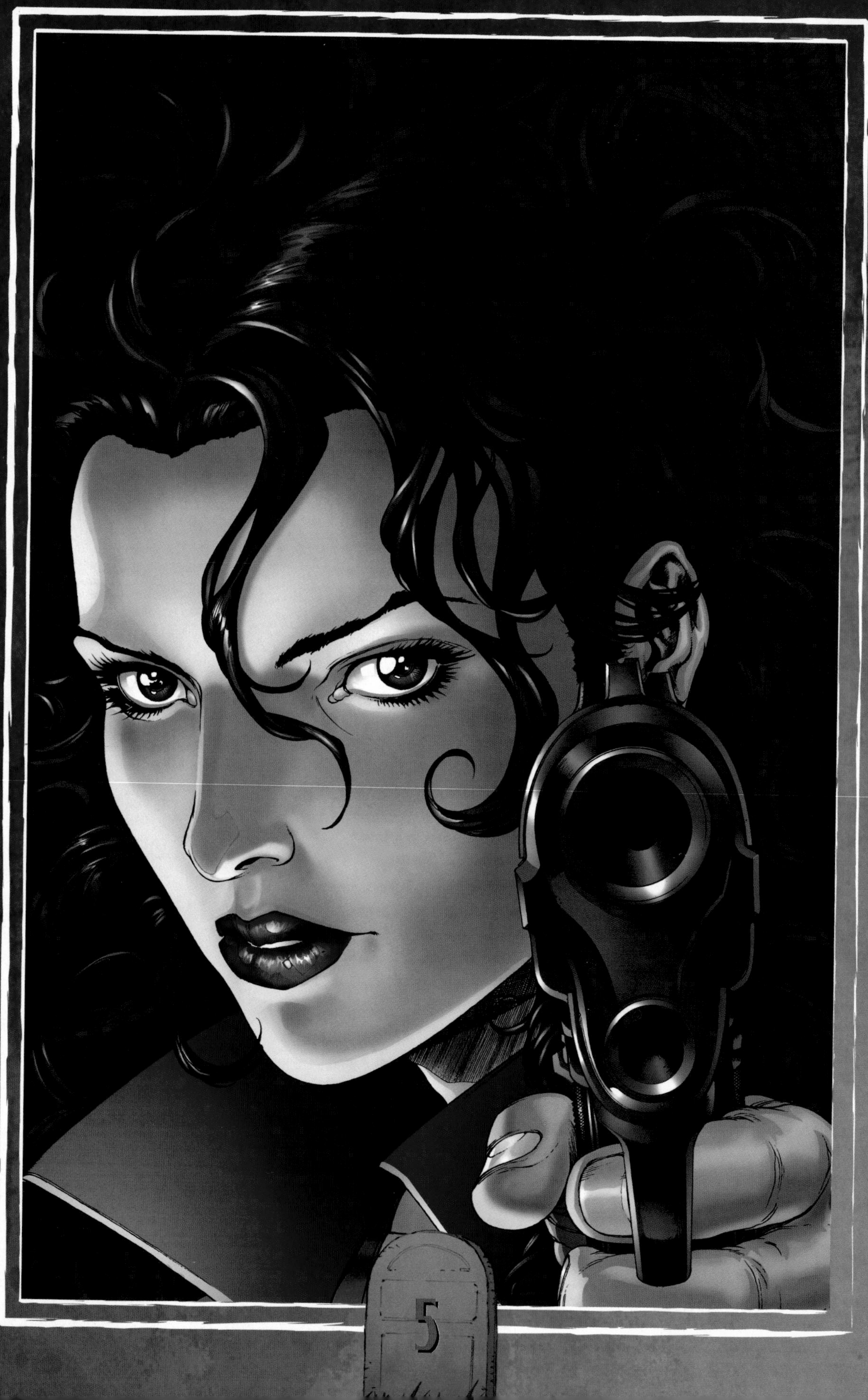
5

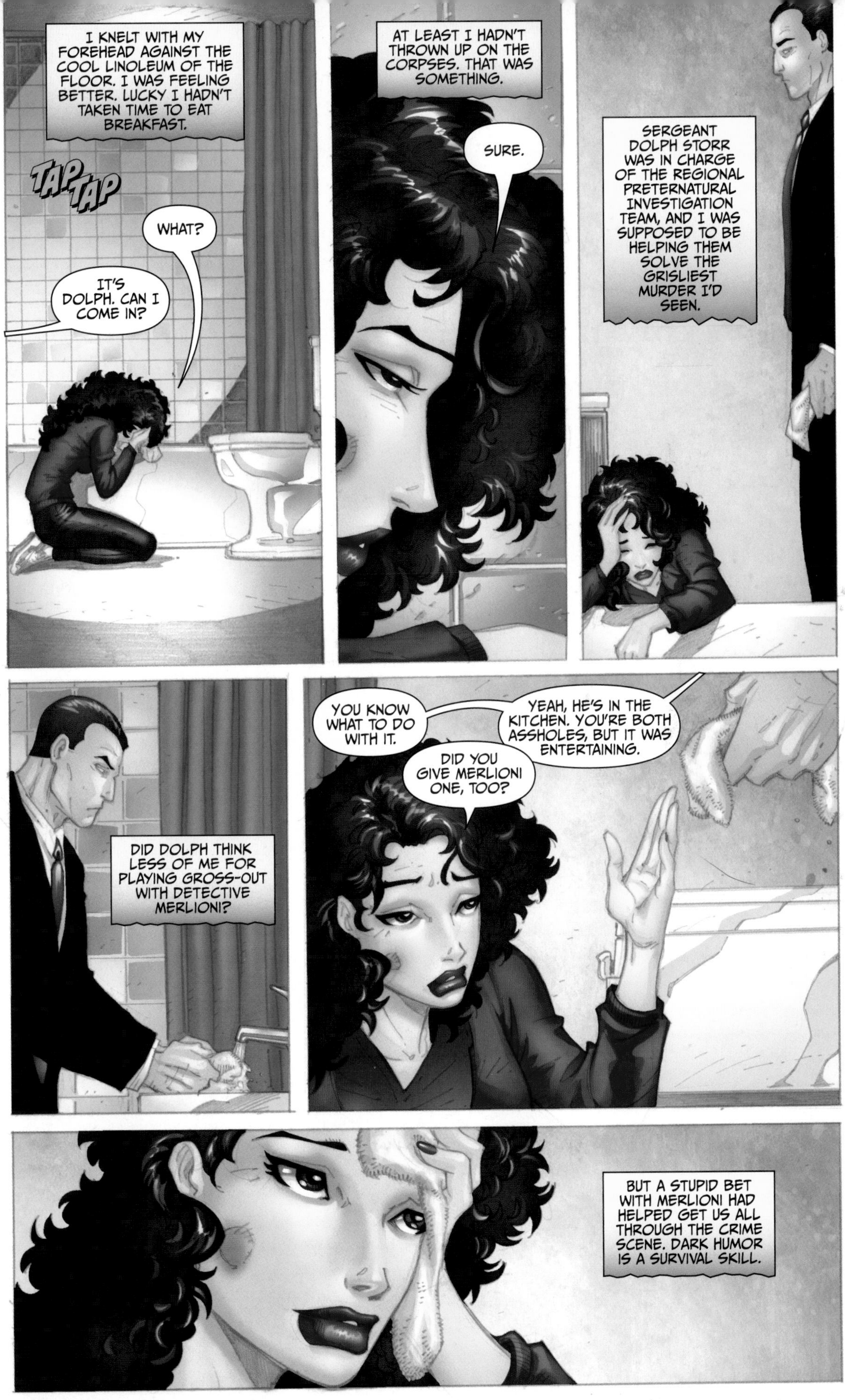
I KNELT WITH MY FOREHEAD AGAINST THE COOL LINOLEUM OF THE FLOOR. I WAS FEELING BETTER. LUCKY I HADN'T TAKEN TIME TO EAT BREAKFAST.
TAP TAP
WHAT?
IT'S DOLPH. CAN I COME IN?
AT LEAST I HADN'T THROWN UP ON THE CORPSES. THAT WAS SOMETHING.
SURE.
SERGEANT DOLPH STORR WAS IN CHARGE OF THE REGIONAL PRETERNATURAL INVESTIGATION TEAM, AND I WAS SUPPOSED TO BE HELPING THEM SOLVE THE GRISLIEST MURDER I'D SEEN.
DID DOLPH THINK LESS OF ME FOR PLAYING GROSS-OUT WITH DETECTIVE MERLIONI?
YOU KNOW WHAT TO DO WITH IT.
DID YOU GIVE MERLIONI ONE, TOO?
YEAH, HE'S IN THE KITCHEN. YOU'RE BOTH ASSHOLES, BUT IT WAS ENTERTAINING.
BUT A STUPID BET WITH MERLIONI HAD HELPED GET US ALL THROUGH THE CRIME SCENE. DARK HUMOR IS A SURVIVAL SKILL.

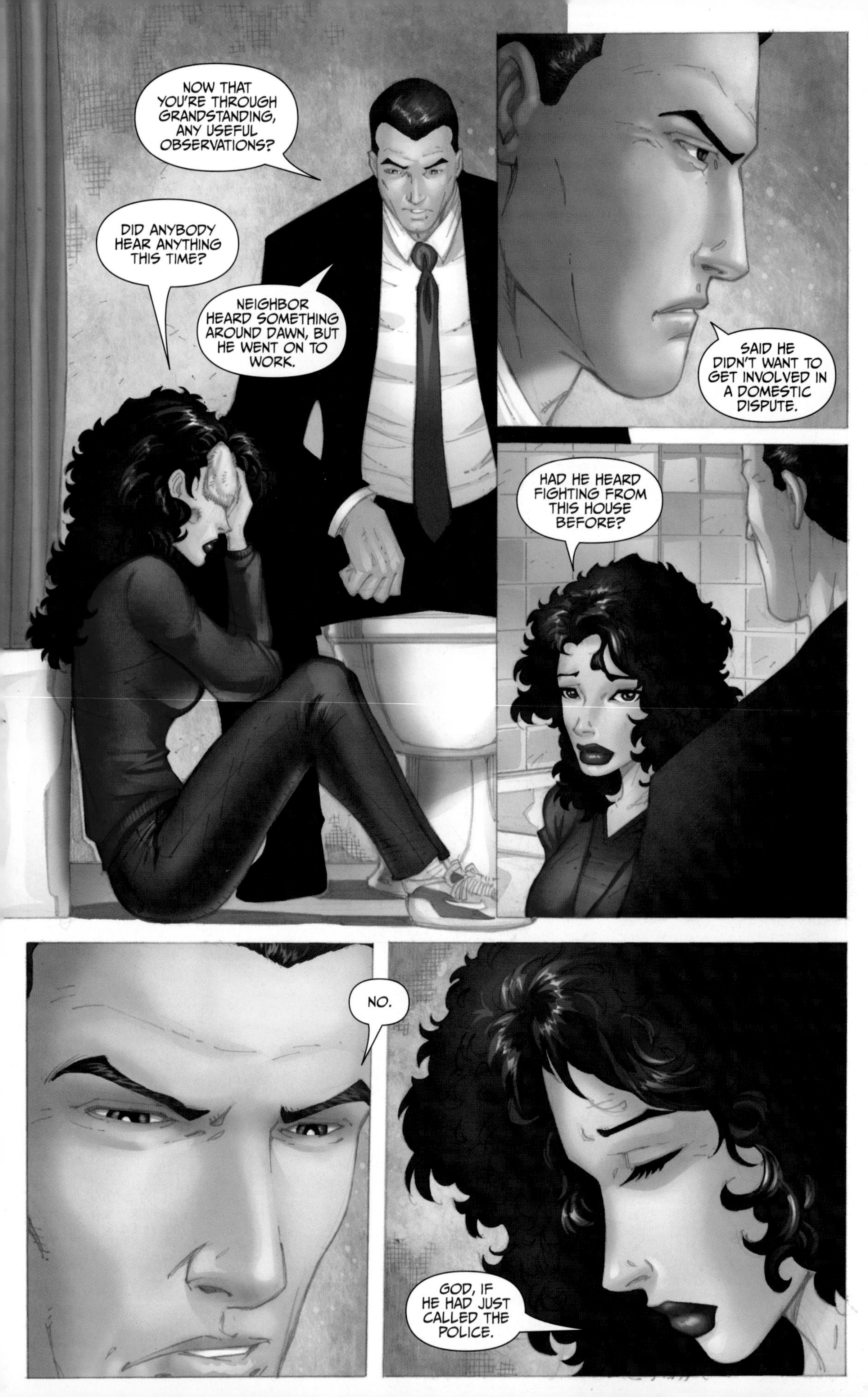
NOW THAT YOU'RE THROUGH GRANDSTANDING, ANY USEFUL OBSERVATIONS?
DID ANYBODY HEAR ANYTHING THIS TIME?
NEIGHBOR HEARD SOMETHING AROUND DAWN, BUT HE WENT ON TO WORK.
SAID HE DIDN'T WANT TO GET INVOLVED IN A DOMESTIC DISPUTE.
HAD HE HEARD FIGHTING FROM THIS HOUSE BEFORE?
NO.
GOD, IF HE HAD JUST CALLED THE POLICE.

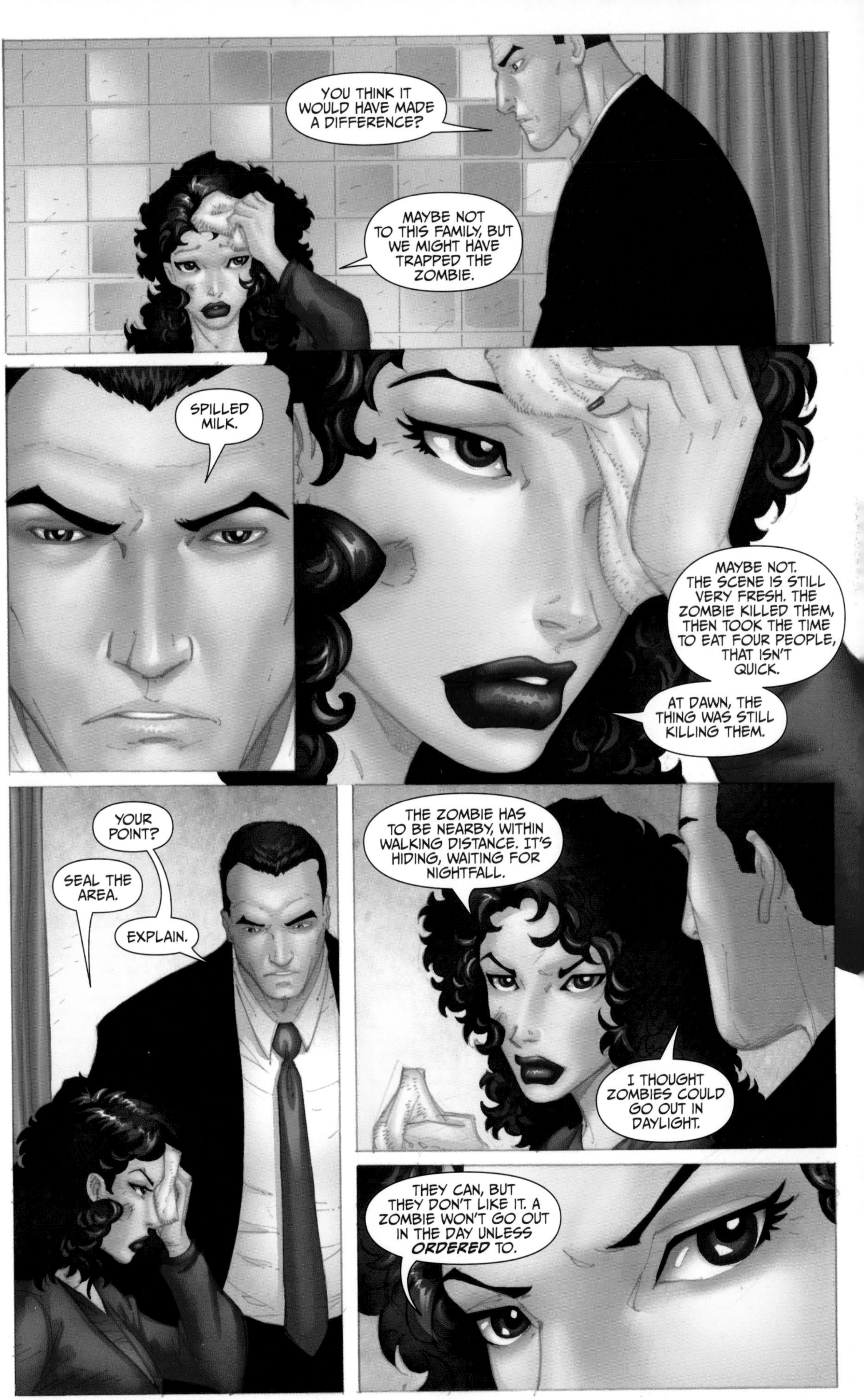
YOU THINK IT WOULD HAVE MADE A DIFFERENCE?
MAYBE NOT TO THIS FAMILY, BUT WE MIGHT HAVE TRAPPED THE ZOMBIE.
SPILLED MILK.
MAYBE NOT. THE SCENE IS STILL VERY FRESH. THE ZOMBIE KILLED THEM, THEN TOOK THE TIME TO EAT FOUR PEOPLE, THAT ISN'T QUICK.
AT DAWN, THE THING WAS STILL KILLING THEM.
SEAL THE AREA.
YOUR POINT?
EXPLAIN.
THE ZOMBIE HAS TO BE NEARBY, WITHIN WALKING DISTANCE. IT'S HIDING, WAITING FOR NIGHTFALL.
I THOUGHT ZOMBIES COULD GO OUT IN DAYLIGHT.
THEY CAN, BUT THEY DON'T LIKE IT. A ZOMBIE WON'T GO OUT IN THE DAY UNLESS ORDERED TO.

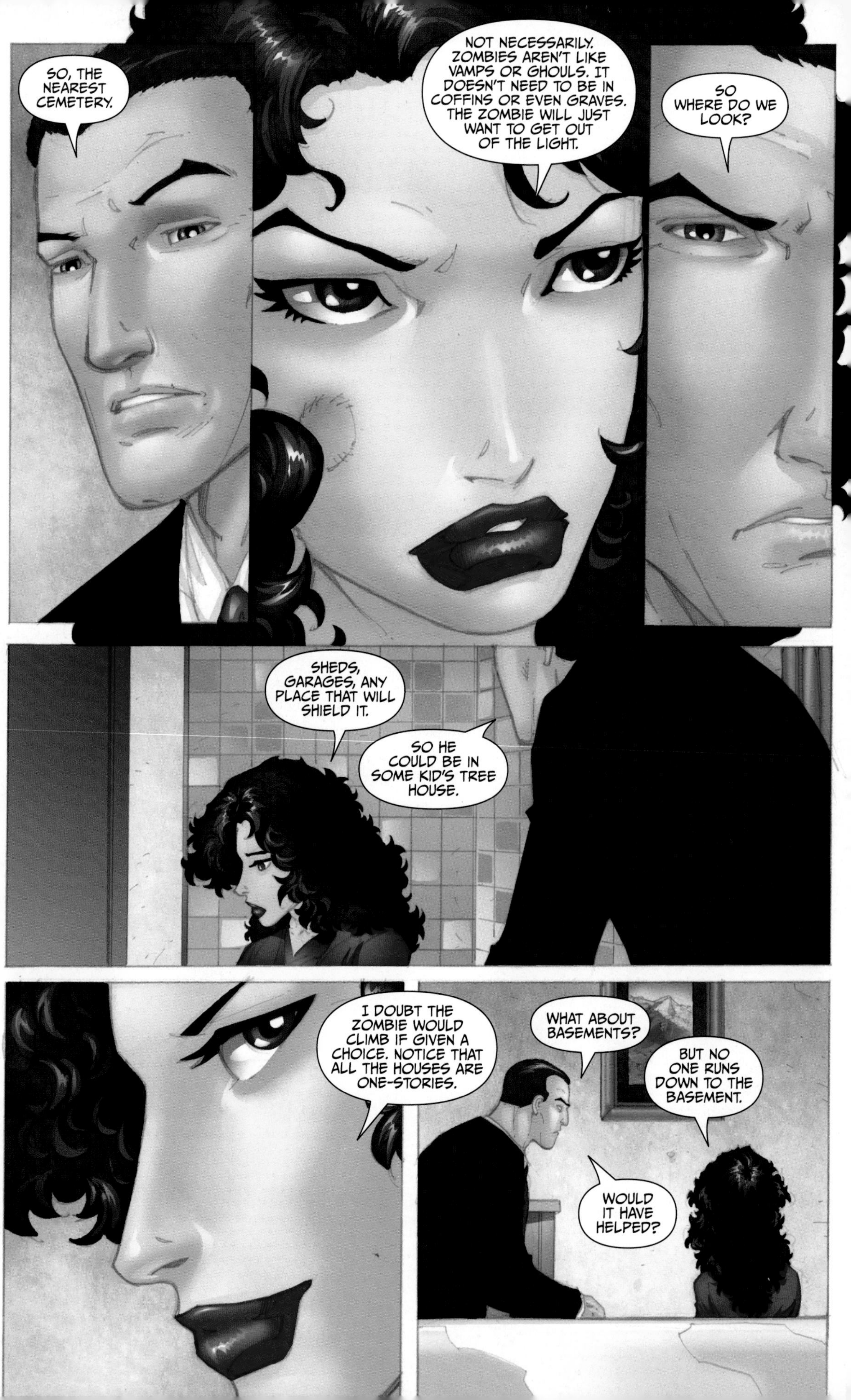
SO, THE NEAREST CEMETERY.
NOT NECESSARILY. ZOMBIES AREN'T LIKE VAMPS OR GHOULS. IT DOESN'T NEED TO BE IN COFFINS OR EVEN GRAVES. THE ZOMBIE WILL JUST WANT TO GET OUT OF THE LIGHT.
SO WHERE DO WE LOOK?
SHEDS, GARAGES, ANY PLACE THAT WILL SHIELD IT.
SO HE COULD BE IN SOME KID'S TREE HOUSE.
I DOUBT THE ZOMBIE WOULD CLIMB IF GIVEN A CHOICE. NOTICE THAT ALL THE HOUSES ARE ONE-STORIES.
WHAT ABOUT BASEMENTS?
BUT NO ONE RUNS DOWN TO THE BASEMENT.
WOULD IT HAVE HELPED?

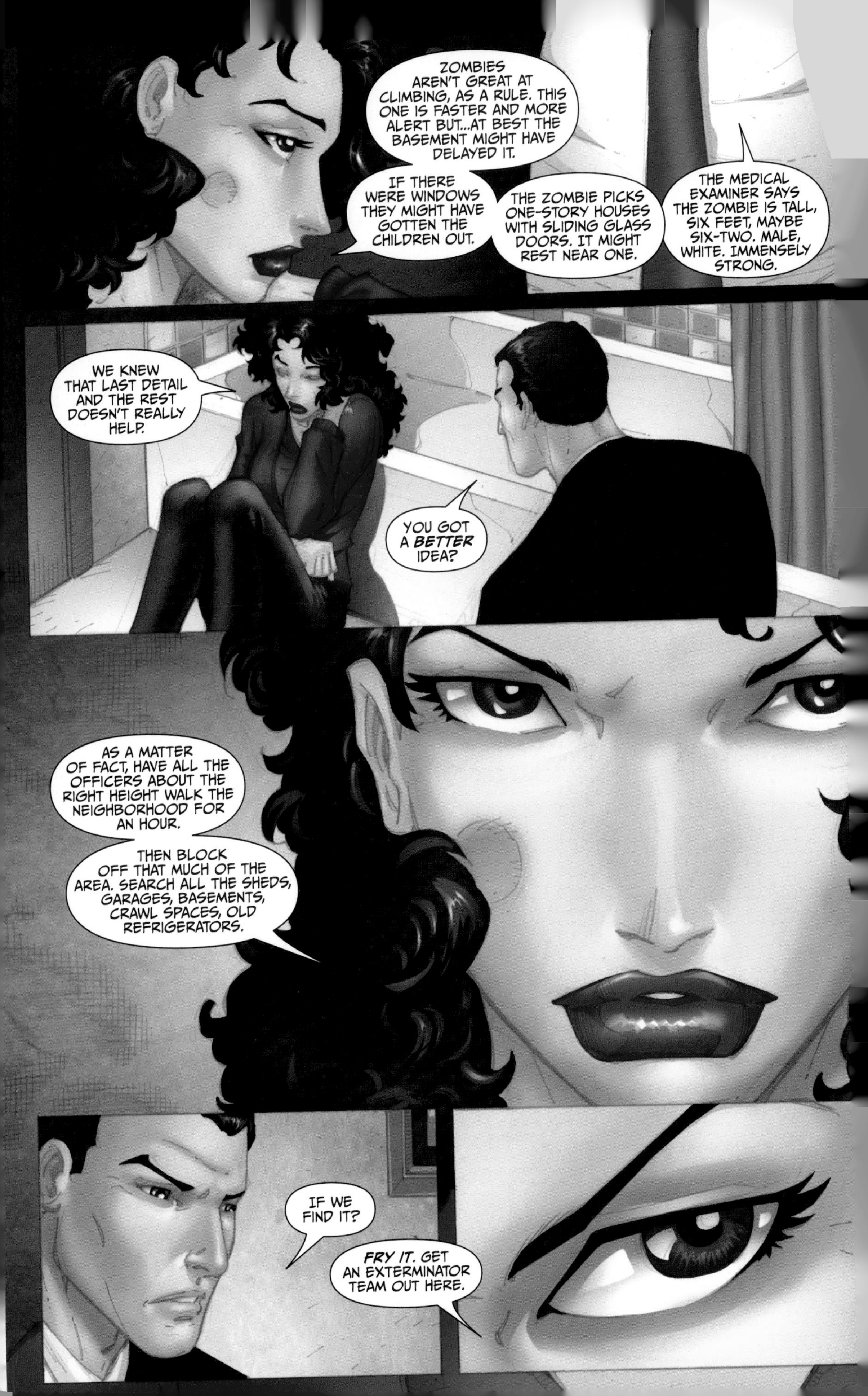
ZOMBIES AREN'T GREAT AT CLIMBING, AS A RULE. THIS ONE IS FASTER AND MORE ALERT BUT...AT BEST THE BASEMENT MIGHT HAVE DELAYED IT.
IF THERE WERE WINDOWS THEY MIGHT HAVE GOTTEN THE CHILDREN OUT.
THE ZOMBIE PICKS ONE-STORY HOUSES WITH SLIDING GLASS DOORS. IT MIGHT REST NEAR ONE.
THE MEDICAL EXAMINER SAYS THE ZOMBIE IS TALL, SIX FEET, MAYBE SIX-TWO. MALE, WHITE. IMMENSELY STRONG.
WE KNEW THAT LAST DETAIL AND THE REST DOESN'T REALLY HELP.
YOU GOT A BETTER IDEA?
AS A MATTER OF FACT, HAVE ALL THE OFFICERS ABOUT THE RIGHT HEIGHT WALK THE NEIGHBORHOOD FOR AN HOUR.
THEN BLOCK OFF THAT MUCH OF THE AREA. SEARCH ALL THE SHEDS, GARAGES, BASEMENTS, CRAWL SPACES, OLD REFRIGERATORS.
IF WE FIND IT?
FRY IT. GET AN EXTERMINATOR TEAM OUT HERE.

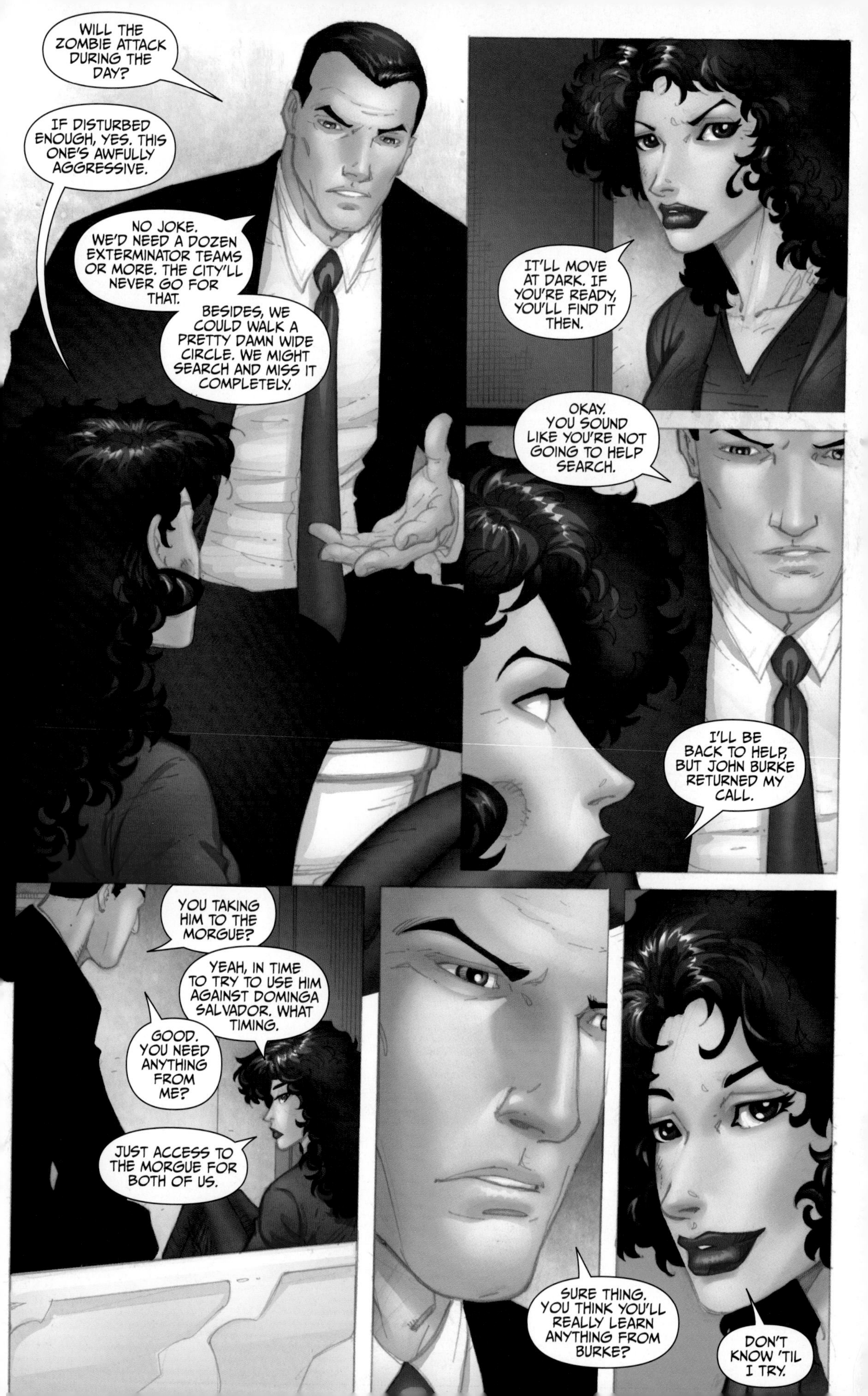
WILL THE ZOMBIE ATTACK DURING THE DAY?
IF DISTURBED ENOUGH, YES. THIS ONE'S AWFULLY AGGRESSIVE.
NO JOKE. WE'D NEED A DOZEN EXTERMINATOR TEAMS OR MORE. THE CITY'LL NEVER GO FOR THAT.
BESIDES, WE COULD WALK A PRETTY DAMN WIDE CIRCLE. WE MIGHT SEARCH AND MISS IT COMPLETELY.
IT'LL MOVE AT DARK. IF YOU'RE READY, YOU'LL FIND IT THEN.
OKAY. YOU SOUND LIKE YOU'RE NOT GOING TO HELP SEARCH.
I'LL BE BACK TO HELP, BUT JOHN BURKE RETURNED MY CALL.
YOU TAKING HIM TO THE MORGUE?
YEAH, IN TIME TO TRY TO USE HIM AGAINST DOMINGA SALVADOR. WHAT TIMING.
GOOD. YOU NEED ANYTHING FROM ME?
JUST ACCESS TO THE MORGUE FOR BOTH OF US.
SURE THING. YOU THINK YOU'LL REALLY LEARN ANYTHING FROM BURKE?
DON'T KNOW 'TIL I TRY.

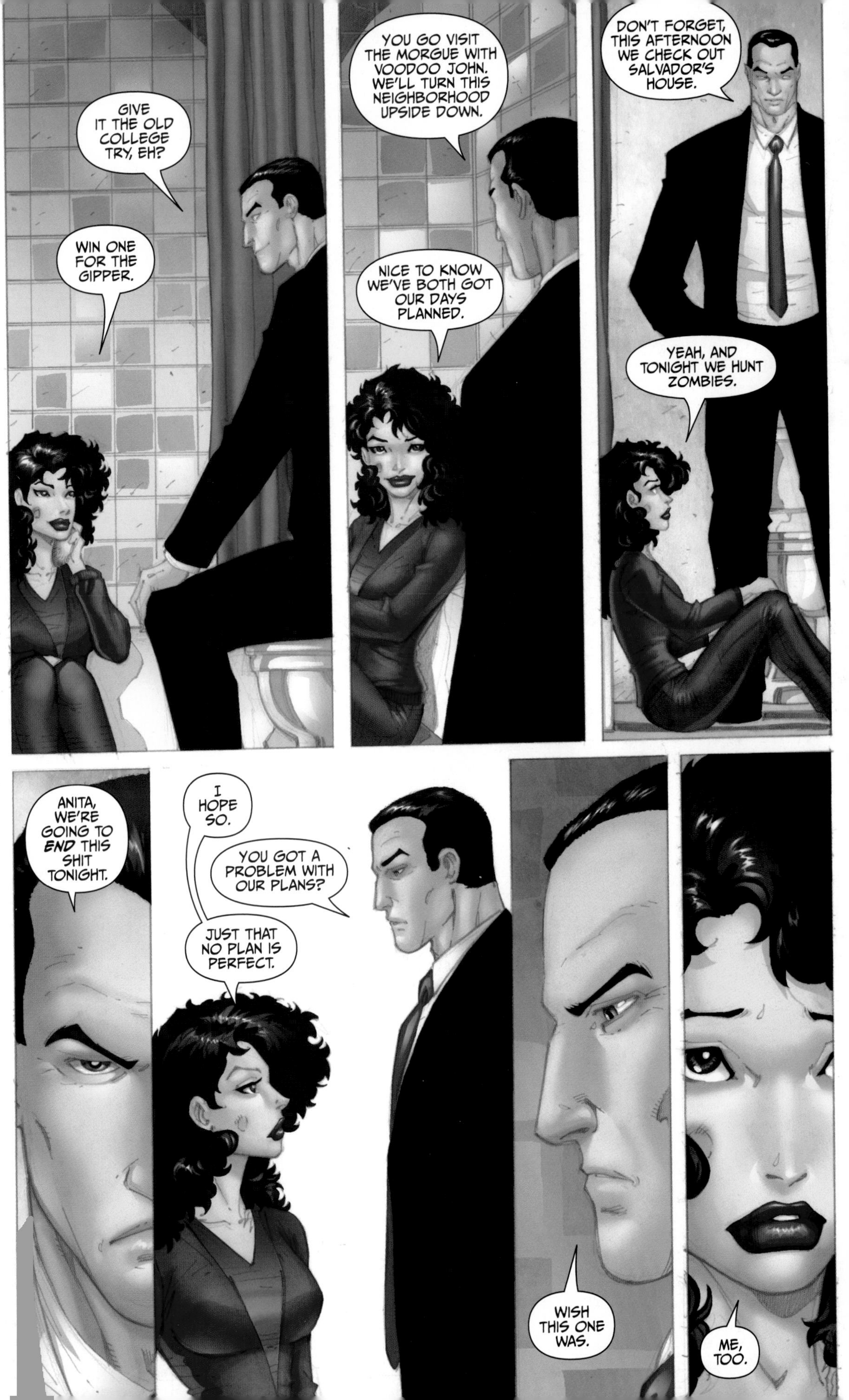

GIVE IT THE OLD COLLEGE TRY, EH?
WIN ONE FOR THE GIPPER.
YOU GO VISIT THE MORGUE WITH VOODOO JOHN. WE'LL TURN THIS NEIGHBORHOOD UPSIDE DOWN.
NICE TO KNOW WE'VE BOTH GOT OUR DAYS PLANNED.
DON'T FORGET, THIS AFTERNOON WE CHECK OUT SALVADOR'S HOUSE.
YEAH, AND TONIGHT WE HUNT ZOMBIES.
ANITA, WE'RE GOING TO *END* THIS SHIT TONIGHT.
I HOPE SO.
YOU GOT A PROBLEM WITH OUR PLANS?
JUST THAT NO PLAN IS PERFECT.
WISH THIS ONE WAS.
ME, TOO.

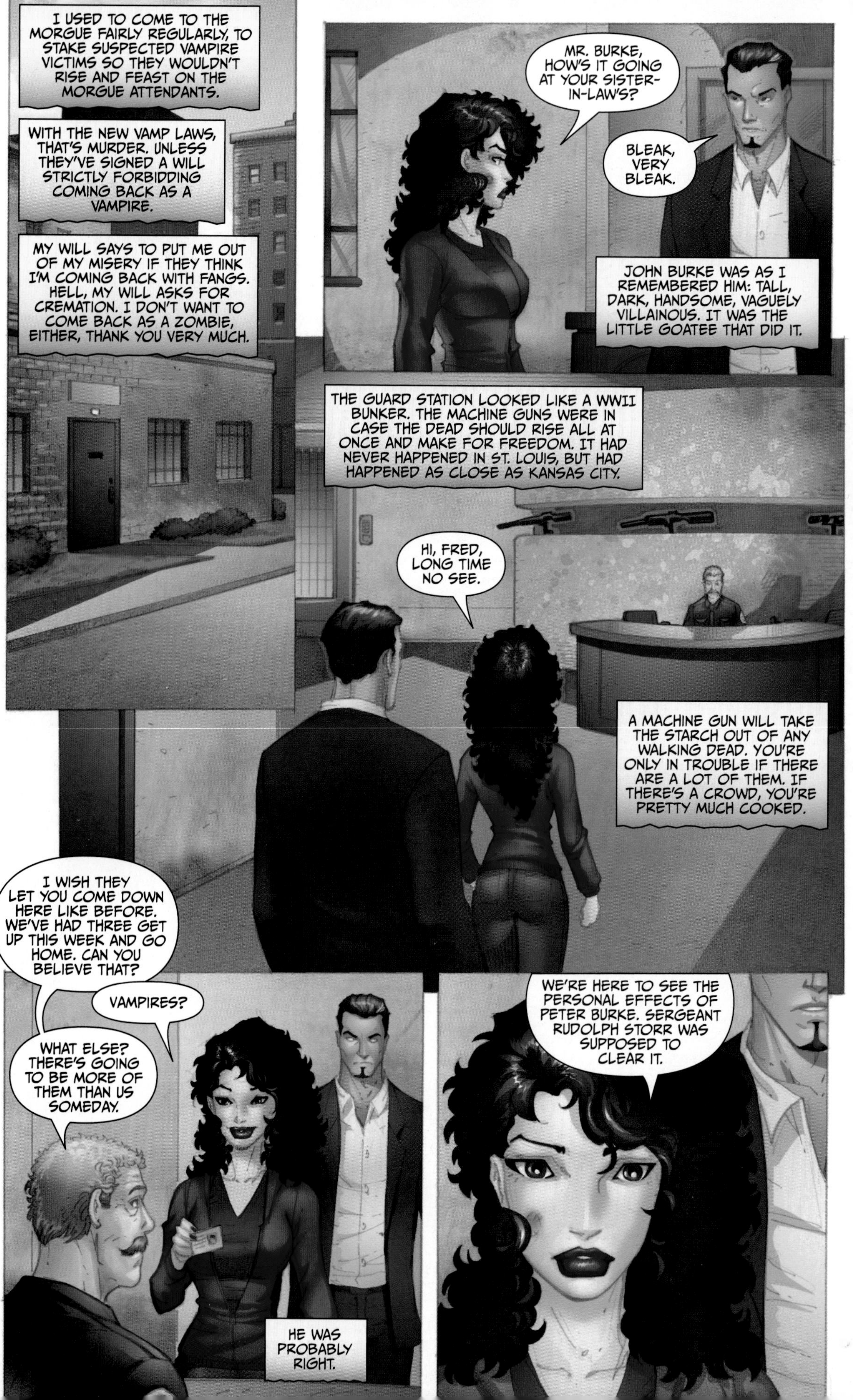
I USED TO COME TO THE MORGUE FAIRLY REGULARLY, TO STAKE SUSPECTED VAMPIRE VICTIMS SO THEY WOULDN'T RISE AND FEAST ON THE MORGUE ATTENDANTS.
WITH THE NEW VAMP LAWS, THAT'S MURDER. UNLESS THEY'VE SIGNED A WILL STRICTLY FORBIDDING COMING BACK AS A VAMPIRE.
MY WILL SAYS TO PUT ME OUT OF MY MISERY IF THEY THINK I'M COMING BACK WITH FANGS. HELL, MY WILL ASKS FOR CREMATION. I DON'T WANT TO COME BACK AS A ZOMBIE, EITHER, THANK YOU VERY MUCH.
MR. BURKE, HOW'S IT GOING AT YOUR SISTER-IN-LAW'S?
BLEAK, VERY BLEAK.
JOHN BURKE WAS AS I REMEMBERED HIM: TALL, DARK, HANDSOME, VAGUELY VILLAINOUS. IT WAS THE LITTLE GOATEE THAT DID IT.
THE GUARD STATION LOOKED LIKE A WWII BUNKER. THE MACHINE GUNS WERE IN CASE THE DEAD SHOULD RISE ALL AT ONCE AND MAKE FOR FREEDOM. IT HAD NEVER HAPPENED IN ST. LOUIS, BUT HAD HAPPENED AS CLOSE AS KANSAS CITY.
HI, FRED, LONG TIME NO SEE.
A MACHINE GUN WILL TAKE THE STARCH OUT OF ANY WALKING DEAD. YOU'RE ONLY IN TROUBLE IF THERE ARE A LOT OF THEM. IF THERE'S A CROWD, YOU'RE PRETTY MUCH COOKED.
I WISH THEY LET YOU COME DOWN HERE LIKE BEFORE. WE'VE HAD THREE GET UP THIS WEEK AND GO HOME. CAN YOU BELIEVE THAT?
VAMPIRES?
WHAT ELSE? THERE'S GOING TO BE MORE OF THEM THAN US SOMEDAY.
HE WAS PROBABLY RIGHT.
WE'RE HERE TO SEE THE PERSONAL EFFECTS OF PETER BURKE. SERGEANT RUDOLPH STORR WAS SUPPOSED TO CLEAR IT.

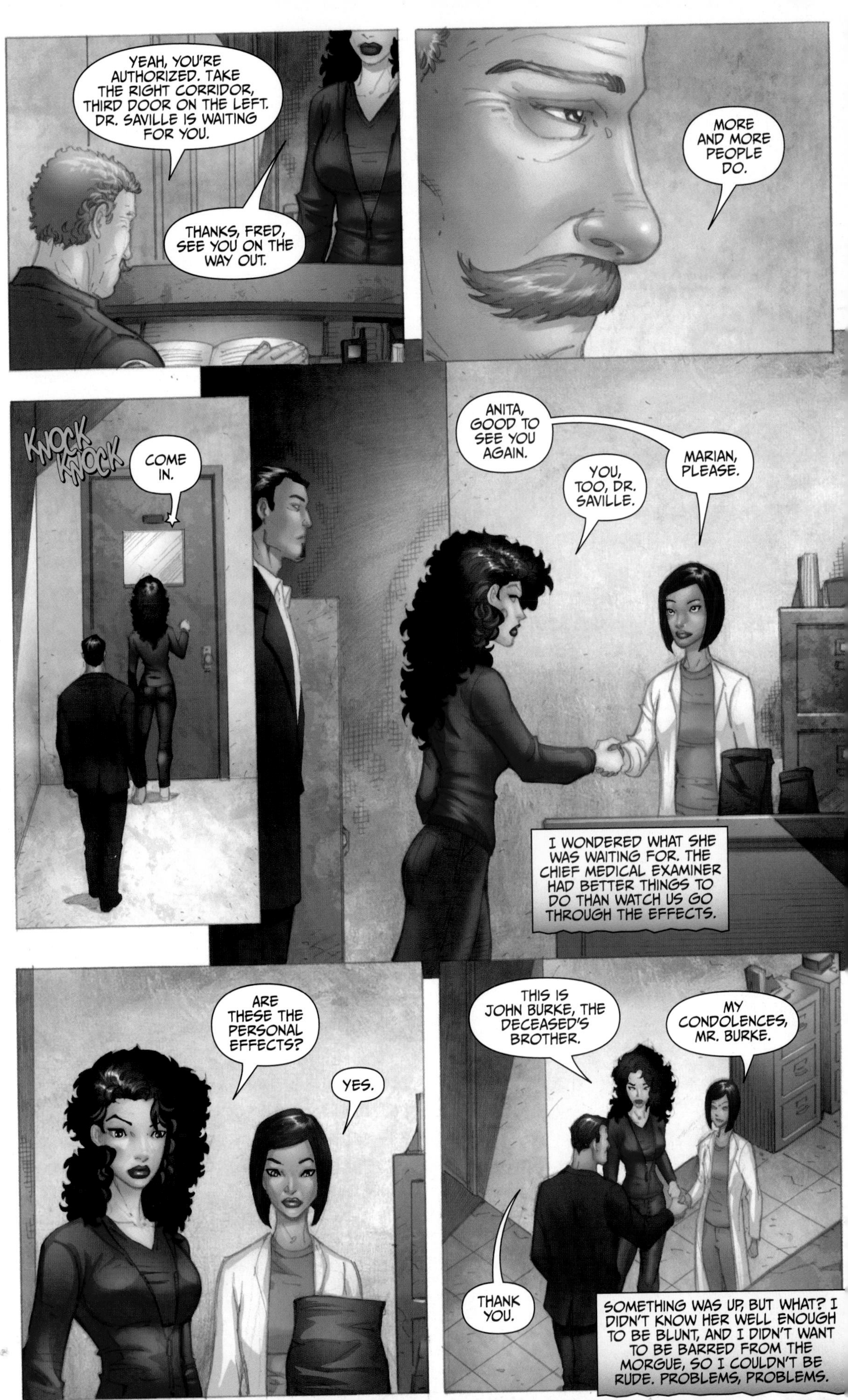
YEAH, YOU'RE AUTHORIZED. TAKE THE RIGHT CORRIDOR, THIRD DOOR ON THE LEFT. DR. SAVILLE IS WAITING FOR YOU.
THANKS, FRED, SEE YOU ON THE WAY OUT.
MORE AND MORE PEOPLE DO.
KNOCK KNOCK
COME IN.
ANITA, GOOD TO SEE YOU AGAIN.
YOU, TOO, DR. SAVILLE.
MARIAN, PLEASE.
I WONDERED WHAT SHE WAS WAITING FOR. THE CHIEF MEDICAL EXAMINER HAD BETTER THINGS TO DO THAN WATCH US GO THROUGH THE EFFECTS.
ARE THESE THE PERSONAL EFFECTS?
YES.
THIS IS JOHN BURKE, THE DECEASED'S BROTHER.
MY CONDOLENCES, MR. BURKE.
THANK YOU.
SOMETHING WAS UP, BUT WHAT? I DIDN'T KNOW HER WELL ENOUGH TO BE BLUNT, AND I DIDN'T WANT TO BE BARRED FROM THE MORGUE, SO I COULDN'T BE RUDE. PROBLEMS, PROBLEMS.

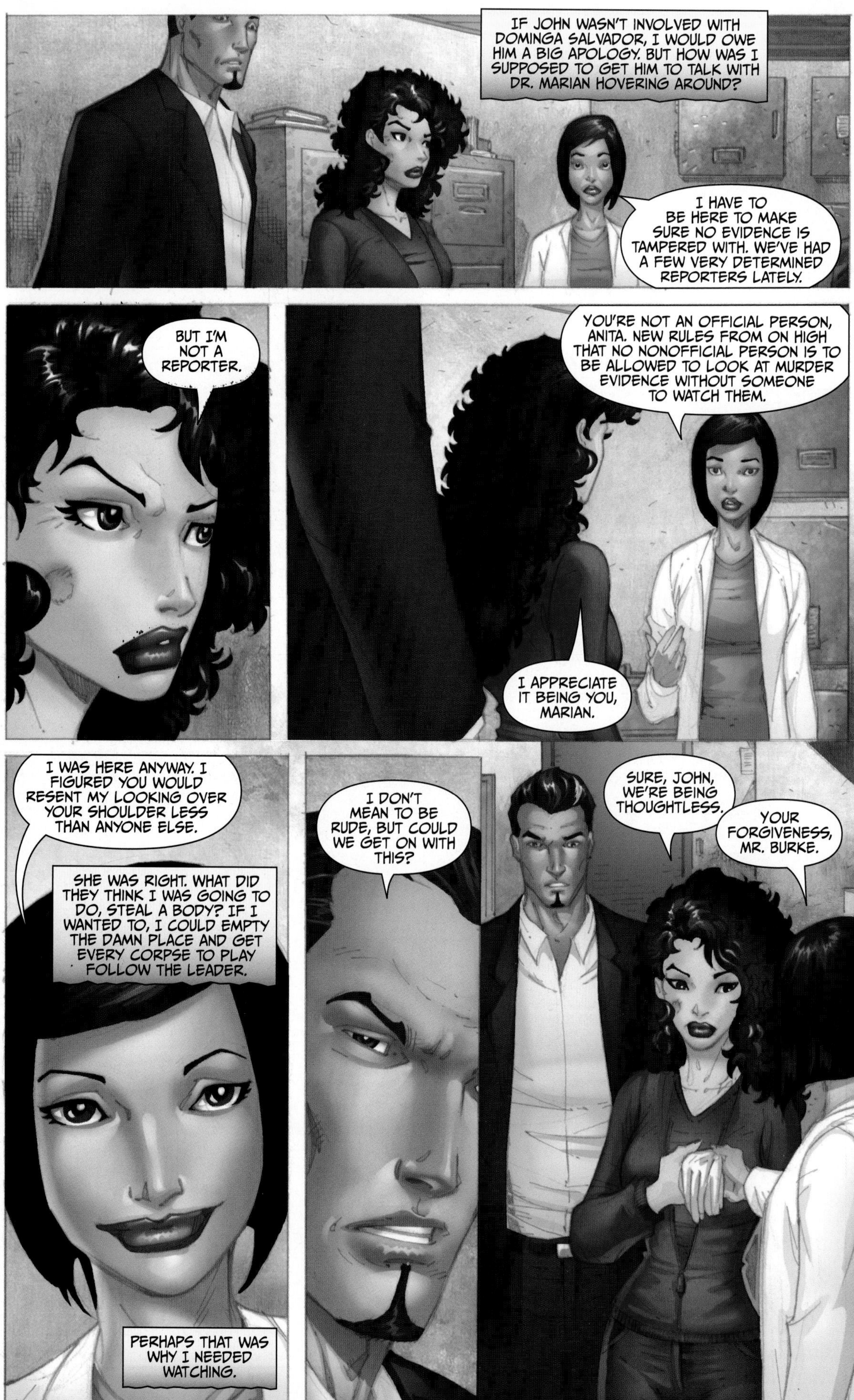
IF JOHN WASN'T INVOLVED WITH DOMINGA SALVADOR, I WOULD OWE HIM A BIG APOLOGY. BUT HOW WAS I SUPPOSED TO GET HIM TO TALK WITH DR. MARIAN HOVERING AROUND?
I HAVE TO BE HERE TO MAKE SURE NO EVIDENCE IS TAMPERED WITH. WE'VE HAD A FEW VERY DETERMINED REPORTERS LATELY.
BUT I'M NOT A REPORTER.
YOU'RE NOT AN OFFICIAL PERSON, ANITA. NEW RULES FROM ON HIGH THAT NO NONOFFICIAL PERSON IS TO BE ALLOWED TO LOOK AT MURDER EVIDENCE WITHOUT SOMEONE TO WATCH THEM.
I APPRECIATE IT BEING YOU, MARIAN.
I WAS HERE ANYWAY. I FIGURED YOU WOULD RESENT MY LOOKING OVER YOUR SHOULDER LESS THAN ANYONE ELSE.
SHE WAS RIGHT. WHAT DID THEY THINK I WAS GOING TO DO, STEAL A BODY? IF I WANTED TO, I COULD EMPTY THE DAMN PLACE AND GET EVERY CORPSE TO PLAY FOLLOW THE LEADER.
PERHAPS THAT WAS WHY I NEEDED WATCHING.
I DON'T MEAN TO BE RUDE, BUT COULD WE GET ON WITH THIS?
SURE, JOHN, WE'RE BEING THOUGHTLESS.
YOUR FORGIVENESS, MR. BURKE.

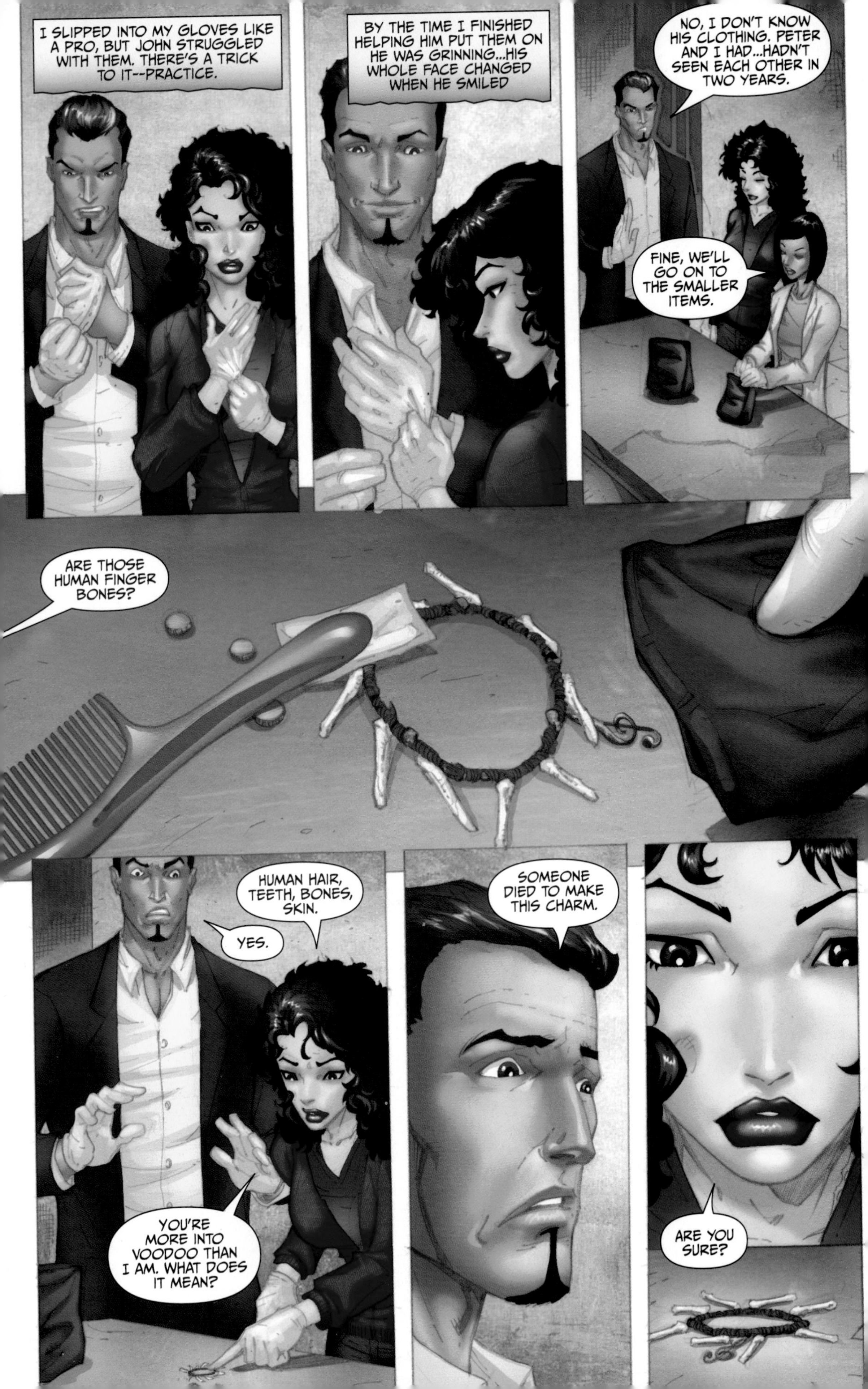
I SLIPPED INTO MY GLOVES LIKE A PRO, BUT JOHN STRUGGLED WITH THEM. THERE'S A TRICK TO IT--PRACTICE.
BY THE TIME I FINISHED HELPING HIM PUT THEM ON HE WAS GRINNING...HIS WHOLE FACE CHANGED WHEN HE SMILED
NO, I DON'T KNOW HIS CLOTHING. PETER AND I HAD...HADN'T SEEN EACH OTHER IN TWO YEARS.
FINE, WE'LL GO ON TO THE SMALLER ITEMS.
ARE THOSE HUMAN FINGER BONES?
YES.
HUMAN HAIR, TEETH, BONES, SKIN.
YOU'RE MORE INTO VOODOO THAN I AM. WHAT DOES IT MEAN?
SOMEONE DIED TO MAKE THIS CHARM.
ARE YOU SURE?

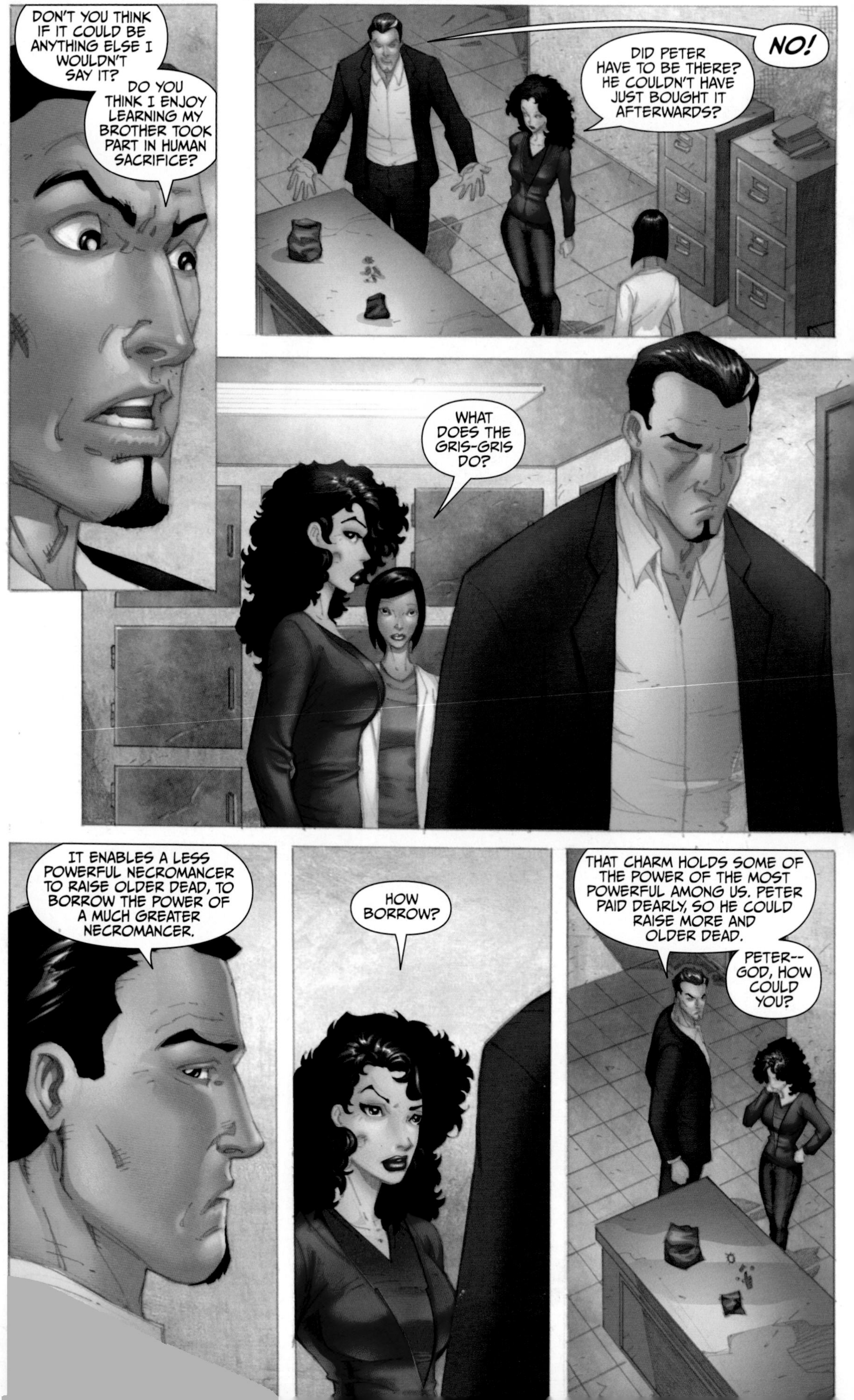
DON'T YOU THINK IF IT COULD BE ANYTHING ELSE I WOULDN'T SAY IT?
DO YOU THINK I ENJOY LEARNING MY BROTHER TOOK PART IN HUMAN SACRIFICE?
DID PETER HAVE TO BE THERE? HE COULDN'T HAVE JUST BOUGHT IT AFTERWARDS?
NO!
WHAT DOES THE GRIS-GRIS DO?
IT ENABLES A LESS POWERFUL NECROMANCER TO RAISE OLDER DEAD, TO BORROW THE POWER OF A MUCH GREATER NECROMANCER.
HOW BORROW?
THAT CHARM HOLDS SOME OF THE POWER OF THE MOST POWERFUL AMONG US. PETER PAID DEARLY, SO HE COULD RAISE MORE AND OLDER DEAD.
PETER-- GOD, HOW COULD YOU?

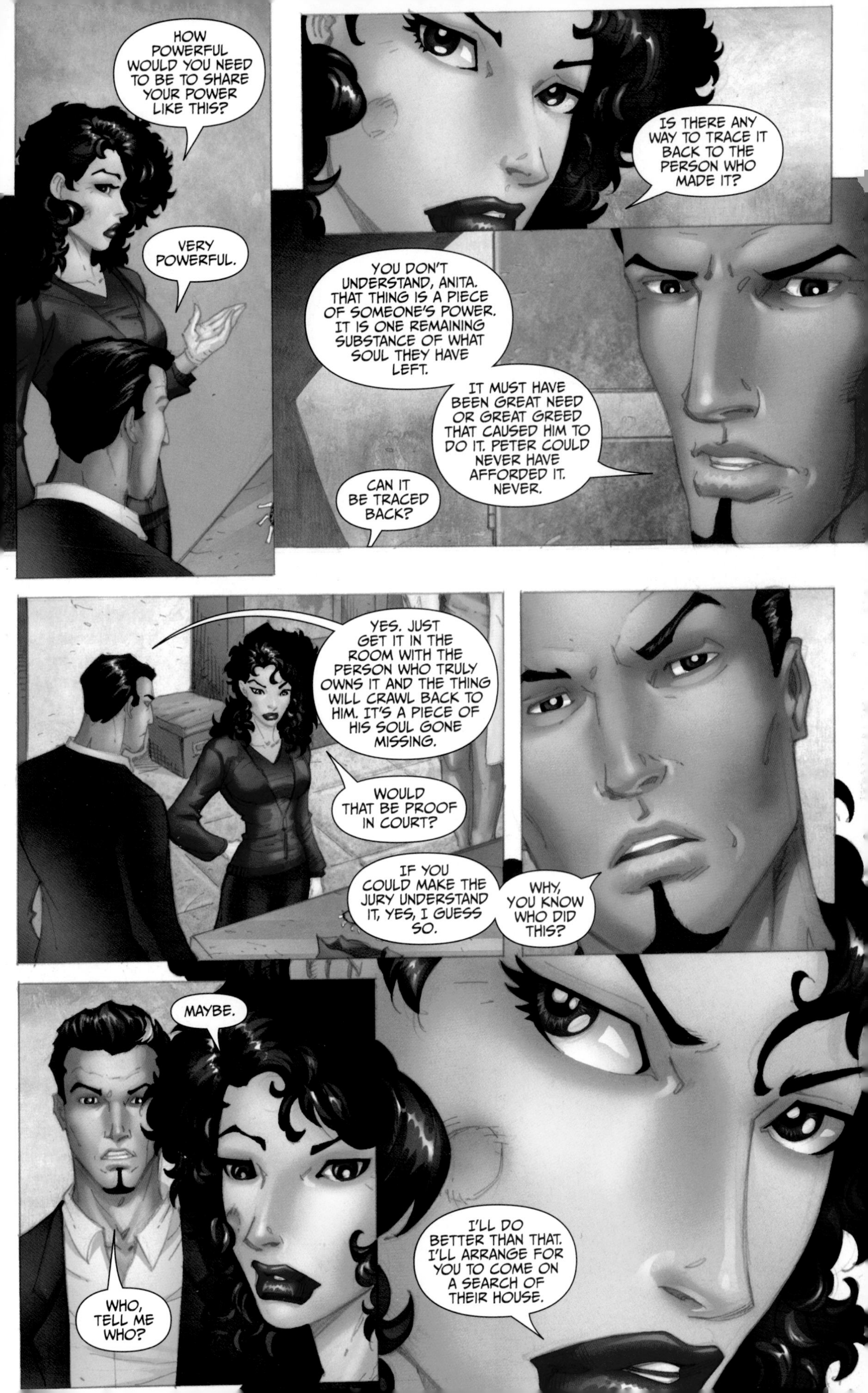
HOW POWERFUL WOULD YOU NEED TO BE TO SHARE YOUR POWER LIKE THIS?
VERY POWERFUL.
IS THERE ANY WAY TO TRACE IT BACK TO THE PERSON WHO MADE IT?
YOU DON'T UNDERSTAND, ANITA. THAT THING IS A PIECE OF SOMEONE'S POWER. IT IS ONE REMAINING SUBSTANCE OF WHAT SOUL THEY HAVE LEFT.
IT MUST HAVE BEEN GREAT NEED OR GREAT GREED THAT CAUSED HIM TO DO IT. PETER COULD NEVER HAVE AFFORDED IT. NEVER.
CAN IT BE TRACED BACK?
YES. JUST GET IT IN THE ROOM WITH THE PERSON WHO TRULY OWNS IT AND THE THING WILL CRAWL BACK TO HIM. IT'S A PIECE OF HIS SOUL GONE MISSING.
WOULD THAT BE PROOF IN COURT?
IF YOU COULD MAKE THE JURY UNDERSTAND IT, YES, I GUESS SO.
WHY, YOU KNOW WHO DID THIS?
MAYBE.
WHO, TELL ME WHO?
I'LL DO BETTER THAN THAT. I'LL ARRANGE FOR YOU TO COME ON A SEARCH OF THEIR HOUSE.

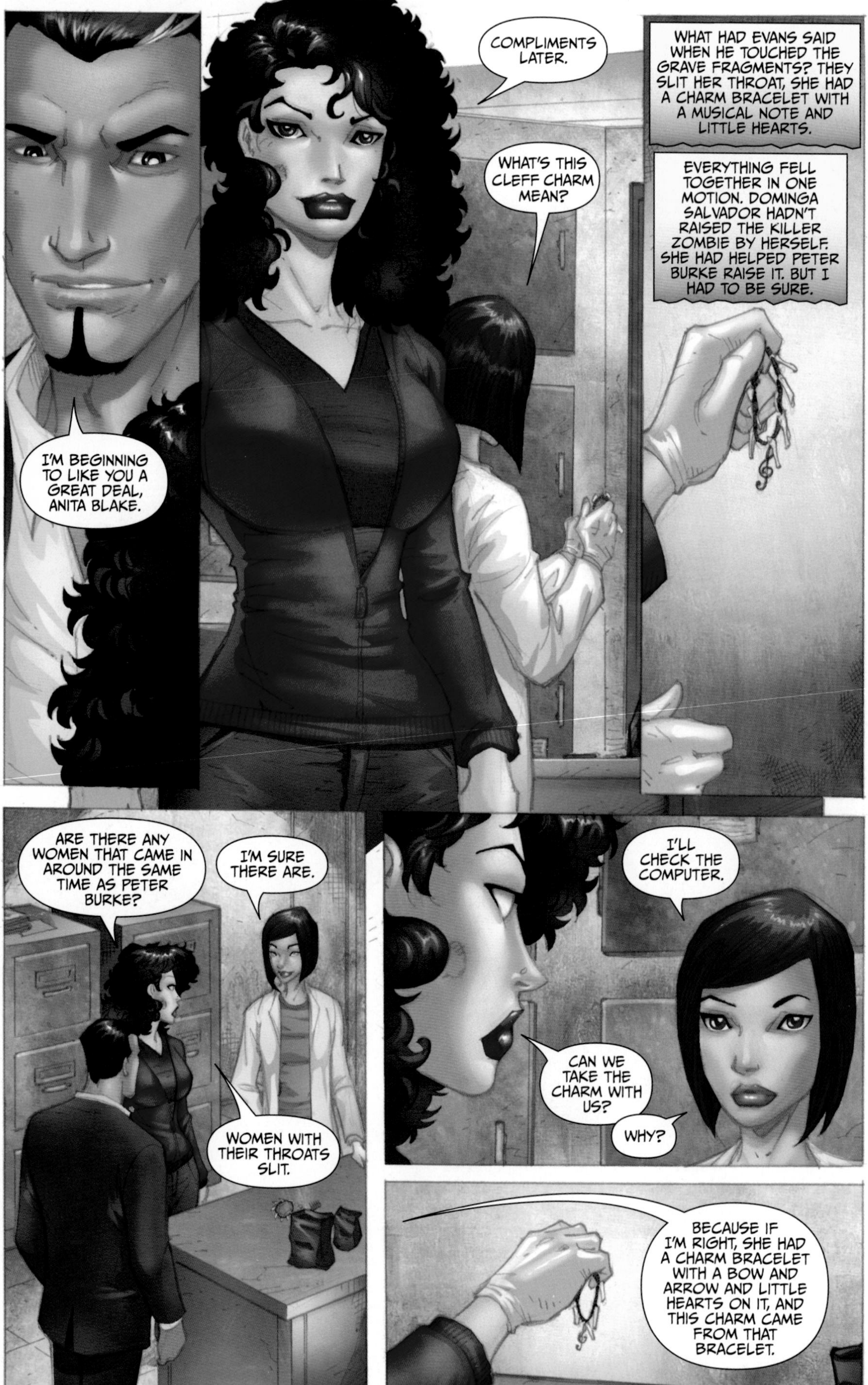
COMPLIMENTS LATER.
WHAT HAD EVANS SAID WHEN HE TOUCHED THE GRAVE FRAGMENTS? THEY SLIT HER THROAT, SHE HAD A CHARM BRACELET WITH A MUSICAL NOTE AND LITTLE HEARTS.
WHAT'S THIS CLEFF CHARM MEAN?
EVERYTHING FELL TOGETHER IN ONE MOTION. DOMINGA SALVADOR HADN'T RAISED THE KILLER ZOMBIE BY HERSELF. SHE HAD HELPED PETER BURKE RAISE IT. BUT I HAD TO BE SURE.
I'M BEGINNING TO LIKE YOU A GREAT DEAL, ANITA BLAKE.
ARE THERE ANY WOMEN THAT CAME IN AROUND THE SAME TIME AS PETER BURKE?
I'M SURE THERE ARE.
WOMEN WITH THEIR THROATS SLIT.
I'LL CHECK THE COMPUTER.
CAN WE TAKE THE CHARM WITH US?
WHY?
BECAUSE IF I'M RIGHT, SHE HAD A CHARM BRACELET WITH A BOW AND ARROW AND LITTLE HEARTS ON IT, AND THIS CHARM CAME FROM THAT BRACELET.

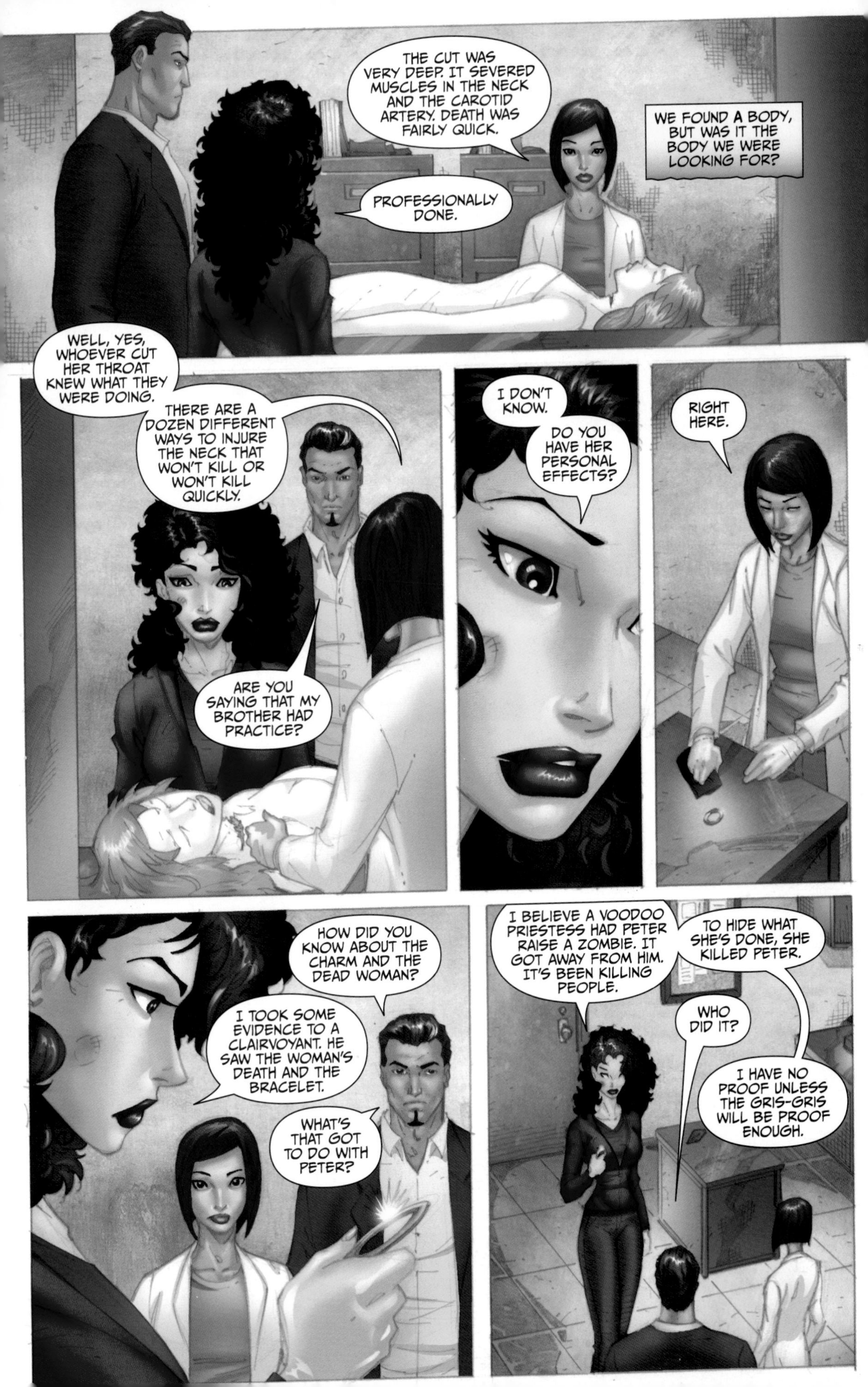
THE CUT WAS VERY DEEP. IT SEVERED MUSCLES IN THE NECK AND THE CAROTID ARTERY. DEATH WAS FAIRLY QUICK.
PROFESSIONALLY DONE.
WE FOUND A BODY, BUT WAS IT THE BODY WE WERE LOOKING FOR?
WELL, YES, WHOEVER CUT HER THROAT KNEW WHAT THEY WERE DOING.
THERE ARE A DOZEN DIFFERENT WAYS TO INJURE THE NECK THAT WON'T KILL OR WON'T KILL QUICKLY.
ARE YOU SAYING THAT MY BROTHER HAD PRACTICE?
I DON'T KNOW.
DO YOU HAVE HER PERSONAL EFFECTS?
RIGHT HERE.
HOW DID YOU KNOW ABOUT THE CHARM AND THE DEAD WOMAN?
I TOOK SOME EVIDENCE TO A CLAIRVOYANT. HE SAW THE WOMAN'S DEATH AND THE BRACELET.
WHAT'S THAT GOT TO DO WITH PETER?
I BELIEVE A VOODOO PRIESTESS HAD PETER RAISE A ZOMBIE. IT GOT AWAY FROM HIM. IT'S BEEN KILLING PEOPLE.
TO HIDE WHAT SHE'S DONE, SHE KILLED PETER.
WHO DID IT?
I HAVE NO PROOF UNLESS THE GRIS-GRIS WILL BE PROOF ENOUGH.

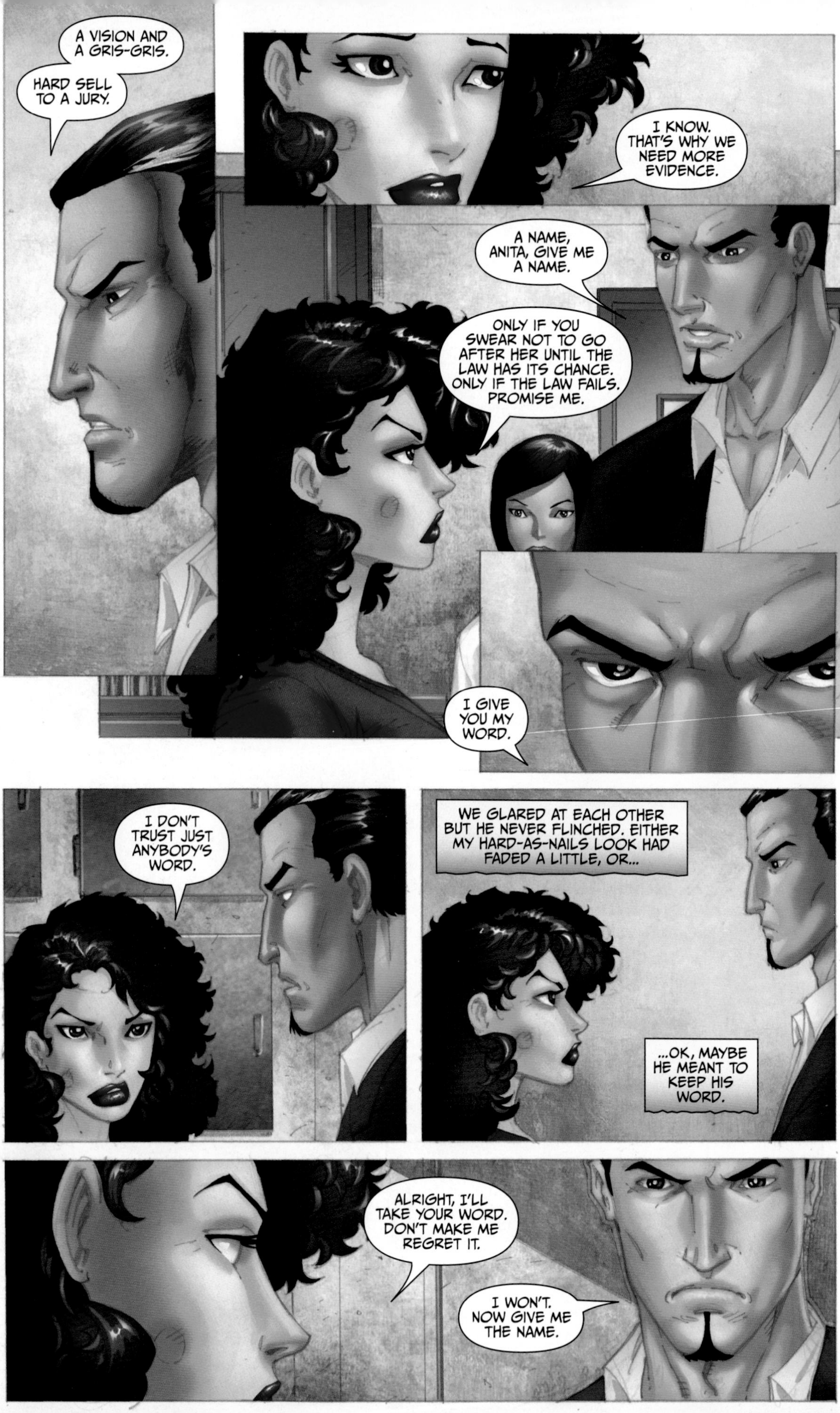
A VISION AND A GRIS-GRIS.
HARD SELL TO A JURY.
I KNOW. THAT'S WHY WE NEED MORE EVIDENCE.
A NAME, ANITA, GIVE ME A NAME.
ONLY IF YOU SWEAR NOT TO GO AFTER HER UNTIL THE LAW HAS ITS CHANCE. ONLY IF THE LAW FAILS. PROMISE ME.
I GIVE YOU MY WORD.
I DON'T TRUST JUST ANYBODY'S WORD.
WE GLARED AT EACH OTHER BUT HE NEVER FLINCHED. EITHER MY HARD-AS-NAILS LOOK HAD FADED A LITTLE, OR...
...OK, MAYBE HE MEANT TO KEEP HIS WORD.
ALRIGHT, I'LL TAKE YOUR WORD. DON'T MAKE ME REGRET IT.
I WON'T. NOW GIVE ME THE NAME.

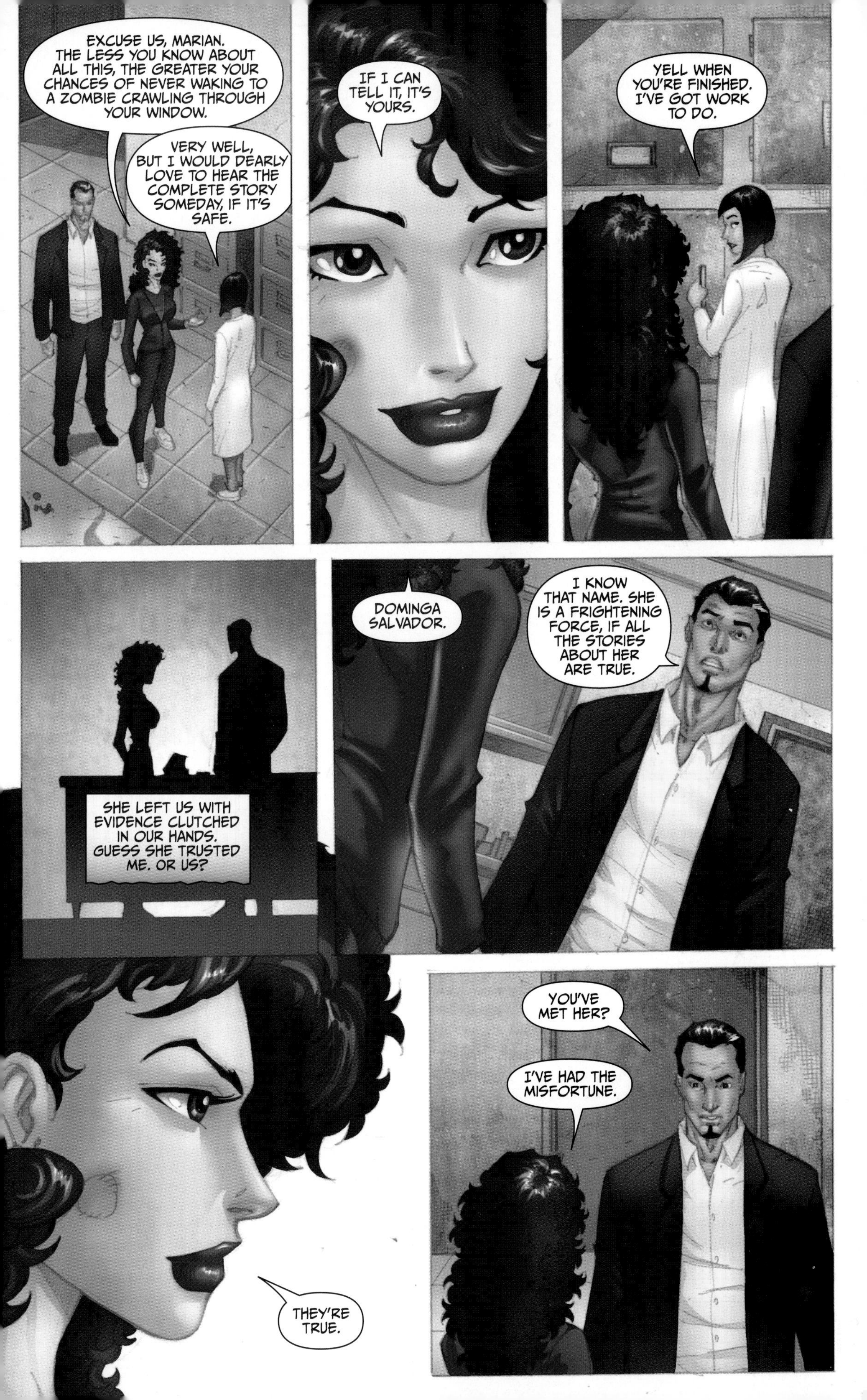
EXCUSE US, MARIAN. THE LESS YOU KNOW ABOUT ALL THIS, THE GREATER YOUR CHANCES OF NEVER WAKING TO A ZOMBIE CRAWLING THROUGH YOUR WINDOW.
VERY WELL, BUT I WOULD DEARLY LOVE TO HEAR THE COMPLETE STORY SOMEDAY, IF IT'S SAFE.
IF I CAN TELL IT, IT'S YOURS.
YELL WHEN YOU'RE FINISHED. I'VE GOT WORK TO DO.
SHE LEFT US WITH EVIDENCE CLUTCHED IN OUR HANDS. GUESS SHE TRUSTED ME. OR US?
DOMINGA SALVADOR.
I KNOW THAT NAME. SHE IS A FRIGHTENING FORCE, IF ALL THE STORIES ABOUT HER ARE TRUE.
THEY'RE TRUE.
YOU'VE MET HER?
I'VE HAD THE MISFORTUNE.

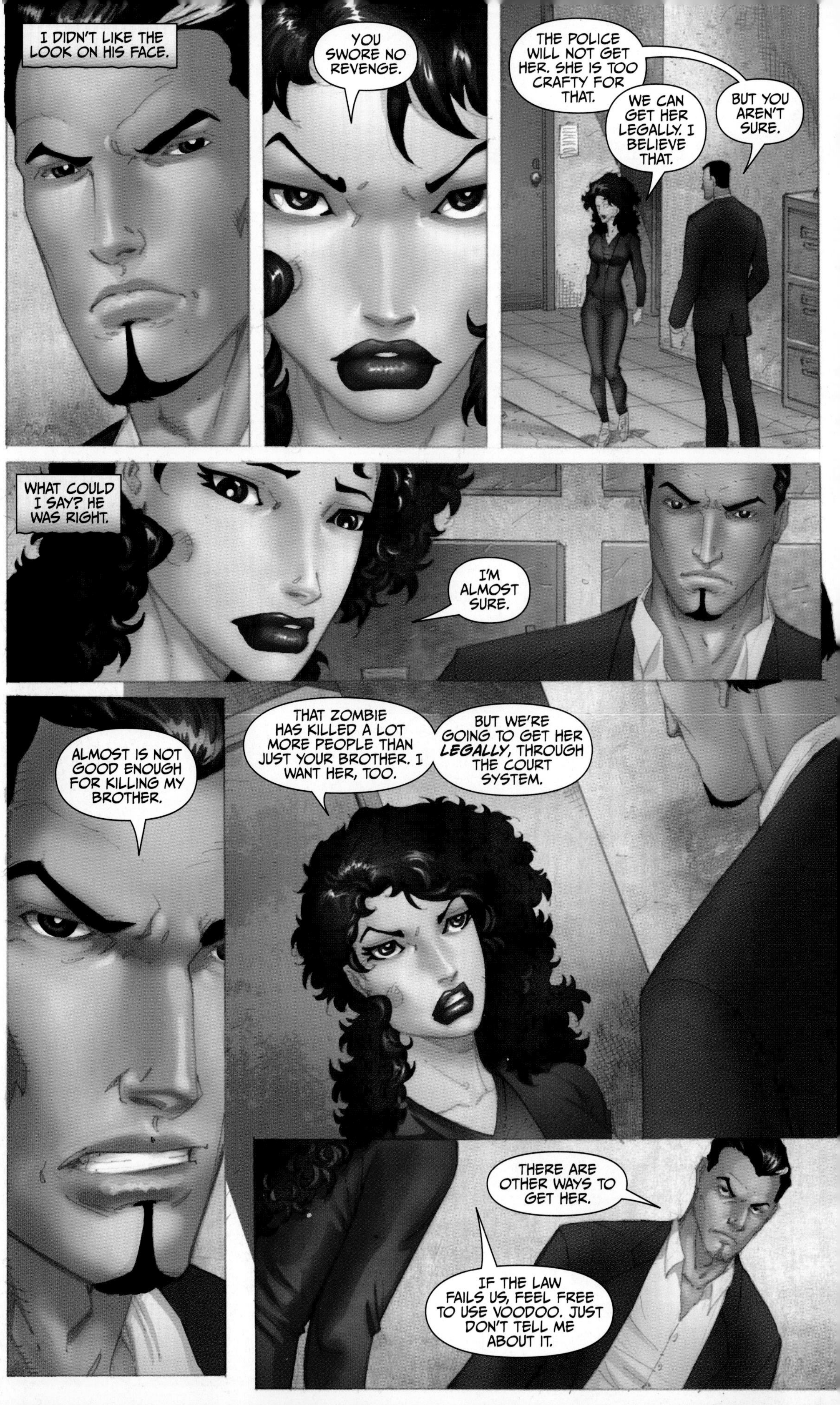
I DIDN'T LIKE THE LOOK ON HIS FACE.
YOU SWORE NO REVENGE.
THE POLICE WILL NOT GET HER. SHE IS TOO CRAFTY FOR THAT.
WE CAN GET HER LEGALLY. I BELIEVE THAT.
BUT YOU AREN'T SURE.
WHAT COULD I SAY? HE WAS RIGHT.
I'M ALMOST SURE.
ALMOST IS NOT GOOD ENOUGH FOR KILLING MY BROTHER.
THAT ZOMBIE HAS KILLED A LOT MORE PEOPLE THAN JUST YOUR BROTHER. I WANT HER, TOO.
BUT WE'RE GOING TO GET HER *LEGALLY*, THROUGH THE COURT SYSTEM.
THERE ARE OTHER WAYS TO GET HER.
IF THE LAW FAILS US, FEEL FREE TO USE VOODOO. JUST DON'T TELL ME ABOUT IT.

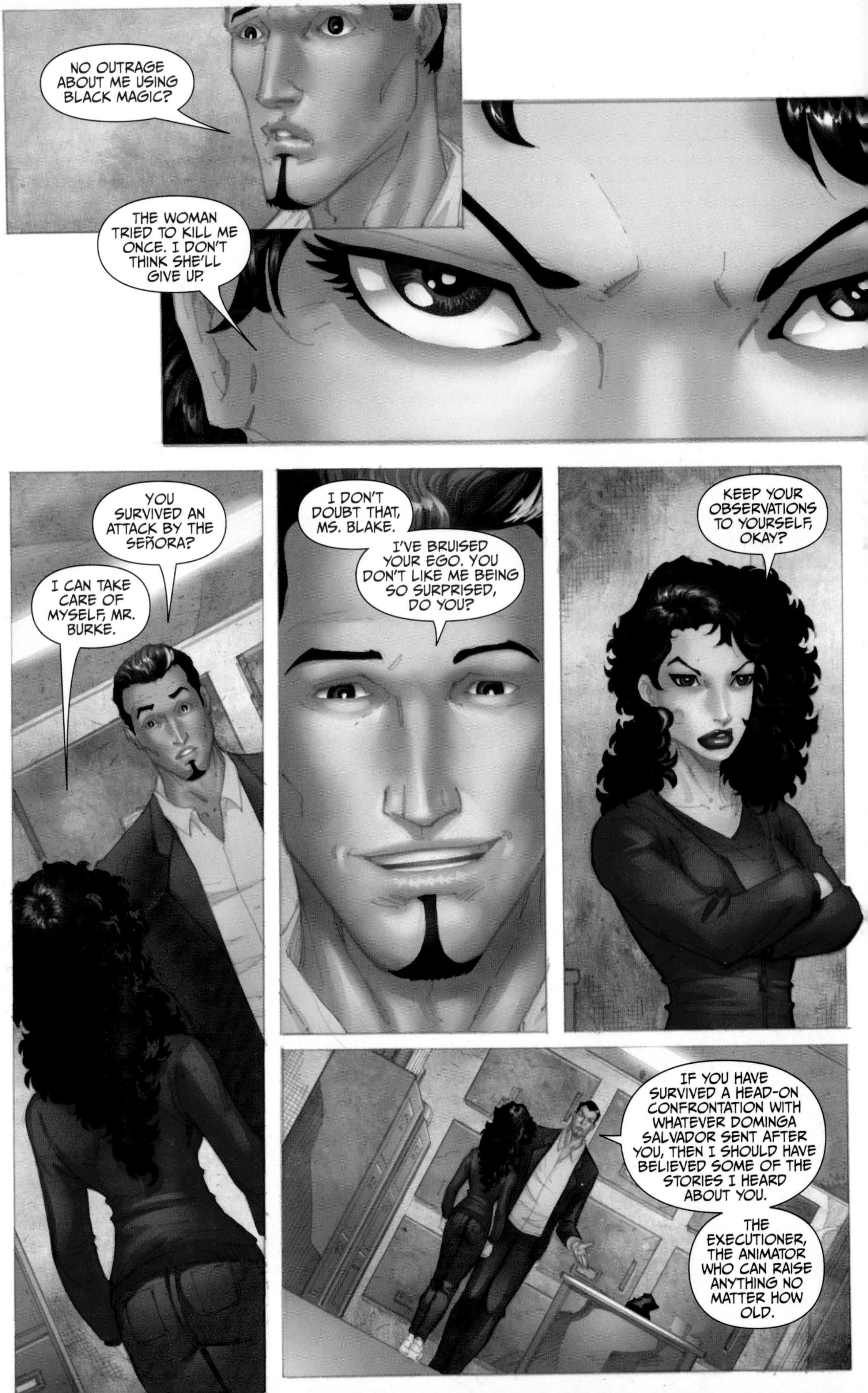
NO OUTRAGE ABOUT ME USING BLACK MAGIC?
THE WOMAN TRIED TO KILL ME ONCE. I DON'T THINK SHE'LL GIVE UP.
YOU SURVIVED AN ATTACK BY THE SEÑORA?
I CAN TAKE CARE OF MYSELF, MR. BURKE.
I DON'T DOUBT THAT, MS. BLAKE.
I'VE BRUISED YOUR EGO. YOU DON'T LIKE ME BEING SO SURPRISED, DO YOU?
KEEP YOUR OBSERVATIONS TO YOURSELF, OKAY?
IF YOU HAVE SURVIVED A HEAD-ON CONFRONTATION WITH WHATEVER DOMINGA SALVADOR SENT AFTER YOU, THEN I SHOULD HAVE BELIEVED SOME OF THE STORIES I HEARD ABOUT YOU.
THE EXECUTIONER, THE ANIMATOR WHO CAN RAISE ANYTHING NO MATTER HOW OLD.

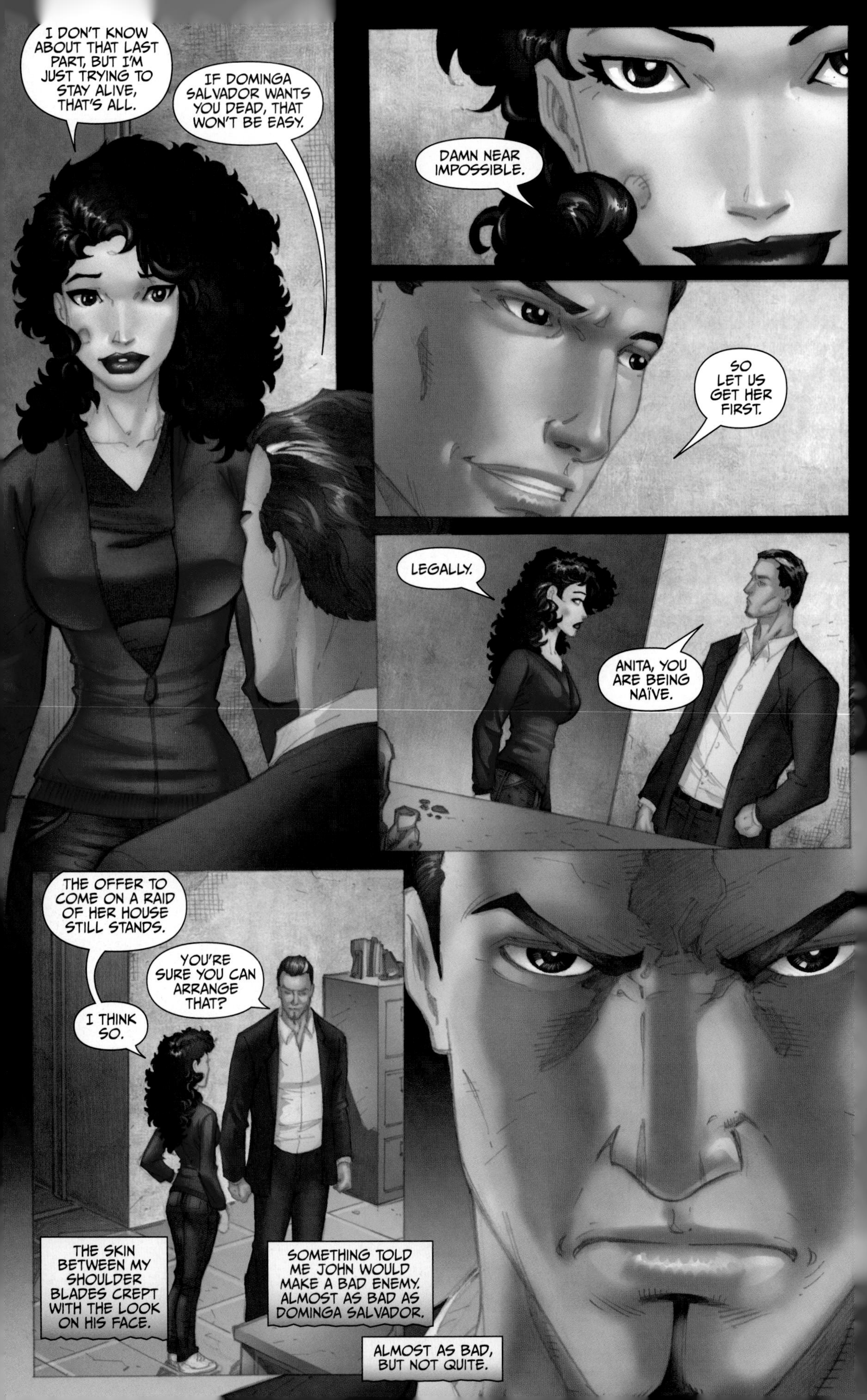
I DON'T KNOW ABOUT THAT LAST PART, BUT I'M JUST TRYING TO STAY ALIVE, THAT'S ALL.
IF DOMINGA SALVADOR WANTS YOU DEAD, THAT WON'T BE EASY.
DAMN NEAR IMPOSSIBLE.
SO LET US GET HER FIRST.
LEGALLY.
ANITA, YOU ARE BEING NAÏVE.
THE OFFER TO COME ON A RAID OF HER HOUSE STILL STANDS.
YOU'RE SURE YOU CAN ARRANGE THAT?
I THINK SO.
THE SKIN BETWEEN MY SHOULDER BLADES CREPT WITH THE LOOK ON HIS FACE.
SOMETHING TOLD ME JOHN WOULD MAKE A BAD ENEMY. ALMOST AS BAD AS DOMINGA SALVADOR.
ALMOST AS BAD, BUT NOT QUITE.

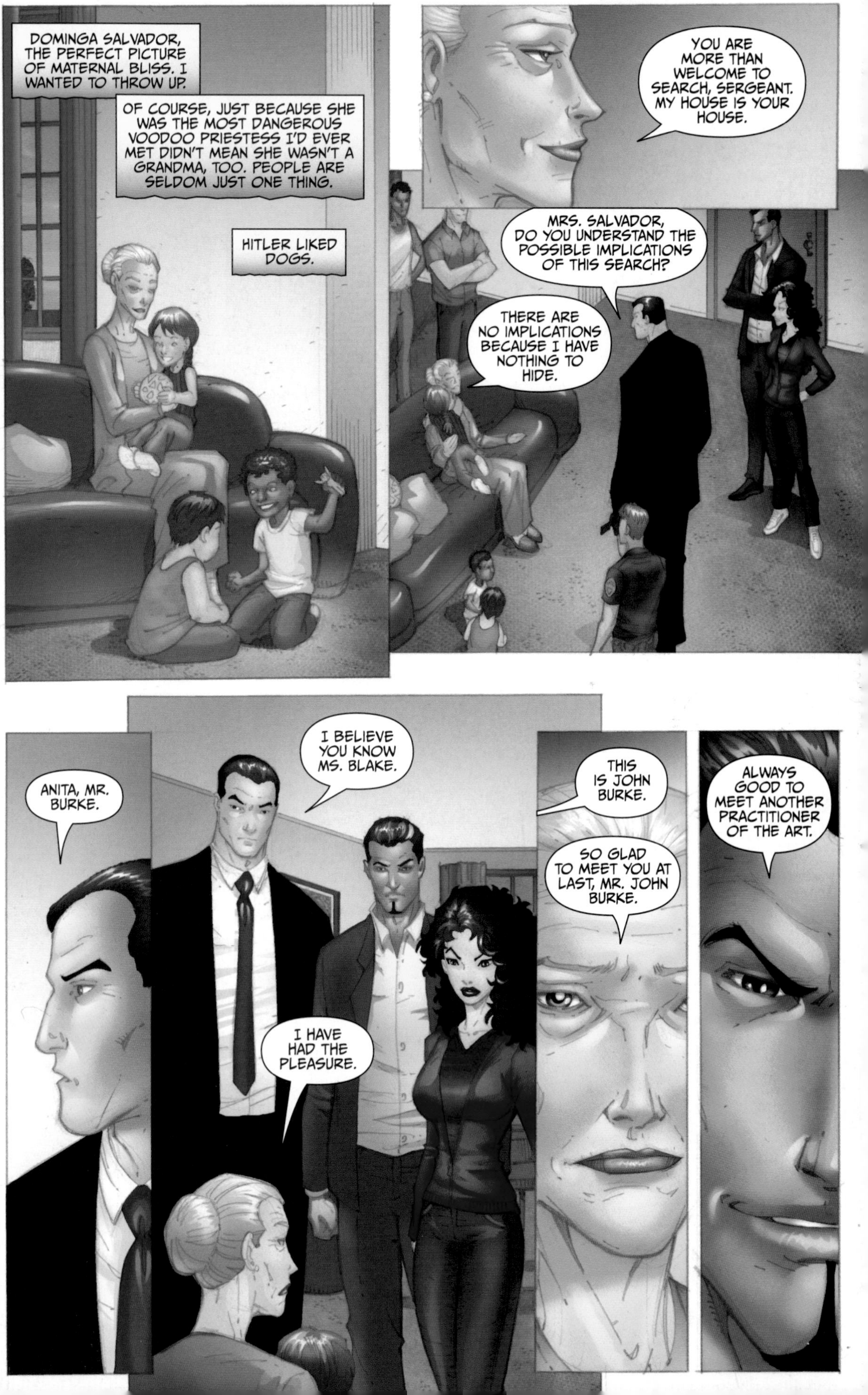
DOMINGA SALVADOR, THE PERFECT PICTURE OF MATERNAL BLISS. I WANTED TO THROW UP.
OF COURSE, JUST BECAUSE SHE WAS THE MOST DANGEROUS VOODOO PRIESTESS I'D EVER MET DIDN'T MEAN SHE WASN'T A GRANDMA, TOO. PEOPLE ARE SELDOM JUST ONE THING.
HITLER LIKED DOGS.
YOU ARE MORE THAN WELCOME TO SEARCH, SERGEANT. MY HOUSE IS YOUR HOUSE.
MRS. SALVADOR, DO YOU UNDERSTAND THE POSSIBLE IMPLICATIONS OF THIS SEARCH?
THERE ARE NO IMPLICATIONS BECAUSE I HAVE NOTHING TO HIDE.
ANITA, MR. BURKE.
I BELIEVE YOU KNOW MS. BLAKE.
I HAVE HAD THE PLEASURE.
THIS IS JOHN BURKE.
SO GLAD TO MEET YOU AT LAST, MR. JOHN BURKE.
ALWAYS GOOD TO MEET ANOTHER PRACTITIONER OF THE ART.